My first night in command was to be like many that followed. At 0200 hours the battalion duty officer called to say that one of my troops was at the MP station. He was under arrest for assaulting another soldier in a downtown bar.

Along with the lack of discipline, the drug abuse, and the general disarray of the company area, other problems had to be dealt with. The annual general inspection (AGI) was scheduled for the end of January. There were only two outcomes of the AGI—pass or fail. Failure usually meant relief from command and a guaranteed spot on the next list of officers being released from military service. After only hours in the company, I was absolutely certain that there was no way we could pass the AGI.

Our only hope lay in the knowledge that division was aware of the situation in the battalion and that it had been at least five years since the ''annual'' inspection was conducted. A week into command I met with the company first sergeant and told him that our objective for the AGI was to keep anyone in the company from going to jail. Beyond that, as he well knew, no other objective would be attainable.

Also by Michael Lee Lanning
Published by Ivy Books:

THE ONLY WAR WE HAD: A Platoon Leader's Journal of Vietnam

VIETNAM 1969–1970: A Company Commander's Journal

INSIDE THE LRRPS: Rangers in Vietnam

INSIDE FORCE RECON: Recon Marines in Vietnam
(with Ray William Stubbe)

THE
BATTLES
OF PEACE

Michael Lee Lanning

IVY BOOKS • NEW YORK

Ivy Books
Published by Ballantine Books
Copyright © 1992 by Michael Lee Lanning

Library of Congress Catalog Card Number: 91-75844

ISBN 978-0-345-48304-1

Manufactured in the United States of America

Cover photo courtesy of Wide World Photos, Inc.

146673257

DEDICATION

to . . .
The parents of soldiers,
especially
James Maurice Lanning
(1912–1989)
and
Alice Coskey Lanning

War after all's but a flash in the pan,
It's the battles of peace that makes the man.

Harry de Halsalle

CONTENTS

THE
BATTLES
OF PEACE

CHAPTER 1

STATESIDE: MOUSEKETEERS, ASSIGNMENT PIMPS, AND BEAUTIFUL BABIES

January–June 1973

Tonight at 2200 hours President Nixon announced that on the 25th a cease-fire will be final and peace will finally come to Vietnam. There is no dancing in the streets, car horns honking or celebration in America of any kind. There is no talk of a VVN day to compare with VE or VJ days—for there is no victory. I feel kind of sad, and a great sense of loss for friends who are not alive to see the war's end.

Captain Michael Lee Lanning
Personal Journal
January 23, 1973

I was driving south on Brett Street [Fort Knox, Kentucky] when word came on the radio that the war was officially over.

Personal Journal
January 27, 1973

I am very pleased the POWs are coming home—it is difficult to express my feelings.

Personal Journal
February 14, 1973

There were far more thoughts than those which ended up written in my journal. I was angry at the American public and leadership because we had abandoned the South Vietnamese—a people for whom I knew the war was not over and a country whose independence had been given away at the conference table rather than defended on the battlefield. I thought about friends, as well as men whose lives had been my responsibility, now resting beneath military headstones in cemeteries across

America. For those soldiers and their families, the war would never be over.

The official announcement of the war's end was no surprise. Our combat divisions had begun withdrawal from Vietnam in 1969, and by 1972 only advisors and a few support units remained in-country. By the time the ironic "peace with honor" was finally declared, we who were staying in the army were already well aware that we were soldiers without a war to fight. It would not be long, however, before I learned that the "battles of peace" are often more difficult than the "battles of war."

After I returned from the combat zone in 1970, like many other professional soldiers, I began to think of a future in uniform without Vietnam. Throughout the army, the word was that counterguerrilla and light-infantry operations would soon be a thing of the past. We believed that the army would not again make the mistake of preparing for the next war by practicing the mistakes of the past one. Official publications, as well as barroom gossip, said the future of the army was in mechanized and armor forces. The greatest challenges in rebuilding the peacetime army would be along the West German border, facing the seemingly limitless hordes of the Warsaw Pact.

By 1972, I was nearing the end of an assignment as an instructor in the Infantry School's Florida Ranger Camp. The next step for a career officer was the advanced course where one supposedly learned the skills to be a staff officer in preparation for promotion to field grade. Each branch (infantry, armor, artillery, etc) offered its own nine-month course. The infantry's was at Fort Benning, Georgia.

I thought that if mechanized infantry and armor were the future of the army, the best place to learn was from the experts. A few telephone calls to my assignment officer in Washington, D.C., finally secured orders for the Armor Advanced Course at Fort Knox, Kentucky. Although I was led to believe at the time that my assignment officer was doing me a great favor, I was later to learn that the army was thinking along the same lines and was looking for infantry volunteers to attend the armor school.

One of the reputed pluses of army schools is that they give families the opportunity to have some time together after separations caused by combat tours, temporary duty away from home, and extended field exercises. That they are a mixed blessing, however, is well substantiated by the number of divorces, affairs, and other matters of the heart that occur during school tours.

My wife Linda and I approached the advanced course for the positive rather than the negative personal aspects. Because I had spent my last two months in the Ranger Department as a class tactical officer, away from home, Linda preceded me to Fort Knox in the fall of 1972. Despite being seven months pregnant, she handled the entire move and drove from Florida to Kentucky with no one except our two-year-old daughter as company.

Arriving at Fort Knox, Linda was informed by a bureaucratic housing officer that dependents could not sign for quarters—the sponsor must do so. Since some wives of infantrymen share much of the personalities of their husbands, Linda calmly threatened to immediately have our baby in the housing officer's office if she was not given quarters. She moved in that afternoon, and by the time I arrived a few weeks later, she was well settled.

Quarters for students at Fort Knox were typical of those of army posts across the United States. Named after a former general, Van Voorhis, they were built along narrow streets in complexes of four to twelve units. The two-level apartments each contained about nine hundred square feet of unair-conditioned living space. Poorly constructed, with little insulation, the walls were so thin that neighbors' arguments, lovemaking, and normal conversations were easily overheard in adjacent units. Except for the occasional jokes at parties about "screamers" or "moaners," we officers and gentlemen rarely remarked on the sounds that drifted through the walls.

My initial impression of the Armor Advanced Course was that no one, student or instructor, seemed particularly interested. Much of our reaction was the result of the ennui of finally being at peace after a decade of war. A more important factor, however, was in the way the advanced course, and most all army schools, was structured and taught. Quite simply, soldiering is not a profession which adapts readily to a classroom.

The military is a hands-on profession in which overhead projectors, long-winded instructors, and popquizzes are not effective. Leadership is not learned at a desk, and management techniques that work in industry will not necessarily motivate men to fight, risk death, and kill.

"The course offers only continued drudgery with little motivation or mental or social stimulus," was typical of the thoughts recorded in my journal over the next months.

Although my fellow students seemed to feel much the same

way about the course, most everyone admitted that the easy schedule and lack of responsibility was a welcome break. And, as bad as sitting in the classroom was, it beat hell out of crossing East Bay Swamp in the Florida Ranger Camp in the middle of winter, while breaking ice and trying to teach a platoon of Ranger students who had not slept for three days nor eaten for two.

Regardless of the relative ease of the assignment, the sad fact is that U.S. Army schools, especially those for midlevel and senior officers, are totally inadequate. In an effort to allow comparison to other institutions of higher learning—so much as to even call the training courses colleges—the military attempts to teach skills as academic disciplines rather than the mechanical skills that dominate on a battlefield. While theories of war and study of great battles may be of interest and even some validity, the fact remains that wars are won in the mud and in the trenches rather than behind a desk or at a chalkboard.

In addition to attempting to teach tactics, maintenance, and logistics in the classroom, each military school dedicates a large part of its time and efforts to teaching leadership—this is like trying to catch fog in a bag. While the principles of leadership and examples thereof can certainly be lectured about from a platform, the ability to lead men in combat and to rally them on to victory—or at least to increase chances of survival—is an ability that is more innate than learned.

Natural deficiencies and pitfalls of the Armor Advanced Course of 1973 were added to—and almost overshadowed by—another phenomenon of the post-Vietnam army. As the military reverted to peacetime strengths, the army found itself with an excess of captains commissioned during the height of the war years of 1965–1969. Although those year-groups had provided more than 80 percent of the officer casualties and almost 10 percent of the army's death toll in Vietnam, too many of us had survived for the available peacetime assignments.*

The army's solution to the excess was simple if coldhearted. Many of the officers had entered the service with commissions in the reserves and remained on active duty by signing "voluntary indefinite" extensions. With little notice, the army announced that all reserve commissioned officer files would be reviewed and those officers with substandard records would be eliminated. This reduction in force (RIF) initially caused little

*Of 3336 army commissioned officers killed in the war, 2973 were lieutenants and captains.

unrest. Most of the individuals on the first RIF list were officers of the poorest quality and motivation, and few could question their dismissal.

Unfortunately, the first RIF was not the last. Several more followed, and each list included the names of more officers who had served well and had proved their merit in combat. Many of those on subsequent lists were former noncommissioned officers who had six to ten years' service before receiving battlefield commissions. The basic message was that regardless of how much the army had needed them, the war was now over. Men with more than fifteen years in uniform and with row after row of service and valor awards were told either to get out or to revert to their prewar enlisted rank.

Particularly hard hit by the RIFs were aviator officers. Vietnam had been a helicopter war, and the ranks of army commissioned aviators exceeded those of the air force. War's end and the focus on mechanized infantry and armor left little room for chopper drivers.

When our course began in August 1973, the official word was that the RIFs were over. Anyone who had survived the lists thus far was safe. We were to learn all too soon the fallacy of that belief.

Other factors also combined to make the advanced course less than a happy time. Many of my classmates recalled that in the last five or six years they had avoided wearing uniforms off of a military installation. Those who did had stories of verbal and even physical abuse heaped upon them by citizens whom they had sworn to defend and protect.

The open contempt for the military caused most of us to withdraw more into our own element. Only fellow veterans seemingly shared our belief in what we were doing. Only our own kind understood our nightmares of combat and would provide natural support groups for continuing in such a difficult profession for such an ungrateful country.

Perhaps this camaraderie among students was the greatest asset of the course. Long hours were spent during classroom breaks, at the club, and in our quarters discussing the future of the army and our places in the postwar era. A major topic of conversation was about the officers and soldiers who were resigning from the army and/or were sending their medals and decorations back to Washington.

One name that kept coming up was that of Col. David Hackworth, who resigned after his second tour in Vietnam. Hackworth, who had served as an infantry battalion commander and as an advisor to the South Vietnamese in the war zone before quitting in protest over the poor training received by replacement troops and the manner in which the United States was conducting the war, had been one of the most respected senior commanders. While nearly everyone sympathized with Hackworth's reasons for resigning, he received little overall support. The consensus was that the way a professional improves his chosen vocation is by remaining with it and working for improvement. Beyond gaining himself a bit of notoriety, Hackworth did nothing but become a part of the problem rather than a part of the solution.*

As for myself, I agreed with the majority. Nothing could be gained or improved by running from trouble or problems. Although sometimes I felt like the old beaten-up, punch-drunk fighter, who—with cauliflower ears, a flattened nose, gaps in his teeth, and a bob to his head from brain damage—would state in an interview, "Boxing has been good to me." Well, the army, despite the hardships, dangers, and sending me to fight a war the country did not intend to win, had "been good to me." It was my army, as well as our army—getting out would do none of us any good.

Despite the content of the course and the overall attitude of the American public about the military, the school months passed quickly and at times were almost enjoyable. In early November, my highlight of the Fort Knox tour occurred with the birth of our second daughter, Meridith, at the post's Ireland Army Hospital. Although the symbolism was lost at the time and remains unexplained to us to this day, Linda's labor pains began late on the evening of November 7 while we were watching the election returns announcing "four more years" for Richard Nixon.

Nixon would not serve his full term, but Meridith signed on for the duration. My second daughter's birth also brought on the rerealization that we were living in times of peace. Less than three years before, I had learned of the birth of our older daughter by way of a radio-relay station while I was between firefights in the midst of the Vietnamese War Zone D jungle. Learning of our second daughter from a white-robed nurse in a hospital waiting room was much the preferred option. Having to wait only

---

*As an aside, several officers who had served under the former commander pointed out that Hackworth had not really quit, he had retired, i.e., was still receiving well over 50 percent of his base salary.

minutes to see her rather than the five months before I saw my firstborn was also much nicer.

Although most of the course curriculum was prescribed, we students were allowed two electives. Although they were at opposite ends of the spectrum of warfare, my selections mirrored the skills I thought officers in the army of the future would need. To cover the possibility of another unconventional, low-intensity conflict, I signed up for a Spanish course. Central America definitely looked like it held possibilities. The second course was at the extreme upper end of the levels of warfare. Commonly known as "Prefix 5" because it offered that numerical addition to a graduate's specialty code, the formal name of the course was Nuclear Weapons Employment. Using manuals, charts, and graphs classified secret, we learned to select the correct yield of artillery and air-delivered nuclear warheads to destroy various targets during offensive operations. In the defensive phase of the course, we learned to plot downwind effects and other dangers of nuclear explosions. Everyone complained about the math requirements of the course and about the long hours that we had to spend in the secure classroom (we could not take the classified data home for study). Interestingly, no one commented about our dealing with facts and figures that would result in casualties measured in the multiples of thousands. In fact, the general guidance was "if in doubt, add another KT (kiloton) to the yield."

Other parts of the advanced course were even more difficult to define as either "good" or "bad." Making a constant effort to keep our morale up was the armor school's assistant commandant, Brig. Gen. George S. Patton. General Patton constantly visited classrooms and on occasion would take over the platform to add his opinion or to tell an off-color joke. Like his father of World War II fame, Patton's speech was liberally sprinkled with obscenities. He also liked to "profile" as much as possible, and while he did not wear pearl-handled revolvers, he did manage regularly to be seen driving around the post in his quarter-ton jeep, accompanied by a large black Labrador retriever.

Like most of us students, Patton's faculty members were a bit unsure of how to take the general. More than one instructor, when using examples of the exploits of the Third Army in World War II, would make reference to the "real General Patton."

Regardless of Patton's influence on us or the army as a whole, there were much more important matters over which neither he nor we had any control. My two years with the Ranger Department at the isolated training camp in the Florida panhandle had exposed me to only the army's top individuals. Only the strongest, smartest, and most motivated students made it to the last weeks of the three-phase, eight-week course. Except for the infantry companies that arrived from Fort Benning with each class to act as aggressors and drivers and to provide various other forms of support, we had little contact with the real army.

Occasional visits to Fort Benning and the move to Fort Knox brought to light some harsh realities of the post-Vietnam peacetime army. Although the draft still existed, more and more of the recruits were from the ranks of the "CAT IV" volunteers. These were the young men who scored in the bottom quarter on standardized tests. Still other recruits were "judicial volunteers," men to whom various judges and correctional officials had given the option of the army or jail.

Along with observing at firsthand the basic-training brigade at Fort Knox, we heard from fellow students about their experiences in recent months with discipline problems, drug use, and racial tensions. "War stories" of drug busts, assaults on superiors, and race riots dominated the classes. As a part of the curriculum, military lawyers and judges lectured for hours on the legal rights of the commander and the soldier.

Around the first of the year (1973), rumors spread that took care of any remaining hope for morale and motivation as students—another RIF was coming in the spring; this time it would include regular officers. All soldiers—professionals as well as recent recruits—soon learn that rumors and scuttlebutt are more often true than not, and are nearly always faster sources of information than official channels. Although experience had taught us to heed the rumor mill, few believed that our class would feel any great effects. After all, why would the army spend all that money getting us to Knox to kick out any appreciable number only a month before graduation?

On the day in early May when the RIF announcement was expected, I noticed that several of my classmates nervously checked their distribution boxes hourly. By our last class at 1600 hours, apprehension had subsided, as we decided that the RIF had either been postponed or, hopefully, canceled altogether. We were wrong. With the true sensitivity of the army and the armor school, our class was interrupted by a call on the intercom. The monotone voice stated that those on the list of names to follow should report immediately to the commandant's office. It did not take long to figure out the message that would then be delivered.

By the end of the announcement, one seat in five was empty. Fully 20 percent of the students were informed that they had been "fired" and had thirty days to prepare for discharge. None ever returned to the classroom. Later that night I ran into a friend in the club who was a "one in five." Still in a uniform that sported aviator wings, a Silver Star, and two Purple Hearts, he offered to buy me a drink. After a prolonged silence, he glanced at me with misting eyes hiding behind a smile as he said, "You know, I had two tours in Nam. Shot down once, wounded twice. God, how I loved the army. Goddamn me if I ever care about another job."

The RIF, and the way in which it was announced, left instructors facing students who paid little attention and participated even less. In an attempt to rouse a response, one instructor posed a question to one of the few battlefield-commissioned former NCOs who had survived the RIF. The officer slowly looked up from the newspaper he was reading. As his Combat Infantryman Badge sparkled over master parachute wings and five rows of ribbons topped by the Distinguished Service Cross (the second highest valor award), he responded, "Sir, you have me mixed up with someone else."

Somewhat taken aback the instructor replied, "No, Captain, I meant to call on you."

After a long pause, the former NCO looked over the top of his newspaper and said, "No, you have me mixed up with someone else—someone who gives a shit."

In the final weeks of the course the instructors chose not to press the issue, but even then they were not safe from abuse. Late in the afternoon on a warm spring day, as a quartermaster major droned on and on about supply rates and requisition procedures, a captain at the back of the classroom raised his hand. As it was by then unusual for anyone to comment or question, it was even more so for this particular individual to request recognition; I could not recall a single remark by him in front of the class in the preceding nine months.

Stories had circulated about this captain having been a "mouseketeer" on the old "Mickey Mouse Club" television show. He never confirmed or denied the rumors, and changed the subject anytime questioned about it. His red-haired, boyish looks and his freckles contrasted with the rows of combat ribbons on his chest; only his cold, penetrating eyes validated the symbols of heroism.

With a smile, our rear-service instructor called on the captain in anticipation of a question or comment on the fine class he thought he was teaching. He got neither. With a straight face and no hint of humor, the alleged former mouseketeer said, "Sir, it's a beautiful day. It's also my dog's birthday; he is two years old. Why don't we all go over to the club and celebrate— I'm sure we would get a hell of a lot more out of it than we are out of this class."

That pretty well ended the session, and although we did not go to the club to celebrate the canine's birthday, we did go home a bit early. My friend was later called to his faculty advisor's office for a counseling session. It made little difference, however, because even the old standby statement of "What can they do, send me to Vietnam?" was no longer appropriate.

Despite our situation—the lack of worth of the advanced course, the general feeling of having been sold out in Vietnam at the Paris conference tables, and out-and-out amazement that "our army" had kicked out fellow officers with no hint of remorse—most of us looked forward to getting back to troops and the "real" army. Assignment officers came from Washington several months before the end of the course to advise us and take requests for our next duty stations. They told us that captains who wanted immediate company command should volunteer for Europe. The RIF had hit hard there, leaving a shortage of captains throughout Germany.

In spite of the knowledge gained from five years in uniform and the notorious reputation of assignment officers for not recognizing—or even knowing the meaning of—truth, I bought the line. With a promise that I would be assigned to an infantry division, I signed up for the United States Army, Europe (USAREUR).

When my orders arrived a few weeks later, I discovered only part of my promised assignment had been met. I was going to Europe all right, but instead of an assignment to an infantry division where I could get command of a company and get back to troops, I was going to a staff job in the VII Corps Headquarters in Stuttgart. Making the assignment even worse was the notice that I would be assigned to the community commander's office—a "mayor's office" for U.S. military and dependents and a liaison between the American and German bureaucracies. After five years in the combat arms, I was doomed to join the ranks of the REMFs (rear echelon motherfuckers) whom I had grown to detest so in Vietnam.

My angry calls to Washington about the "promise" by my assignment officer brought only the explanation that I had already commanded an infantry company in combat. Command slots were being given to officers who had not yet had the opportunity to command a company and, therefore, needed the "ticket punch." The patronizing assignment pimp concluded by telling me, "Once you get to Germany, you'll be able to work yourself into a company."

Beyond slamming the phone receiver down, I made no final comment. I knew he was right—after I got to Europe, I could find a command. Men who wanted companies so that they could be with soldiers, rather than just to get a ticket punched, could always find work. After all, the army had been good to me so far, and I had no doubt that it would continue.

CHAPTER 2

PRELUDE TO COMMAND—VII CORPS AND PAYING DUES

July 1973–October 1974

The differences between going overseas to a war zone and journeying to a peacetime assignment were soon quite apparent—going to war was a hell of a lot easier. I had departed for Vietnam with a duffel bag containing a single change of clothes and a shaving kit. Going to peacetime Germany was not so simple.

In preparation for Europe, Linda and I had to determine what few items we and our daughters could not do without for the next three years—while remaining under the four-thousand-pound weight limit. Our other household items would have to go into storage. We had to get photos, passports, and various immunizations as well as decide how to get our car to a port in New Jersey for transport. Linda shopped for children's clothes for advancing ages, as several couples we had met at Fort Knox reported the difficulty in finding the proper items in the European post exchanges.

Other concerns also surfaced. In Vietnam, I had gotten by on less than fifty dollars a month; there had not been many places to spend money in the paddies and jungle. Facing rent on the German economy meant that our financial planning would have to be a little more regimented. Not helping at all was the devaluation of the dollar to the deutsche mark. In the last three months of our time in the States, in the spring of 1973, the conversion of DMs to dollars fell from 4.24-1 to 2.7-1; what a dollar had bought in Germany only months before now purchased only 65 percent of the same product or service. Defending freedom and democracy in Europe apparently had its price—and it was going up daily.

More bad news soon arrived from my new assignment headquarters. My request for concurrent travel—authorization for my family to accompany me—was denied. According to the letter, on-post quarters, as well as housing on the German economy, were in short supply. Families were not authorized travel until the sponsor arrived in-country and secured living accommodations. This news brought wonderment along with disappointment: wonderment was based on the knowledge that the U.S. Armed Forces had been sending families to Germany for nearly three decades—ample time to solve such basic problems as housing; as for disappointment, after six years of marriage, Linda and I had been together less than half of that time due to Vietnam, schools, and training exercises.

The denial of concurrent travel caused other difficulties in addition to separation. Although no quarters were available at my next assignment, our apartment at Fort Knox had to be vacated for a student in the next class. Fortunately, our daughters were not yet of school age, so transfer to new schools was not a problem. Linda and the girls would be forced to move in with her parents in West Texas until I found a place in Germany. This going back home was a typical solution for families of many of my classmates. As I'd had transfers every twelve to eighteen months and we were now enroute to Germany, buying a home or even considering a permanent residence was out of the question. We accepted living a vagabond existence as just another part of being a professional soldier and family.

My leave back home in West Texas before departing for Europe reminded me of the time I had spent there prior to going to Vietnam. If something did not concern weather, the church, or high-school football, it was of little concern or importance to the locals. Most had been able to avoid any contact with the war in Vietnam and were of the opinion that all the GIs had come home from Europe after World War II to enjoy parades and the adoration of the American public. Few realized or cared that American soldiers were still stationed in Germany. I suppose that where social life revolves around the local Dairy Queen, one could not expect much interest in my impending journey to Europe.

Regardless of the conditions at home, leave-time was most welcome and, like all vacations, came to an end much too soon. On July 14, 1973, I flew to McGuire Air Force Base, New Jersey, to catch a chartered civilian airliner. Despite the fact that the aircraft was owned and crewed by civilians, the air force was in charge of boarding and seating. In typical air force fashion, the passengers were allowed to sit for four hours in a waiting

room between the time of initial manifest call and final boarding. Actually, I suppose we were lucky. At other air bases and
strips around the world, I had joined fellow soldiers in waits of
six to eight hours before the boys in blue finally decided it was
all right for us to load.

Another great "advantage" of flying air force charters was
the throngs of children accompanying their mothers to join husbands who had also failed to receive concurrent travel. With
seats configured even closer together than on commercial air-
lines, and with each of those seats filled, no one could think of
anything good to say about the Military Airlift Command and
the United States Air Force.

We took off at dusk, but the night was short because we
crossed six time zones to meet the sunrise. At Rhein-Main Airport, near Frankfurt am Main, we were quickly placed on busses
and transported to the 21st Replacement Battalion. After a half-
hearted "Welcome to Germany" speech by a rumpled captain,
I met with a personnel NCO to confirm my assignment. Despite
diligent efforts to get my orders changed to an infantry division,
I soon found myself on the way to Stuttgart and VII Corps
Headquarters.

Meeting me at my new office was Capt. Domi Yacapin, whom
I was replacing. Domi, a decorated infantry veteran of Vietnam,
had been commissioned from the ranks through Officer Candidate School and was a victim of the most recent RIF. Born in
the Philippines, Domi was old enough to recall the Japanese
occupation during World War II. With an ironic laugh he related
that his most vivid memory of the period was of constant hun-
ger. According to Domi, during the entire occupation, he recalled only one meal with enough food for everyone in the
family. The disappearance of the family dog the day before the
feast had a connection not thoroughly understood by Domi until
years later.

Yacapin eventually had made his way to Hawaii, and it was
to the islands that he intended to return upon his discharge.
Somewhat bitter about his RIF, he turned down an opportunity
to revert to his precommissioning NCO rank. Despite his feelings about being "fired" as an officer, Domi was quick to admit
"that the army had been good" to him. With a grin he explained, "All I ever wanted out of the army—and out of life for
that matter—was a good-looking blonde and a fast car. I've married a blue-eyed, Nordic German girl and will drive out of the
service in a new Porsche fresh from the factory, so I guess that

this 'coconut head' has done all right for himself, considering the circumstances.'' But in a whisper, the RIFed captain concluded, "Still I'm going to miss it. I was a good soldier and officer. I paid my dues in combat, but I guess that doesn't really count anymore.''

Domi spent his last few days on active duty out-processing and showing me around my new home. The VII Corps Headquarters was located just south of Stuttgart in the village of Möhringen. Built in the late 1930s, it had served during World War II as a headquarters and coordination center for the various batteries of Nazi antiaircraft guns that took on allied aviators during bombing runs of the area.

My temporary quarters were on the second floor of the Kelley Officers Club. Though not overly comfortable or overfurnished, the room was at least well located. Complete with an Italian bartender, who had the uncanny knack of being able to remember everyone's favorite drink, the club bore distinct reminders of an earlier age. Above the entrance was a stone portal roughened by the removal of the swastika and eagle emblem of the Third Reich. Two heavy hooks, from which a large painting of Herr Hitler had once hung, were still in place above the main dining-room fireplace.

My initial reaction to my new assignment was not as positive as the assessment of my quarters. Everything I had ever heard about the actions of a senior headquarters appeared to be absolutely true. Day-to-day activities were characterized by a total lack of urgency. Except for uniforms and tape-recorded bugle calls, the headquarters could easily have passed for the corporate offices of a branch of any large overseas U.S. firm—or for one back in the States for that matter.

My new boss, Col. Theodore C. Biel, fit well into the nonmilitary facade. Biel's first tour in Europe had been nearly a quarter century earlier when he was assigned as a lieutenant in the occupation forces at the end of World War II. Since that time, Biel had transferred from armor to the chemical corps, somehow avoided the unpleasantness of the Korean Conflict, and managed to "homestead" at his alma mater—the United States Military Academy—as an instructor for more than ten years. He had only left West Point to go to Vietnam during the last year of U.S. involvement so he could get his "ticket punched" as a prerequisite for his promotion to bird colonel. Biel was a brilliant, intellectual officer who was quite gifted as a writer—all great characteristics, but unfortunately, not enough to make up for his total lack of leadership, military bearing, and tact. The colonel had spent so long as an instructor that anything outside the classroom was no longer familiar to him. Theory was his forte, reality a stranger.

Our shared office seemed about as foreign to my idea of the "real" army as was Biel. The office of the community commander was an organization new to the U.S. Army in Europe, duplicated nowhere else on the globe. Its stated purpose was to "coordinate all military activities within the community, regardless of commands, and to improve the quality of life for soldiers and family members."

The origin of our organization was to be found in recent lengthy studies which had noted the poor living conditions and the army's apparent lack of concern for soldiers and families. The office of the community commander was to alleviate that situation by crossing command and installation lines to coordinate overall efforts to improve the quality of life—housing, post exchanges, commissaries, recreation facilities, and information sources. Indeed, our function was similar to that of a mayor's office in a metropolitan city back home.

Although the new organization had inherent problems as well as obvious merits, its principal strength was the community commander himself, George S. Blanchard. With the three stars of a lieutenant general on his collar and as the highest ranking U.S. officer in southern Germany, he saw that we received the proper support for the program, which he originated.

Nevertheless, and without regard for whatever interesting aspects the assignment might offer, at each stop during the corps in-processing procedure, I let it be known that I wanted a transfer to an infantry unit as soon as possible. The personnel managers, or "manglers" as they were not-so-affectionately known, were somewhat encouraging, saying, "Do well on the staff and we will get you a company in eighteen months or so." They also mixed their comments with outspoken doubts about my sanity. The "eight to five—or less" corps staff was considered to be one of the cushiest positions in Europe, and the local warriors were amazed that anyone would want to go to where they called "down range."*

---

*"Down range" is the area forward of the firing line on a live-fire range. To the typical staff officer, anyone wanting to go down range was obviously reckless, naive, or just plain dumb. I, perhaps, was guilty of all three charges.

Lack of appreciation and respect for line service was not all that I discovered was different about the occupants of higher staffs. I had been with the 82d Airborne Division as a paratrooper, the 199th Light Infantry Brigade as a platoon leader and company commander in combat, and the army's Ranger School as an instructor; life at the corps level, however, was an entirely new experience. For the first time during my service, I was working with service and support officers and NCOs* who shared the benefits but little of the danger and hardships of combat soldiers. Many of them seemed to see the army as a job similar to industry or a business—dealing with statistics and paper—rather than a profession of arms confronting blood and death.

While my new job was providing daily—and at times, hourly—disappointment, not everything was going wrong. With assistance from the local housing-referral office, I was able to find an apartment in a village only a few kilometers from the main gate. Except for the initial surprise that "unfurnished" means just that in Germany—no closets, light fixtures or any other "frill" beyond walls and floors—the apartment appeared comfortable.

Once I had secured quarters, the army officially granted me permission to bring my family over from the States. In typical army fashion, however, the paperwork, flight scheduling, and various notifications would add several more weeks to the separation before Linda and our daughters would be able to begin their journey.

Meanwhile, I was finding that the work of a staff officer followed generally the same procedures as other assignments. I spent much of my time writing and coordinating staff papers which were teletyped to the subordinate units and/or subcommunities. My first effort to write a directive in message format produced unusual results. As was frequently the case, Biel was absent when I finished drafting the message, so I just sent it to the corps command group. A few hours later I received a call from the command group secretary saying that Brig. Gen. Allan Toffler, the assistant corps commander, wanted to see me. Since

---

*Combat support and combat service support are all those branches of the army other than infantry, armor, and artillery. To most good infantrymen, even the latter two branches are support arms, since everything in the army exists to support the infantryman.

it was my experience that generals rarely deal with captain staff officers, I thought that an ass chewing would be awaiting me.

Toffler, a tall, thin, graying man with a thin mustache—rare for a general officer—politely but firmly informed me that my message was a disaster and there was no way he would approve its release. I responded with the only acceptable answer, "Yes, sir." Toffler then pulled a chair up beside his desk and told me to sit down. For the next thirty minutes, he rewrote the message with his red pen, explaining as he went why he was making various changes, additions, and deletions. The brief one-on-one session taught me more than nine months of the advanced course and won my respect for a man who would take time to teach rather than criticize.

A short time later I had another interesting experience with General Toffler. I had arranged for him to welcome new soldiers and their families at Panzer Kaserne in the nearby subcommunity of Böblingen. On behalf of the local Germans, a city official by the name of Dr. Kramer made a few remarks. His heavily accented English had lost most of the crowd's attention until he mentioned that during the same week twenty-nine years earlier, he had been a young lieutenant in a Wehrmacht tank unit preparing to counterattack the allies at what would later be known as the Battle of the Bulge.

Toffler followed the German and with a smile remarked, "Sir, I did not know that we had met before today. You see, twenty-nine years ago I also was a lieutenant and was serving as an artillery forward observer in the Ardennes Forest where the brunt of your attack took place."

Following the welcoming ceremony, the two old soldiers talked for a few minutes before returning to their duties. I was fortunate to overhear their conversation, which ended with both acknowledging that their second meeting had been much more pleasant than the first.*

Another major portion of my duties was establishing liaison with the various German civic and community leaders in the

---

*A few months later Toffler failed to be selected for promotion to major general and shortly thereafter retired from active duty. Despite the fact that everyone in the army, save the chief of staff, eventually gets passed over for promotion, I wondered at the time, and still do today, why Toffler did not get his second star. Perhaps, it was his mustache, or maybe it was that he was the kind of officer who would take time to teach a young captain how to write a message properly.

Greater Stuttgart area. This ranged from hard work to harder play. As for work, there was much to do in setting up meetings, putting together "talking papers" to prepare the participants before they met, and arranging for translators of conversation and documents. Typical of most such diplomatic maneuvering, the meetings were scripted through the entire agenda. Everything was agreed upon beforehand, including who would say what, when, to whom, and what decisions would be made. The briefing packets were often six to eight inches thick for a meeting as short as an hour.

A meeting between the corps commander and the mayor of Stuttgart, for instance, took several months of preparation. Briefing papers for the general were almost identical to those prepared for the mayor by his staff. Opening and closing statements were written and continually revised until they included marks for where to pause for translation. The key to success was that there be no surprises for general or mayor. If it was not in the premeeting briefing packet, it did not and, more important, would not exist.

The fun part of such tedious tasks was the fact that it was impossible to conduct any meeting with the Germans without beer, wine, and schnapps flowing freely. Most business was accomplished in the morning, and adjournment to the nearest *gasthaus* followed, generally, at noon. The lunch of too much wurst, bread, and booze occasionally lasted through dinner and on into the late evening. It was a given in the office that if we went to lunch with the locals, we would not return until late that afternoon and that if we did make an appearance, we would be worthless the remainder of the day.

In today's army, such drinking and partying during duty hours is extremely frowned upon. During the early 1970s in Europe, it not only had official approval but also had official funding so we could return the favors of our German hosts.

I was fairly familiar with my new job and with the local environs by the time Linda and our two daughters finally arrived. After a thirty-hour trip with a baby in arms and a three-year-old on a short leash, Linda looked as if air force charters were no better for dependents than for soldiers. I made a brief protest about my firstborn being on a dog leash but quickly learned that it is not wise to question the decisions of someone who has just completed a transcontinental, transoceanic flight with two small children.

Over the next months, Linda and I would have the opportunity to see much of Germany, Western Europe, and a few points beyond. Always short of time, and usually money, we made a maximum effort to take advantage of our location. We soon developed a routine—seeing local sites on weekends and taking advantage of every minute of three-day holidays. Either leaving the girls with friends or taking them with us, we could be on a train within an hour of the end of the duty day and arrive at places like Paris, Zurich, or Vienna the next morning. After three days of frantically seeing the sights, we would board another train or bus at the last possible moment to get us back home in time to change clothes and make it to work.

Every two or three months I would take a week's leave, and we would extend out travels to places like Italy, Spain, and North Africa. We did our best to see and do everything and usually arrived home exhausted and broke.

Despite the travel opportunities and fraternizing with the Germans, I continued to miss the infantry. All I could get from the personnel folks was advice to be patient. That was difficult at times, because despite the relatively relaxed atmosphere at VII Corps, the rest of the world was not so peaceful. The first shots of the Arab-Israeli War had not ceased to echo before U.S. troops all across Europe were placed on full alert. But, except for causing a muster to confirm off-duty telephone numbers, the war had little direct impact on the corps staff warriors other than to serve as a reminder of the real world beyond the gates of Kelley Barracks.

Over the next weeks we closely followed the war's progress through the corps's classified message center and through AFN (Armed Forces Network) radio and *Stars and Stripes* (the army's official newspaper). As usual, the latter two were generally more current and often more accurate than the official sources. Ultimately, a major impact of the war was the worldwide gasoline shortage. While the folks back home had to cope with high prices and long lines, we in Europe had to deal with those irritants and a driving ban on Sundays. The first day of the week meant stay at home, take a walk, read a book, or find some other activity. With no delivery of an American newspaper or English-language television, even more than usual Sundays did not resemble what we had known back in the States. Of course there were ways to pass the day. I wonder if anyone ever did a study to see if the birthrate made a sudden jump about nine months after the no-drive rule.

After about six weeks of the carless Sundays, the rule was modified to allow cars with an even/odd last digit on its license plates to drive on alternate Sundays. Since a close friend had evens while I had odds, our transportation problems improved.

One aspect of the community commander's office that made it a bit more tolerable—at times even enjoyable—was Colonel Biel's avoidance of staff meetings. An interesting characteristic of the colonel was that, by his own admission, he never shined his shoes unless he was in trouble with his boss. Despite the fact that his shoes usually glistened while I worked for him, Biel nonetheless did his best to avoid large meetings—particularly the weekly corps staff meeting. Sent in his stead, I was frequently the junior attendee at the gathering of colonels and generals.

Although I am not much on meetings myself, the opportunity did offer insights into the corps and its leaders not usually available to a lowly captain. One thing I quickly learned was how to judge the feelings of the corps commander, Lieutenant General Blanchard. The general seemed to have the respect of his staff for more than just the stars that he wore. His genuine caring about his soldiers and his logical, unemotional decision-making were impressive. The only indicator that the general was upset or was losing his patience was when he took his pipe (those were the days before the near zealous avoidance of tobacco by the military in offices and meetings) and tapped it against his West Point ring to loosen the ashes. A good indication of his mood was the strength and the frequency of the taps.

The "Biel-less" staff meetings also provided me a detailed look into the discipline, morale, and training of the corps's subordinate infantry division, armor division, separate infantry brigade, cavalry regiment, and various support units. Since no combat troops were assigned to Kelley Barracks, and the corps support troops who lived there were relatively handpicked, we staff officers had little or no day-to-day knowledge of what was going on in the line units. Briefings and reports delivered at the weekly staff meeting by the corps provost marshal, surgeon, and drug and alcohol prevention officer offered unique insights into what was going on in the field units.

While I was well aware of the impact of the shrinking dollar on my personal finances, its effect on younger, lower ranking soldiers—especially those with families—was particularly critical. From across the corps area, we received reports that many enlisted soldiers were sending their families back to the States and were moving back into the troop barracks. Married and single soldiers alike were selling their cars because of the increase in the cost of fuel and insurance since the dollar bought fewer deutsche marks.

Drug abuse by U.S. troops was on the increase all across Germany. Most critical was the increased use of heroin—not only was the corps suffering casualties from the drug itself but also from the nearly two thousand cases of hepatitis in the first half of 1973 caused by the use and sharing of dirty needles.

Racial incidents among Americans and between U.S. soldiers and German civilians mounted in number and intensity. Reports ranged from isolated one-on-one occurrences to full-scale riots requiring military police and local law-enforcement officials.

Many of these problems were not only characteristic of the army in Europe at the time; they were common on the streets back home. As with all other periods of military history, the army merely reflected the society from which its soldiers came. Social problems manifested themselves in the isolation, loneliness, and financial difficulties of an army six thousand miles from home.

Complicating the situation was the end of the draft.* Although the sons of the Ivy League crowd, moneyed families, and influential citizens were able to avoid conscription, the system had still provided a fairly equitable cross section of young men. Now the army faced filling its ranks with all volunteers (it would be termed VOLAR, for "volunteer army").

Even without the draft, the army continued to be a mirror image of the society that provided its members. The only problem was that now instead of reflecting all facets of the population, the mirror reflected only the bottom of society. Under great pressure to make their quotas, recruiters had to take whom they could get and often signed up ex-offenders, the medically impaired, and the mentally or educationally deficient. In their search for "volunteers," recruiters sought out judges who would

---

*Since conscription had first been authorized by President Abraham Lincoln during the Civil War, more than 17.5 million men had been drafted into the American Army. History does not note the name of the first draftee, but according to military recruiters of the 1970s, the last official conscriptee was Dwight E. Stone of Sacramento, California, who was inducted on June 30, 1973.

propose jail-or-the-army deals in their courtrooms and high-school counselors who could refer potential dropouts to their offices. Recruiters did what was necessary to keep the induction centers filled.

By mid-1973, fully 30 percent of the enlistees were from the bottom 25 percent (called Cat—for category—IVs) of intelligence scores. Even during the height of the Vietnam War, the number of Cat IVs—volunteers or draftees—was kept to a minimum. While the U.S. population was then about 12 percent black, in the all-volunteer army, blacks were 35 percent, and 40 percent of army volunteers were minority members.

Discussion about drug abuse, racial unrest, poor quality of recruits, and the financial difficulties of living in Germany dominated staff-meeting and officer-club gatherings alike. Yet the official army was not yet ready to face up to the facts. Army personnel chief, Lt. Gen. Bernard Rogers in the summer of 1973 sent a message to his subordinate personnel managers worldwide, directing them to "quit bad-mouthing Europe." In a letter to the military personnel center, Rogers explained that he wanted more attention paid to seeking volunteers for Europe. The general also lamented that the press was giving service in Germany a bad name by discussing drug and racial problems and the rising cost of living.*

The recurring problems naturally led to an increase in crimes of various types and severity. Concern about serious incidents—murder, arson, aggravated assault, rape, armed robbery—was the subject of the most interesting staff meeting I attended for the absent Colonel Biel. Statistics gathered by the corps provost marshal indicated an increase in the rate of serious incidents and that the local German government was demanding something be done to protect its citizens. The corps commander opened the meeting by mentioning his concern about the mounting rate of serious crime. He emphasized the impact not only on relations with the Germans but also on the general poor state of morale and discipline in the corps. As a captain, and the lowest-ranking person in the room, I remained quiet and listened as

---

*Rogers's techniques of talking away a problem or of ignoring it altogether were apparently successful methods of operation. They might not have done anything to help the situation, but they apparently assisted the general in realizing his own ambitions. Rogers went on from personnel chief to four stars, chief of staff of the army, and, incredibly, commander in chief of all NATO forces.

the colonels and generals discussed the issue, searching for possible solutions. After about an hour of much talk and little agreement, a graying, obviously past-his-prime colonel took the floor. His solution to the increasing rate of serious incidents was simple. "Sir," he began, "I suggest that we rewrite the criteria of what we define as a serious incident and throw out a few of the categories like aggravated assault or rape—that should bring the rate down."

At first I thought the colonel was joking and almost laughed. Fortunately, I suppressed it; unfortunately, the colonel was serious. Gen. Blanchard apparently did not embrace the colonel's idea nor share my sense of humor. With a look of perplexity, the general soundly rapped his pipe against his academy ring, and dismissed the meeting. Of course, I was not privy to what Blanchard might have said to the colonel after our dismissal. I did observe a continuing increase in the rate of serious incidents over the next months but no change in our criteria for defining them.

As with any army assignment—staff or unit—what made work bearable at the office of the community commander was the people. Without a doubt, no other job or profession anywhere brings together people of such diverse origins and experiences. From the colorful and flamboyant, to the shy and reserved; from the winners with futures, to the worthless with pasts; there is no greater melting pot than the United States Army.

Though the office of the community commander was a miniscule portion of the army, it, too, provided a sampling of interesting characters. Biel, idiosyncratic in his own right, and I were initially the only office occupants. The staff grew when General Blanchard decided to establish an army community services (ACS) center. This organization, headed by an officer and operated by volunteer wives, would provide loan-closet assistance for new arrivals, food-locker resources for the needy, emergency loans, and information programs. Blanchard directed the personnel manager to secure an ACS officer to head the new center.

Orders were soon cut, and for two months we awaited our new ACS expert from the Stateside replacement pipeline. We made plans for his arrival and promised the various wives' clubs on the post that all their requests would be taken care of "when the ACS officer arrives." His arrival seemed to offer the solution to all present and future problems.

I suppose I should not have been surprised when the ACS officer arrived without any idea what his job was. He did not even have a clue what ACS stood for. Capt. Frederick G. Wong, like myself, was an infantry officer who had volunteered for Europe to get back to troops. Instead, Fred found himself on the corps staff in charge of forty volunteer wives. He also found lines of soldiers and their dependents needing all types of assistance. After hearing the personnel manager's refrain, "Do a good job, and we will get you to a unit in eighteen months," Fred accepted his temporary fate and began finding his way around the office and learning the nuances of being in charge of the ACS.

Wong, a native Hawaiian of Chinese descent, was an immediate asset at work and a good friend off duty. Blending an excellent sense of humor with stereotypical inscrutability, Fred was equally adept with staff papers and with people. Operating under the philosophy—which he repeated at least a dozen times a day—of "Whatever's fair," he could always be depended upon to make timely, sound decisions. Calm in practically every situation, one of the few things that irritated Fred was his official record which classified him as a member of a minority: Wong was quick to point out that Chinese was not a minority but rather the world's majority race.*

Rounding out the office's personnel were individuals who were fairly typical of the army of the early 1970s. Hired to work in our office was the wife of a young soldier who was assigned to the corps headquarters transportation company. A veteran of a previous marriage with two small children, she offered excellent office skills and a cheerful attitude toward work.

Despite her demonstrated abilities, there were detractors to her overall proficiency. The usual difficulties of a new marriage were compounded by the declining dollar, extreme distance from friends and family, and the ready availability of drugs of all types. That things were not going well at home for our office worker were first indicated by bruises on her face that did not come from running into a door. Eventually her hus-

---

*Despite much maligning, the army's way of advancement has its proven merits. In fact, nice guys do not necessarily finish last. Fred Wong (with successive assignments and promotions in the infantry after leaving the office of the community commander) was selected for advancement to brigadier general in September, 1989.

band volunteered for referral to a drug rehabilitation program.

As the responsibilities of our office grew, so did our staff. We were soon assigned two enlisted soldiers trained in the military operational specialty (MOS) of 71B (clerk-typist). The first to arrive, PFC Mark Bishop was a long way from his small-town, midwestern upbringing in Keokuk, Iowa. Intelligent and a good worker during duty hours, Bishop was frequently found at the wrong place at the wrong time once the bugle had blown retreat. Caught up in a barracks racial brawl, he reported to work one morning with multiple knife cuts on his face and arms. A few weeks later, Mark was rolled up in a crackdown on drug dealers and found himself arrested by the military police. But the MP investigators were apparently convinced that he had been an innocent bystander, who had no idea that the others with him were buying, selling, or dealing. Somehow Mark was able to consistently stay out of real trouble while constantly romancing the narrow edge between the good, the bad—and the caught.

The second enlisted clerk in the office did his best to emulate Mort Walker's cartoon character, Beetle Bailey. PFC Larry Dickerson had attended the University of Texas, but when his grades slipped, he came to the unwanted attention of his local selective-service board. Although he had a good sense of humor and was generally respectful to those who outranked him, Dickerson was convinced that the only way to strike back at the draft was to do the minimum work necessary to stay out of major trouble. Larry yearned to return to the Austin campus life, and he was quick to tell anyone, whether we had heard it many times before or not, that "the army will never be all volunteer until they let me out."

Rounding out the office staff was SFC Ralph Norris as the NCO in charge (NCOIC). I assisted in his assignment to our office, and that later paid great—if unexpected—personal dividends. Norris had had difficulties with a former boss in the corps's adjutant general section. Knowing that sergeants always lose conflicts with majors, Ralph had sought another job before he was in his old one long enough to get an efficiency rating. My assisting Norris had been no great favor because he proved to be an excellent worker and supervisor of the enlisted men.

By the summer of 1974, I was nearing the completion of my first year in Germany. Despite the many difficulties of adapting to living in a foreign country on an extremely limited budget and to a job I did not want, the months had gone fairly quickly. The regular hours of corps-staff duty and the frequent socializing with the Germans, combined with visits to nearby countries, had made the year tolerable.

In spite of several disappointments and some downright disasters, I could reflect with some satisfaction at the accomplishments of the office of the community commander. During the twelve months, we had made significant progress in improving the quality of life for the soldiers and their families in the Greater Stuttgart area. In addition to establishing the ACS, we were now publishing a weekly community newspaper, had increased the hours of post exchanges and commissaries, built a launderette, added lighting to housing complexes and high-crime areas, and written and coordinated a long-range plan that would continue to make improvements as funding became available over the next five years.

Many of the improvements were the direct result of General Blanchard's involvement. I was quickly learning that what Three Stars wants, Three Stars gets—regardless of bureaucracy or the lack of resources. A prime example of the problems we were facing and how the general was able to force solutions was in the "Master Five-Year Construction Plan."

Major construction projects—defined as those that cost more than $100,000—were approved five years before any work actually began. Each subcommunity and unit submitted a list of proposed projects to our office, where, with help from the regional engineers, they were assigned a priority. The system seemed quite simple at first glance; the problem was that it was too simple. My first Five-Year Construction Plan board meeting was short. We listed and ranked the community's top fifty projects only to learn from the engineers that sufficient funds were available for only one project. The other forty-nine proposals would have to wait another year for the slim possibility that they might eventually be funded to begin a half decade later.

Another problem with the "simple" procedures behind the five-year concept was that previous plans—devised during the height of the Vietnam War—were still on line for funding. Not only were we getting further behind in the present year, we were doing nothing to make up for the ten years of negligence in housekeeping of the United States Army in Europe. Compounding our frustration was that the single project for which we did have approval was to build and illuminate a motor pool for a unit that was no longer assigned to the area. Five-year plans may

make sense in ivy-walled business schools and might possibly
have some application in a long-term peacetime army, but in the
constant change of a military transitioning from war to an un-
easy peace, they had little practical use.

Fortunately, Three Stars came to the rescue. Rather than build
an unneeded project, the funds approved for the motor pool
were applied to the building of sidewalks in highly trafficked
housing areas, troop barracks, and the various service facilities,
as well as for lighting in areas where darkness had fostered crime
and drug sales.

Enough money was left over to build a security fence around
a storage area and vehicle park, which had required six guards
each night and additional personnel on weekends. As fulfilled,
the project was on none of the master plans; it surfaced when
Blanchard had asked a private during a visit to a unit how to
best improve his quality of life. The young soldier replied that
he thought it was a waste of his and his buddies' time to guard
a site that could just as easily be secured with a fence. Three
Stars agreed. The fence was built in short order.

Progress and minor victories notwithstanding, I continued
to lobby the personnel office to be reassigned to the infantry.
Prospects were promising until a series of events conspired to
delay me further. Biel put in for retirement; Wong, selected for
promotion to major, transferred; and Blanchard decided to reorganize and relocate the office of the community commander.

Blanchard's decision to combine two 0–6 level (colonel) commands into one headquarters left a colonel and his staff with
nothing to do. The general saw this as an excellent opportunity
to expand the community commander's staff and to take on even
greater problems and challenges. As the only remaining member of the office with any experience, I would be responsible for
ensuring a smooth transition. Because Kelley Barracks had no
room for an augmented staff, the new office of the community
commander would be at Robinson Barracks (RB) on the northern edge of Stuttgart—nearly an hour's commute through the
heart of the city. I dreaded the daily drive, and feared the new
job would jeopardize my chance of getting back to the infantry.
However, much to my relief, my request for transfer was finally
approved, and I was expected to fulfill my new duties for only
ninety days.

More good news awaited me when I reported to Robinson
Barracks. The new deputy community commander—my new

boss—Col. Jack C. Woods was a level-headed gentleman, not long separated from the field artillery and the real army. Woods seemed to respect the expertise I had developed during fourteen months in the community commander business, and he completed winning me over when he assured me that he would support my impending transfer.

Other perks went with the new job location. In addition to a much larger office, I was assigned my own personal secretary—a stunning Australian woman. Although she had no experience working for the military, she had worked as a government employee in Australia before she and her husband had come to Europe on a year-long holiday. The vacation was curtailed when their car was totaled in an accident, and the couple took jobs and decided to view their extended stay on the continent as an adventure.

In addition to her wonderful accent and quite Australian name, Dawn Toddhunter, my new assistant, was a fantastic typist, office organizer, and project coordinator. I was not at all surprised to learn that upon my departure, Ms. Toddhunter would move to the front office to work for Colonel Woods.

As with most situations in the army, the good is always accompanied by the bad. Along with other extraordinary office staff, I was assigned an experienced military office clerk—unfortunately, none of his experience had anything to do with being an office worker or a good soldier. A hard-core drug abuser as a civilian, the young man had continued his habits after joining the service, using everything from airplane glue to heroin. Nearing his separation date, the soldier assured me that he was clean and would stay that way—at least until he got an honorable discharge.

Quite open about what he called his "former use," he frequently told stories about the ease of securing drugs on U.S. installations and on the German economy. According to the soldier, it was not uncommon for troops to extend their tours so that they could stay near the "candy store" of drug availability. With a laugh, he would add that all that was behind him—despite the still-distinct needle scars on his arms—and that all he really missed were the LSD trips. With great animation, he would describe former visits to the local produce market to admire the hues and symmetry of oranges, apples, and other fruits and vegetables while tripping on LSD. Sadly, beyond telling drug stories, the soldier was virtually useless for anything but the simplest tasks. His brain was so fried from acid and other drugs that his attention span was minimal and his ability to learn new skills nonexistent. In this case, America's finest was no more than a washed-up former junkie—and the "former" was in some doubt.

With Three Stars's backing, the expanded community staff assumed more responsibility in coordinating and managing all aspects of troop and dependent support in the Greater Stuttgart area. In a matter of weeks we were consolidating our community-action plans and exporting our quality-of-life improvement models to other communities in VII Corps.

Now with a staff of more than a dozen to accomplish what formerly Wong and I had been responsible for, I was quickly able to work myself out of a job. With less to do and more time in which to do it, I began to look for additional duties to pass the time. One interesting extra duty was a monthly inventory of the criminal investigation division (CID) evidence room. Containing items from crimes under investigation, at trial, or under appeal, the tightly secured room contained more than five hundred numbered exhibits in bins, racks, and lockers.

The warrant officer in charge of the room and I began with a serial-number inventory of the various pistols, revolvers, shotguns, rifles, machine guns, and automatic rifles. Each weapon came with a story—one used by a GI to kill his wife and her boyfriend, another used to rob and kill a German taxi driver, still another relieved from a drug runner. Other weapons included knives, brass knuckles, straight razors, and improvised clubs ranging from iron pipes to wooden table legs—the latter stained with blood and embedded with bits of hair and flesh.

Next on our checklist were lockers containing drug-case evidence. Hash and heroin had been confiscated by the gram and by kilo, and pills of all types ranged from pouches of a few to bags of thousands. Most interesting were kilos of hash wrapped in aluminum foil, with logos imbedded in the bricks. The evidence agent identified the design of various Turkish manufacturers reputed to distribute only the very best.

Alongside the drugs was a safe containing plastic bags of cash ranging from $100 to $10,000. All totaled, we counted in excess of a quarter-million dollars that had been confiscated in less than six months. I found myself wondering. If the CID, which had no great reputation as crime busters, could catch so many pushers with so much money, how many and how much were still out there?

We saved the physical-evidence lockers for last. Airtight plastic bags could not completely contain the odor of blood-soaked clothing and other personal effects. Although it certainly would have been much easier to merely count the bags and consider the inventory completed, we followed the procedures and opened all the bags to compare the contents with the list provided for each.

After a day lasting long past retreat, the inventory was complete. Fortunately, everything tallied. It had made for a memorable day—both because of what I had seen and the better understanding I had about the wave of drugs and crime across the U.S. Army in Europe.

Despite promises, I still had no official ticket out of my present job by the end of the summer of 1974. Then I was informed that I had an interview with the commander of the 3d Infantry Division's 1st Brigade in Schweinfurt on September 13. Schweinfurt and neighboring Bamberg shared the reputation of being the least friendly cities and the worst places in Germany to be assigned. Even so, I was happy with the news because I knew that for two primary reasons subordinate commands rarely protested the assignment of officers from higher-level staffs—first, line units were always short of their authorized numbers, and second, ambitious brigade commanders did not usually say no to corps commanders' recommendations.

After interviews with the brigade commander and two infantry battalion commanders, I was informed that I would be welcomed. I was not going to question their decision, whatever their reasons. My exact reporting date and unit assignment would depend on the corps personnel officer cutting orders. All I could do was return to Stuttgart and wait.

Also coordinated during my visit to Schweinfurt were the plans for me to attend the two-week USAREUR Company Commander's Course at the Vilseck Combined Arms Training Center in early October. Offered as a refresher on subjects taught—or subjects that should have been taught but were not—at the advanced course and for procedures and regulations specific to Europe, the classes were generally well done. I am certain that some of my appreciation for the course came from my immediate need for the information. Still, the ten days of classes taught me more than the entire nine months of the advanced course had. I was reminded again of the uselessness of the army officer-school system, because one more time I had seen that unit-schools are far more useful than the attempt to take non-academic subjects into classroom disciplines.

In the Company Commander's Course we reviewed mainte-nance records and procedures, personnel administration, and supply operations. Of real interest were the sessions instructed by lawyers and military police on legal requirements of search and seizure, health-and-welfare inspections, and administrative and judicial punishments and procedures. The only thing that detracted from our appreciation of otherwise good information was the apparent neurotic need for each instructor to remind us that our chances of successful command were less than fifty-fifty. They warned us that we would be relieved for cause, re-ceive low efficiency reports, and likely see our careers thrown on the growing garbage heap of those who attempted to lead troops in peacetime, post-Vietnam Germany.

The MPs talked about the frequency of assault on and ha-rassment of company commanders by unhappy soldiers. They recommended we locate desks near windows for quick escape in case of fraggings. They also showed us how to check our cars for bombs and booby traps.

The Vilseck classes* proved useful not only for the infor-mation they offered but also for the sobering insight they provided into discipline and morale levels. In addition, the school provided us the opportunity to meet and exchange ideas with thirty-five other captains who were soon to take command.

I returned to Stuttgart from Vilseck with only one obstacle blocking my infantry assignment—I still did not have official orders in hand. Daily phone calls to the personnel office assured me that the orders would be cut any day. Word from Schweinfurt that I would be going to the 1st Brigade's 2d Battalion, 30th Infantry, was encouraging, but I was well aware that without hard-copy orders promises did not mean a move.

*The worst part of the Company Commander Course was its location. Vilseck is in a drab, remote portion of Germany, surrounded primarily by the Grafenwöhr and Hohenfels firing and maneuver ranges. The USAREUR staff had recently moved the instruction from Oberammergau in southern Baveria—home of the world famous passion play and one of Europe's most scenic regions. Beyond expending training funds that were already in short supply, the move accomplished little. Officially, the transfer was conducted to consolidate assets; unofficially, it was known to all that several senior officers had complained about the luxurious surroundings provided mere captains in Oberammergau.

My concern proved to be well-founded. On my way home from Robinson Barracks in mid-October, I heard an AFN radio newscast announcing an immediate freeze for in-theater transfers because of a cutback in transportation funds. I immediately drove to Kelley Barracks in hopes that my orders had been signed before the deadline. The personnel office was already closed for the day when I arrived.

I had been in the army long enough to expect the unexpected, and I was well aware that the needs of the service are far more important than those of the individual. Knowing that did little to lessen my disappointment, however. The irony was that I was not attempting to get a cush assignment or get out of a difficult one. All I wanted to do was go down range and do the things that I had stayed in the army to do. When I found the personnel office closed, I decided to go to the club to at least soak my troubles in drink. On the way I noticed the post theater was open. I entered to escape into the fantasy and darkness of whatever was showing.

While I waited for the movie to begin, SFC Ralph Norris—whom I had helped change jobs months before—walked down the isle and slid into the seat beside me. When the community commanders's office transferred to Robinson Barracks, Norris had remained at Kelley, and I was not sure where he had been reassigned. After a brief greeting as he sat down, he said, "I thought I saw your car outside. I've got something you might like to see."

He handed me a piece of paper. Even as I unfolded it, I could see the magic words, "Following reassignment directed: Individual will procede no later than 19 October 1974 to 1st Brigade, 3d Infantry Division, Schweinfurt, Federal Republic of Germany." At the top of the page were my name and, more importantly, the date of the day before—twenty-four hours before the transfer freeze was effective.

I let out a loud "Yes!" and waved a clenched fist in the air to the amusement and curiosity of the other movie patrons. Norris explained, "I started working in the personnel office a few weeks ago and saw your request for orders. Through the good-old NCO grapevine, I heard about the freeze coming, dug your request out of the pile, and hand carried them through. Got them signed a few minutes before we received the official freeze message."

I mumbled thanks to Norris, skipped the movie, and headed

home. The incident reminded me of two things. First, favors never go unrepaid in the army. Second, if something needs doing, finding a good sergeant is the answer.

CHAPTER 3

ASSUMPTION OF COMMAND— THE BATTLES OF PEACE, FIRST SHOTS

November 1974

Who hath not served cannot command.

First Fruits
John Florio, 1578

On the morning of November 29, 1974, I assumed command of Company A, 2d Battalion, 30th Infantry, 1st Brigade, 3d Infantry Division.* The ceremony took place during a battalion formation, accompanied by the division band. Family members and staff officers from senior commands made up the sparse audience. Proceedings took place indoors in a cavernous gymnasium because of gusty winds and intermittent snow flurries. Such accommodation was made not for the infantrymen in formation but rather for the family members and uniformed dignitaries in the stands.

Along with A Company, the battalion's headquarters company and Charlie Company changed command at the same time. While much of my overt patriotism and misplaced sentimentalities had been lost or at least forgotten on battlefields in Vietnam, I nevertheless felt a great sense of pride while the band played the national anthem and finally, finally the company guidon passed into my hands. A lump in my throat accompanied an acute awareness of the huge responsibilities now on my shoulders.

Six years earlier, I had assumed command of my first rifle

---

*Organization, mission, and capabilities of the company and battalion are detailed in Appendix A as well as in the following chapters. Specifically, the company and battalion, as parts of the brigade and division, were charged with being ready to defend a line along the East and West German border against an attack by the Warsaw Pact.

company. With sixteen months in the army and less than five months in grade as a first lieutenant, my primary qualification for the job had been that I had survived six months as an infantry and reconnaissance platoon leader in combat. While experience and survival were no small feat, they certainly could not make up for the captain's rank and years of experience expected of a peacetime commander.

In combat, experienced junior leaders are always in short supply. There had been no weeks of Company Commander Course or months of advanced course training before taking command in Vietnam. Although I had been told several weeks prior that I might get a company, when the time came, I had only a few hours warning before I was in command and leading well over one hundred infantrymen in the jungle against the VC and NVA.

Since that time I had learned—and relearned—that everything moves at a much slower, more complacent, bureaucratic pace when no real bullets are in the air. Well over a month passed between the time I received my transfer orders and the time I actually had been passed the company guidon. Weeks of out-processing in Stuttgart were followed by days in-processing in Schweinfurt. In addition to briefings at my new duty station, I again had to attend an eighteen-hour race relations seminar and a forty-hour German language course—both duplicates of classes mandatory when I arrived at Kelley Barracks.

Another difference between assuming command in peacetime and during war was not really all that bad—my family would be able to join me in Schweinfurt. Of course, because of the usual military paperwork drills, that was not as easy as it might seem. Despite the fact that I merited priority for on-post housing because I was in a command position, the wait for vacant quarters was still to be nearly a month.

The first few weeks in Schweinfurt again found me staying in a room on the second floor of an officer's club; not until a few days before I was to take command did an apartment finally become available. In my absence from Stuttgart, Linda had to take charge of supervising the loading of our household goods for yet another move. She, the girls, and our furniture all arrived in Schweinfurt at the same time.

As usual, Linda did a good job of managing the move. Of course, she did have experience, it being our ninth move in six years. This time, however, my eyes had been only on command. When Linda arrived, she saw not the company but the four-story, barrackslike apartment buildings, each with three stairwells of eight units. One of the buildings would have looked bad enough, but ours was one of more than twenty in a row. Containing nine-hundred square feet, our apartment's only redeeming feature was its ground-floor location, which did not require the negotiation of the narrow stairwell to get "home." I suppose that I should not have been surprised by Linda's tears on her first—and second—observations of our new home, but I was. How could anyone be unhappy with such glorious challenges ahead? Of course, my challenges were accompanied by command and, hopefully, rewards; Linda's tribulations were in many ways even more taxing but brought little public recognition for a job well done.

Once the formal change of command was completed, I thought little about the wasted weeks of repeated classes or about the poor quarters that would be my family's home for the next eighteen months. My mind was on the company: it had priority and would be the center of my every effort for the next year and a half. Even an amateur psychologist can easily determine that so concentrated a focus is not healthy for a good family relationship. To counter that thesis, however, I need only say that damn few psychologists ever got the privilege of commanding an infantry company—and if they did, especially in those dark, post-Vietnam days in Germany, they would have had to think my way instead of theirs—or not stayed in command for long.

Immediately after the change of command, I returned to the company area with the rest of the troops. Although the ceremony had taken place on a Friday morning, there was much to do before the weekend.*

One of those pressing duties was to take a look at my new unit—and, unfortunately, my initial impressions were not positive. Alpha Company occupied the second floor of Building

---

*In the "old army," which is usually defined as any period before the present but more specifically refers to the time before World War II, officers came in late, left early, and spent weekends at socials and polo matches. The NCOs ran the company, and they and the soldiers worked long hours to accomplish whatever was required. In more recent times—especially after Vietnam and as a result of VOLAR (the Volunteer Army)—soldiering for the troops, unless in the field, was often an eight-to-five job. But by late 1974, additional paperwork, the necessity to write reports, and discipline problems had officers and NCOs staying late, with few days or hours off.

#209, a multistory complex at the southwest edge of Ledward Barracks. Charlie Company of our battalion was on the ground floor, and a company of the division's engineer battalion occupied the third. The concrete-walled, slate-roofed barracks had been built during the rise of the Third Reich in the 1930s. The swastikas that had originally adorned the building had been removed, but above each entrance was still a statue of a muscular Nordic soldier in the "Kraut" helmet of World War II infamy.

Except for the arms and supply rooms located in the basement, the entire company—including living quarters and administrative areas and my office—flanked an eight-foot-wide hallway that extended the entire length of the fifty-yard-long building. Niches that had been designed for storage of rifles belonging to a Nazi air-defense unit were still present. Our modern, all-volunteer army was in such a state, however, that all weapons had to be kept under triple lock and key unless checked out for training or maneuvers under supervision of an NCO. The wall niches now held platoon bulletin boards.

Most of the rooms were painted a dingy shade of gray. Window panes at the end of the hall and in a couple of the rooms were broken. Some had been covered with poorly cut cardboard, but others had been left open to the icy wind. At least a quarter of the light fixtures were inoperative—either broken or simply burnt out; I could not determine which at first glance.

In the latrines at each end of the hallway, at least one commode or urinal was stopped up or broken. The walls and the partitions around the commodes were painted a flat black. When I asked, "Why black?" I was informed that it cut down on the graffiti. On further inquiry, I learned the previous company commander had ordered the paint job because of references to unnatural or impossible sexual acts the writers recommended he perform. But even the black paint could not hide a fresh track of blood sprayed across one of the latrine walls. A broken syringe and needle on the floor suggested the source of the blood was a junkie who'd popped his tourniquet at the same time he withdrew the needle from his arm.

After the brief tour of the barracks, I walked into my new office to find that my predecessor had followed the advice of the Company Command Course—the desk was next to the windows, despite its second-floor location. At the same time I realized that my immediate predecessor might not be responsible for the location of the desk—or for that matter the commander before him. Neither had been around long enough to worry about rearranging furniture. Both were in command only months before receiving RIF notices and being discharged within ninety days thereafter.

Although the "last" of the RIFs had supposedly been executed while I was in the advanced course, another had been announced in the summer of 1974. The A Company commander twice removed had been in the position only weeks when he received his pink slip. He had not even completed his inventory of the company's weapons, vehicles, and equipment—and not surprisingly, had failed to do so once he learned of his RIF.

My immediate predecessor had assumed command with the promise that the recent "ultimate RIF" was indeed the last. Less than two months later the army announced that it still had too many captains, and another elimination list was released. Despite a respectable combat record, my predecessor, too, was RIFed.

Once I had my desk back in the center of the office, facing the entrance where I thought it belonged, I sat down to talk with my first sergeant, Pedro A. Carrasco. A veteran of multiple tours in Vietnam with Special Forces, Carrasco had been the company first sergeant for the past two years. Of medium height and build and in his late thirties—an old man for the infantry—Top spoke articulately in an English accented with the Spanish of his Mexican birth.

My initial conversation with Carrasco had me immediately wondering why the battalion commander had claimed to have little confidence in the first sergeant, recommending that I find a replacement as soon as possible. It would not take long to determine that if Carrasco had a fault, it was one that in my mind was not really negative. Experience would prove that Top was a loyal first sergeant. Whatever his company commander desired, Top delivered. He had stood loyally behind a succession of less than adequate commanders. If I was good, so would he be.

During that first conversation with my top NCO, I emphasized that my priorities were to focus first on discipline of the soldiers and then on maintenance and accountability of the company's arms, vehicles, and equipment. We would concurrently and ultimately concentrate on training readiness to assume our combat mission along the border that then separated the two

Germanies, less than an hour's tank ride away. At the same time we were accomplishing those objectives, we would improve the quality of life in the barracks—by making them clean, attractive, and safe. I concluded my part of the talk by stating that the key to all the objectives was an active, operative, concerned chain of command, where NCOs demanded and earned the respect of their soldiers.

When asked for his evaluation of the company, Top was at first reluctant to speak. After prodding, he responded in a matter-of-fact tone, "Sir, there are lots of problems—you have seen the barracks; the equipment is in the same shape. Few funds have been available to train, much less to take care of housekeeping. The NCOs don't understand or appreciate the new leniency under VOLAR and feel that no one backs them up when they make a stand."

After a brief pause to see if I wanted him to go on, Carrasco continued. "With all of that, the worst problem is the drugs. I'd say that well over thirty percent of the company has experimented with heroin. We've got at least ten men hooked on junk, maybe more. Half the men at one time or another have tried speed, LSD, or a local, across-the-counter pill called Mandrex. The troops call it 'mad dog' for good reason. Apparently—at least by the actions of guys I've seen trying to tear up the barracks, the MPs or anything else that gets in their way—all it does is make you go crazy; there's no high or low to it. As for marijuana and hashish, well, sir, everybody in the company smokes it but me and you—and I'm not sure about you."

Top again hesitated, but I reassured him that he was telling me what I needed to know. He continued by again reflecting on the poor condition of the unit's vehicles and equipment. Finally, with a shake of his head he said, "You know, sir, I hate to say it, but the troops are not much better than everything else around here. The ones who are good or who have potential have never really been challenged. To fill the VOLAR ranks, the recruiters have had to scrape the bottom of the barrel. Lots of the men were policed up in courtrooms, where they had the choice of us or jail. Some seem to have regretted their decision."

Top was on a roll by then and seemed glad to be getting what he was saying off his chest. "Most of the troops don't know their jobs and couldn't care less about learning. As far as fighting the Commies, many of the sergeants and officers are more afraid of their own men than the enemy. And it's not just us.

The rest of the brigade and probably the division and maybe the whole goddamn army is in the same shape.''

Another long pause followed before Top concluded. ''We're on our ass, sir, but there's nothing we can't fix, or at least improve. The men want to be in a good company whether they know it or not. Just let me know what you want, and support me when I do it.''

Immediately following my session with Carrasco, I met with the company's executive officer and platoon leaders. As with every meeting I was to hold in the company, Top was invited to sit in. I was not surprised to find only three of the company's five authorized lieutenants. Two of the platoons were led by their platoon sergeants, who were also included in the meeting.

First Lieutenant Dick Earle, the executive officer, had been in the company as a platoon leader and had then been the battalion motor officer before returning as the XO. Short and stocky with ruddy complexion and prematurely thinning red hair, Earle was quick-tempered and even faster to offer his opinion—requested or not. He was extremely enthusiastic, the kind of person who enjoys being a soldier. His knowledge of maintenance and overall leadership ability would prove invaluable.

Leading the 1st Platoon was 2d Lt. Doug Musser. Tall, thin, and looking younger than his twenty-two years, Musser was new to the company and to the army. Whatever his capabilities, I would have to hold myself responsible; I had been his tactical officer when he had gone through the army's best and toughest training in Ranger School. None of my students earned the Ranger Tab unless they deserved it. Musser was wearing his at the proper place above the division patch on the left shoulder of his uniform.

First Lieutenant Jim Clark was in charge of the weapons platoon, which operated the company's three tubes of 81mm mortars and the two TOW antitank missile launchers. Clark had the ability and knowledge but was not yet long enough out of West Point to have the flexibility to help turn the company around. On the Hudson River, Clark had learned that everything is black or white with no grays. From my observations, cadets at the Point were taught to be generals rather than to be lieutenants. Clark would have to learn quickly that the Plain of the Military Academy was a long way from Schweinfurt, Germany—or look for a job somewhere other than in A Company.

Sergeant First Class (SFC) Dick Arford, a twenty-year-plus career man, led the 2d Platoon. A veteran of the occupation of Germany after World War II, Arford had lots of stories to tell. The problem was that he would much rather relate tales than run his platoon. As a result he had already been fired as a platoon sergeant in our sister infantry battalion on Ledward. Despite his record, Dick Arford was basically a good soldier with untapped leadership potential. If he did not produce, it would be my failure as much as his.

In charge of the 3d Platoon was SFC Wolfgang Hans Liebrich, a native of Germany who had immigrated to the United States as a teenager. Drafted after only months in the States, Liebrich had spent most of his fourteen years in the army in Vietnam and back in his native Germany. The epitome of a German military man, his attention to detail made his the best platoon in the company. With an NCO like Liebrich, I knew at least one of my platoons could get along fine without an officer assigned.

More help arrived a few days after my assumption of command. Second Lieutenant Gary Gaal, direct from college ROTC in Missouri and the infantry school at Fort Benning, reported for his first troop assignment. Gaal had much to learn, and was at times too stubborn to learn quickly. Eventually, however, he proved to be a key officer in improving the company. I assigned Gary as leader of the 2d Platoon, with SFC Arford returning to his regular job as platoon sergeant.

My initial meetings with the first sergeant and company officers took place in my office. For the meeting with the company NCOs, we assembled in the company day room on the fourth floor of the barracks. Varying in age from nineteen to forty and in experience from two to twenty years, these men would be the key to whatever we accomplished or failed to accomplish over the next months. As I expected, there were far more young sergeants with stripes barely sewn on their sleeves than the grizzled old veteran NCOs who are depicted in novels and movies. In the officer clubs at the time, a popular question was "What has happened to the NCO corps? Where are all the sergeants?" For anyone who had been around for a while, the answer was obvious. Many of the senior NCOs with years of experience were occupying billets where they would get no older: ten years of repeated tours to the Vietnam War had many sergeants on the list of the dead and missing. During the war the ranks of experienced NCOs had further been depleted by direct commissions and officer candidate schools which made sergeants into lieutenants—a rank that produced a vast majority of the war's officer casualties. Many of the sergeants-turned-officer who had survived Vietnam were to fall to postwar RIFs. Lying under a headstone or kicked out after the war in the officer reduction measures, *that* was where all too many of the NCOs had gone.

Despite the rarity of senior NCOs, I was not overly concerned. I had fought a war with a rifle company, where at twenty-three years of age, I was the second oldest man in the unit. If nineteen- and twenty-year-old NCOs could be proficient in combat, then there was no reason they could not be the same in peacetime. The NCOs were still the backbone of the army—VOLAR or not.

I promised my sergeants that, in front of the troops, I would support them whether they were right or wrong. But if they were wrong, they would pay the price to me later. Their place in the chain of command would be honored both up and down. No soldier would question a sergeant's word or action. At the same time, each NCO would be held totally responsible for the actions, good and bad, of his subordinates. If they could not perform as NCOs and deliver as NCOs, then they would no longer be NCOs.

The duty day was nearly over before I talked to the company as a whole. Carrasco assembled all 145 men* on the street in front of the barracks. Each squad leader accounted for his men and reported their presence or absence to the platoon sergeant, who in turn reported to Carrasco. As Top reported to me, he saluted and turned the formation over to me. The platoon leaders took over from their sergeants as I returned Top's salute.

There was not much I could say to the company that those assembled had not heard many times before. Changes of command and new commanders were becoming almost monthly events. However, soldiers are always curious about what the Old Man—the company commander—is going to be like. Though I detected the usual curiosity, there also seemed to be a sense of general malaise. Even with a weekend beginning as soon as the

---

*Authorized strength of the company was 156 officers and men. The 5–10 percent shortage at my assumption of command was typical of my time with the company. For a complete list of authorized personnel and positions, see Appendix A.

formation concluded, most of the men seemed bored and disinterested.

My remarks were brief. I did not mention my initial impressions of the unit—nothing could be gained by looking backward
when so many challenges lay ahead. I emphasized that I was
glad to be in command of the company and that I would do my
best to meet the needs of the soldiers. I explained that foremost
of those needs was to prepare them to fight, if that became
necessary, and to win, and hopefully to be so prepared that no
aggressor would be tempted to take us on. Adding that I would
also be attentive to their professional and personal needs in garrison, I told them that a high state of discipline would be demanded and expected. I concluded by stating that the chain of
command would work, up and down, to ensure the company
was prepared to meet all missions.

When I had completed my remarks, I turned the formation
back to Top, who dismissed the troops. A few minutes later
Carrasco, Earle, and I met back in my office for further discussion. In the change-of-command formation earlier that day, the
company had been assembled with the tallest at the front, the
shortest in the rear. The formation just completed had been
assembled by platoon, allowing me to notice for the first time
that most of the thirty-five percent of the company who were
black were assigned to the 1st Platoon.

Top answered my questions about the concentration by telling
me the last three company commanders had believed the black
soldiers worked better together and got along easier if assigned
together. Feedback from rap sessions monitored by the division
race relations office had also been positive about the arrangement. As for the racial situation overall, Top said that the men
got along fairly well during the duty day and especially during
field maneuvers. However, after hours everyone socialized only
within their ethic group. While full-scale race riots, which had
been common a few years before, were probably a thing of the
past, small fights still occurred, and individual confrontations
based on race were common.

By Carrasco's tone, I could tell that he did not agree with the
assignment policy but because of his loyalty to previous commanders would not articulate his objections. Despite my disagreement—revulsion really—I decided not to conduct a
wholesale transfer of personnel within the company to achieve
an immediate racial balance. With completion of tours and arrivals through the replacement system, we could remedy the

situation in a few months without calling attention to the problem. I also mentioned to Top my observation that, except for a few junior sergeants, none of the company's NCOs or officers were black. One of our priorities would be to secure black leaders through the replacement pipeline. In the meantime within the company, we could actively pursue promotion of blacks to sergeant and staff sergeant. Ranks higher than that were out of our control because the army's central promotion system assigned grades of E-7 (sergeant first class) and above (master sergeant, first sergeant, and sergeant major).

The sun had already set, and I could hear the laughter and horseplay of soldiers departing for the night spots of Schweinfurt before Top and I prepared to handle the day's last bit of official business. During the change of command that morning, I had noticed a soldier in the front rank wearing a Silver Star (the third highest valor award), a Purple Heart, and several rows of "I-was-there" ribbons from Vietnam. The medals had caught my attention along with the fact that instead of the crossed rifles of infantry, the soldier wore the flaming bomb of the ordnance corps on his dress-uniform collar.

At my request Top had secured the man's official file from the local adjutant general and pulled his personnel records from the company files. The company records revealed a stack of letters from finance companies, jewelry shops, and furniture stores, requesting help in securing payment or return of goods. A detailed check of the official records noted that the soldier had been in Vietnam, but there were no accounts of a Silver Star or Purple Heart.* I had the soldier report to my office.

The soldier—a vehicle mechanic and a member of the headquarters platoon—entered, stopped one step in front of my desk, and reported as he saluted. I returned the salute with a question about when and where he had been awarded the medals. After a lengthy pause, the soldier said he had been a truck driver in

---

*"PX heroes," as they were called (because they bought their medals at the post exchange), were not unusual in the years immediately after the end of the Vietnam War. This trend has grown during the last decade to the point that individuals who were never in the service claim to be Vietnam vets with high decorations. For those of us who really did answer the unpopular call to fight in Vietnam and had to wait until the 1980s for any recognition, the desire to share our pride in being Vietnam veterans seems a bit strange coming from those who did everything possible to avoid their responsibilities at the time.

Vietnam and had been in a road ambush sprung by the Viet Cong. He had been wounded, and while in the hospital, a general, whose name he could not recall, pinned the two medals on his hospital gown.

I explained to the soldier the severe consequences of wearing unauthorized decorations and informed him that he had thirty days to produce written orders, medical reports, or other information confirming the awards. If none were found in his personal files at his quarters or from the addresses in Washington DC we provided, I would proceed with judicial action. Although I was nearly certain that no such awards ever had been made, the man would have the chance to back up his claims. Part of this opportunity was based on fairness, but the majority was the result of Top's informing me that the soldier was married with two children and, as I had already noted from his file, in debt so deep there was little chance he would ever again be solvent.

After a final walk-through of the barracks, I headed home, where Linda was attempting to make some order out of the boxes and furniture overflowing our apartment. During the day she had managed to buy bunk beds for the girls—not out of any desire on her or their part but simply because their bedroom was not large enough for two regular beds.

My first night in command was to be like many that followed. At 0200 hours the battalion duty officer called to say that one of my troops was at the MP station. He was under arrest for assaulting another soldier in a downtown bar. I was beginning to understand the trials of peacetime command.

CHAPTER 4

IF THE RUSSIANS COULD SEE THIS, THEY WOULD ATTACK TOMORROW

December 1974–January 1975

Offenders must be punished, unless some reason be presented which will enable me to be lenient without creating a bad precedent, and encouraging others to be offenders.

Robert E. Lee

I don't know which is more dangerous—those that write regulations, or those who interpret them.

Personal Journal
January 10, 1975

Along with the lack of discipline, the drug abuse, and the general disarray of the company area, other problems had to be dealt with in the initial days and weeks of command. Equipment, arms, and vehicles had to be accounted for, training schedules planned, and daily activities monitored.

Two major issues also lay in the immediate future. For the next month the company and the rest of the battalion were assigned to "installation support." Instead of training to fight Communist or other transgressors, we would guard gates, stock commissary shelves, pick up debris along the roadways, and perform any other ash-and-trash details that came along. None of these were jobs which prompted men to volunteer for the army. The support duties were notorious morale busters—assuming there was any morale to be damaged. Second, and much more critical, was the annual general inspection (AGI) scheduled for the end of January. The AGI, conducted by the division inspector general's office would check maintenance records, conditions of arms and vehicles, supply procedures, training schedules, billets, and soldiers. There were only two outcomes of the AGI—pass or fail.

From past experience I was aware that passing an AGI allowed a commander to "continue the march." Failure usually meant relief from command and a guaranteed spot on the next RIF list. The hazards of going down range were becoming quite real. After only hours in the company, I was absolutely certain that there was no way that we could pass the AGI; after several days in command, I wondered why my initial conclusion had been so optimistic.

Our only hope lay in the knowledge that division was aware of the situation in the battalion and that it had been at least five years since the "annual" inspection was conducted. Evidently no one at division had been willing to discover and document just how bad things really were. A week into command, I met with Carrasco and told him that our objective for the AGI was to keep anyone in the company, present or past, from going to jail. Beyond that, as Top well knew, no other objective would be attainable.

Another requirement also had priority: within thirty days, I had to account for and sign for the more than a million dollars' worth of property assigned to the company. If I did not sign the master hand receipt at the end of a month, my signature would make no difference—any person in command for that length of time was automatically responsible for the property.

My "great property hunt" began by a meeting with the company supply chief, S.Sgt. Richard Cook. Supply sergeants are a breed apart—somewhere between clerks, traders, thieves, and con artists. If a supply sergeant cannot get it, it cannot be gotten—or one needs a new supply sergeant.

In addition to having current printouts of everything the company was supposed to have, Cook had stacks of sub-hand receipts which recorded the distribution of equipment to users. I looked over the master list. It contained items as detailed as 153 plastic canteens at $0.44 each, 139 M-16A1 rifles at $142.00 each, and 15 M-113A1 armored personnel carriers at $34,678.00 each. Totaled, the list contained nearly 11,000 items valued at more than $1.38 million (for a complete list of company property, see Appendix B).

I asked the supply sergeant about accountability. Cook, medium height, with pasty skin from too much time spent in the basement supply room, twitched his small mustache and answered, "Well, sir, my ass is covered (a typical supply sergeant response), everything on the property list is signed for by someone. The problem is a lot of it is missing. As I'm sure you know, you can put a report of survey or statement of charges against whoever signed for anything missing. Much of it can be charged to the previous commander or the one before him. Neither ever signed the master list, but the thirty-day rule will put their asses and pocket books in a sling. Some things I can make up, others I can trade for if you want to give them a break, or we can just do the paperwork. With both of them being RIFed, I doubt if Uncle Sam will ever get much out of them. One problem with the paper route is that we will do without whatever is missing until all the paperwork goes through channels. You and me will both likely be gone or maybe retired before that's all completed."

I was well aware that almost any item in the army inventory could be "made up" except weapons. Even those could be recovered if one still had the receiver group with the serial number. Parts could be ordered, exchanged, or swapped. Any good supply sergeant, and I could already tell I had one, could make anything appear or disappear given enough time. With a smile of reassurance—which by the book might not have been the best course of action—I told Cook, "You probably already know about many of our shortages. Start making them up. If you need some assistance, check with Top. As I complete each line item on the master property list, I'll let you know what we're short. Whoever is signed for it can assist in the hunt if they're still around."

I concluded with a question to which I already knew the answer. All supply sergeants, even the not-so-good ones, have excess equipment (items not included on the inventory lists) that makes good trading material. Cook did not disappoint me. When I asked if he had any excess, he responded, "Of course not, sir, that's against regulations."

I continued, "Well, Sergeant Cook if you had any, what would you have."

Almost giggling, Cook explained, "About a month ago we received new spare barrels for the company's twenty-two M-2 .50-cal machine guns. Somehow the requisition got mixed up, and we got a double issue; also the guys at ordnance screwed up and didn't make us turn in the worn-out barrels. *If* I had any excess it would be in the way of forty-four machine gun barrels worth a little over $1,100 each. Unless we are missing a weapon, or maybe a vehicle, I can trade for it."

There was no reason to make any more comments to Cook except to tell him that I was heading to the arms room to conduct a serial-number inventory. No question of ethics or honor had crossed my mind. If I tried to live solely within the army system and its reams of regulations, I and my command would accomplish little. Another important factor in my reasoning was that very little of the company's property had any value except to soldiers doing soldierly things. Missing items had probably been traded or given to other companies facing the same problems we were. There was also a good chance that items had been turned in to ordnance with no credit, just as we probably had received items for which we were not accountable.

More important, paperwork charging present and past members of the company for losses that they may or may not have been responsible for would be bad on morale—and the equipment would still be missing. Once everything was accounted for, it would be sub-hand-receipted to the users, who would be held responsible for future accountability and maintenance.

The A Company arms room resembled a bunker with concrete-block walls. It had a three-lock steel door with a log book attached that noted each time and by whom it was opened and closed. An additional sheet was for the initials of the charge of quarters (CQ) who checked the door hourly during nonduty hours. This last measure was in lieu of an electronic intrusion-detection device that was due to be installed whenever funds become available.

Inside the arms room was an inner room formed by steel mesh walls. Racks, each with its own locks, shared the inner room with locked steel cabinets containing sensitive items. No weapon or piece of equipment left the arms room without being signed for.

The inventory of the arms room was accomplished by checking the serial number of each of the rifles, machine guns, mortars, binoculars, and night-vision devices. Sp4 Robert W. Peterson, the company armorer, assisted in the lengthy process. Peterson, a Vietnam veteran who had left the army for several years after his combat tour, had returned because of the poor job prospects back in his hometown, Chicago. Although still an infantryman by military occupational specialty (MOS), he had volunteered to take over the arms room when no trained armorer was available. Peterson was intelligent and a voracious reader of military manuals and civilian books on weapons. When I asked if he planned to reenlist, Peterson laughed and said there was no way he was staying in. He continued, in a tone that betrayed no humor, saying, "I know what I'm doing; this tour I'm getting a skill. There are lots of folks back in Chicago who need a weapons expert. I won't have any trouble finding a job this time."

Security of weapons and sensitive items was a priority and one that could lead to a captain's termination of command about as quickly as any other issue.* Whereas there was little market or demand for most of the things we used day-to-day, military automatic weapons were easy to sell almost anywhere.

Despite his lack of formal training, Peterson had learned his job well. With the exception of two numbers that had been transposed on the master hand receipt—which could be fixed with my final report before signature—everything was accounted for. While most of the weapons were not as clean as they should have been, and certainly could not have passed the AGI, I felt that the arms room was the first bright spot on my dismal first tour of the company.

The next stop on my inventory inspection made the arms room look all that much better. About two hundred meters from the barracks, the motor pool consisted of three covered maintenance bays with a cobblestone workspace outside. Another hundred meters up a slight rise was a large concrete-covered hardstand where the vehicles were parked in surveyor-straight lines.

The company was assigned twenty-one tracked vehicles, two trucks, two quarter-tons (jeeps), a Gamma Goat** and four trailers of different sizes. I had ordered all the various tools and

---

*Division and army regulations called for a serial-number check of weapons and sensitive items monthly. This once-a-month inspection was supplemented by identical checks at least once a week and often twice that frequency while I was in command. My policy was that anytime I discovered that one of my lieutenants had nothing to do, I would send him to the arms room for an inventory.

**The M-561 Gamma Goat was a one-and-one-quarter-ton, all-wheel-drive, troop and cargo carrier that was designed to navigate rough terrain, swim rivers, and be air-droppable. The Gamma Goat had been described as early as 1972 as a "dog" by House Armed Services Committee investigators, but army officials in Washington were still defending the vehicle when I took command in 1974. While army officials said they were "satisfied" with the Goat, we in the field felt differently. Some of the Goat's problems were merely irritating: its engine noise was so loud that we had to wear ear plugs to prevent hearing damage and one had to be a contortionist to get in and out of the small cab. More severe were its mechanical problems and the difficulties in securing spare parts for the one-of-a-kind vehicle. During the year and a half I commanded A Company, the Gamma Goat was operational for less than three months. Eventually the army agreed with field commanders: the Gamma Goat went the way of other well-meant but worthless projects.

authorized equipment laid out with each vehicle in the motor pool.

Before I began on-site inspection of the vehicles and their basic issue items (BII, pronounced Billy), I reviewed the company's daily DA (Department of the Army) Form 2406 for the past few months. The 2406 is a list of vehicles that will not run or are too dangerous to drive. Parts needing replacement but not causing the vehicle to be deadlined and entered on the 2406 were recorded in the vehicles' logbook. The daily 2406 revealed that on inspection day well over a quarter of the vehicles, track and wheel, were deadlined—several had been for as long as three to four months.

Closer inspection revealed that the inventory on the 2406 was optimistic at best. Several of the vehicles not on the report had obvious oil or fuel leaks that were deadlining faults. Not a single vehicle had all its tools or even a list of the shortages and requisition numbers for replacements. Inboard and portable fire extinguishers were missing, not at the correct charge, or lacking safety devices. Vehicle logbooks revealed a lack of quarterly overhauls or, even worse in some cases, that overhauls had obviously been performed with an "M-1 pencil" rather than with tools and proper procedures.

I doubted if a single vehicle could pass the AGI, and I was well aware that my experience with, and knowledge of, mechanized vehicles was limited. In peace and war I had served with airborne, airmobile, ranger, and leg infantry where a jeep and a deuce-and-a-half or two were the unit's total rolling stock.

Despite my inexperience with mechanized infantry, I felt that I could take care of any maintenance problems that came up. While I was extremely critical of army regulations (ARs) which governed personnel and administrative procedures, I placed a great deal of confidence in the army's maintenance technical manuals (TMs) and tactical field manuals (FMs). TMs and FMs were simple, by the numbers, and accompanied by pictures for the completely uninformed. As I inspected each vehicle, I had in hand the correct TM-10 (operators manual), which had a checklist for pre- and postoperation checks as well as pictures and lists of each piece of equipment and tools which were supposed to accompany the vehicle.

Two deficiencies that were apparent during the vehicle inspection would be easy to fix and would make great strides in improving the company's maintenance posture. First, there were no drivers, assistant drivers, or tactical commanders (TCs) assigned to each vehicle. Once that situation was remedied the crew could develop the pride of "ownership" and receive the rewards of a well-maintained vehicle. At the same time the responsibility of "ownership" provided someone who was directly in charge when things did not go so well. The second deficiency was really a part of the first. Many of the vehicles were missing their TM-10 and the accompanying lube order, which illustrated and outlined when and where lubrication was to take place. Even more revealing, those that were present were in mint condition, with clean covers and pages. If they had been used at all, they would have shown the wear, with oil splatters and grease stains.

I concluded my track and truck inspection with one last count of the vehicles—followed by another and then another. No matter how many times I counted, I continued to come up one M-113 armored personnel carrier (APC) short and with a serial number on my master list with no check mark along side it. Cook, Earle, each platoon leader, and the motor sergeant joined me in the maintenance office in an attempt to figure out how one could lose a thirteen-ton tracked vehicle.

S.Sgt. Delbert Thomas, the company motor sergeant for more than two years, finally broke the silence. He said that he might know the location of the missing 113. Thomas, career mechanic on his final tour before retirement and with little use for the infantry and our lack of mechanical knowledge, said, "There are several APCs with battalion markings over at the ammo dump. We've been cannibalizing [stripping parts] off them for more than six months. They were originally kept up-loaded with ammo for alerts and in case the balloon went up, but a while back all the ammo was moved to a regional dump."

Earle, resignation in his voice, added, "Oh, shit, sir, battalion said they were responsible for the tracks when they went to the ammo dump years ago. They were supposed to turn them in for salvage, but I bet they've transferred them back to our books. If they have, we have a real dog waiting for us."

A short jeep ride later proved Earle's description of the 113 as a dog was too kind. At first glance, I saw that a track was missing and two road wheels gone. When we opened the engine compartment, wires and hoses were intertwined and ran from nowhere to anywhere. A check of the data plate provided a matching serial number. The dog was ours. I turned to Earle and told him to get Thomas and the M-578 track retriever and take our 113 home. I added that I wanted a list of missing and inoperative parts, along with an estimate of how long it would take to get the track operational, on my desk by 0700 the next morning. My only solace, was that the three other similarly sorry 113s sitting in the ammo dump belonged to other companies in the battalion.

I spread the rest of the inventorying out over the next two weeks as I attempted to get preparation underway for the AGI. More shortages appeared: missing blankets, sheets, and body armor (flak jackets)—none of which would be any problem to make up, especially with S.Sg. Cook's supply of .50-caliber barrels. Other missing items—such as a typewriter, a few protective (gas) masks, and communications wire and reels—would be difficult but not impossible to find. And I learned we had an extra VRC-46 radio—used in command vehicles—which was even better than machine-gun parts for trading.

Many shortages were in the mechanic tool chests and in the motor-pool toolroom, which contained the Common Tool Set Number One (all the tools needed to keep a mechanized infantry company operational). We could trade for some, and others could be requisitioned against the company's spare parts budget. A few missing tools could be charged to the individuals signed for them, but the records were poor, where they existed at all.

Another sign of the unit's poor maintenance posture was that there was plenty of money in the spare parts budget. Few parts had been ordered and the company prescribed load list (PLL) had less than twenty items listed. The PLL was supposed to itemize parts which frequent requisition had proved necessary to be kept in stock. A decent PLL for a mech infantry company should have well over one hundred line numbers, each spare part being numbered and kept in a bin for immediate use when needed. During a field problem, or in combat, the PLL would offer spare parts with no delay in ordering from the rear or a theater warehouse.

In addition to accounting for weapons and equipment that were poorly cared for, the inventories of the arms room, motor pool, and track park revealed an even more startling deficiency in the company's ability to defend its segment of the border separating the two Germanies. After finally finding the stripped M-113 hulk at the ammo dump, I inquired about our basic load of ammunition and explosives. To my amazement I discovered that the company's go-to-war ammo package was stored at the Kist Ammunition Storage Area—more than sixty miles away—and across at least two major rivers. Questions to Capt. Nick Bozick, the battalion S-4, who was responsible for supply and ammunition, produced the explanation that division and higher commands had decided that a surprise attack by the Warsaw Pact countries was unlikely. Ample time would be available for him to truck ammo from Kist to our staging areas.

The S-4 had no response to my query about the expected use of Soviet special forces to destroy bridges and rail lines—and probably ammo storage areas—in advance of attacks. He also had nothing to say about the fact that well over one half of his five-ton ammunition trucks were deadlined—some of which had not been operational for more than ninety days. It did not take long to realize that Bozick had asked the same questions of higher commands and had received equally inadequate answers.

After nearly an hour of discussion with the S-4, our conversation had degenerated to comments about fighting Communists with bayonets and taking on tanks with rocks. Nick said aloud what I had begun to realize but was unwilling to say myself. "Lee," the S-4 said, "no one is willing to admit it, but lots of us supply types think the reason that ammo is no longer readily accessible is that the big guys in Heidelberg (USAREUR Headquarters) don't trust the troops with live rounds."

With a shake of my head, I headed back to the company. As I passed through the outer room of the supply office, I noticed a sign taped to a senior NCO's desk. In crude letters it warned, "If the Russians could see this shit they would attack tomorrow." With a red pen the "tomorrow" had been scratched out and replaced with "today."

During my inventories, we were also making plans and preparation for the installation-support-battalion duty we would pull over the Christmas and New Year's holidays. Training and normal administration continued as well. Immediately upon assuming command, I had worked with the battalion S-3 (operations) section to get a few days in the field before we took over our garrison support responsibility.

At the end of my second complete week in command, I led every vehicle that would run and every soldier who was not in the hospital or jail out the back gate of Ledward Barracks. Our destination was the ten-square-kilometer local training area just fifteen minutes by M-113 from the motor pool. Preparation for the three-day, two-night field exercise provided the most encouragement I had yet received during my short period of command. For the first time, I sensed enthusiasm on the part of the troops. Field training and maneuvers were what many of the men had expected when they volunteered for the infantry—not garrison duty of picking up cigarette butts, raking gravel, and painting rocks.

While the field training did seem to raise morale, it also confirmed the low level of discipline in the unit. Soldiers wore a mixture of uniforms, some even sporting items of civilian cold-weather garb. Many had brought along garrison, baseball-type caps, which they wore rather than the steel pot. Despite the company SOP clearly outlining that the field uniform included web gear and that weapons would be carried at all times, many of the soldiers wandered about the German forest as if they were on nature hikes instead of preparing for future battles.

Of course, none of these things by itself, is a basis for concluding how well an individual or company could fight. Yet, they were certainly good indicators. If soldiers did not follow simple orders for dress and equipment, how could they be expected to follow orders given in the heat of combat to perform difficult and often dangerous deeds? Of even more concern was the fact that it was not just the soldiers who were negligent. Many of the younger NCOs had no better work habits than their soldiers and, more important, placed no demands on and made no checks of their subordinates.

Even with the lax field discipline and despite the several vehicles which broke down during the brief exercise, I felt better about the days away from garrison than about any other part of command thus far. Unfortunately, I knew that my good feelings were not the result of anything going right, but rather the fact, like the rest of the company, I was enjoying the opportunity to be a soldier in the field.

We returned to Ledward for a few days of cleaning up from the field before joining with the rest of the battalion for the installation-support detail. Since the beginnings of armies, soldiers have been required to perform jobs outside the combat missions for which they enlisted or were drafted. A certain amount of housekeeping, security requirements, and ceremonial duties are as much a part of soldiering as physical conditioning and marksmanship.

Unfortunately, the U.S. Army in Europe in the mid-1970s was so strapped for funds—and had been for well over a decade with the tremendous expenditure of resources in Southeast Asia—that many functions normally performed by civilian employees or contract labor were left to the soldiers. In addition to the traditionally despised peeling of potatoes and scrubbing of pots in the mess hall on KP and the daily police calls around the barracks area, installation support put the battalion on a "hey, you" roster for any dirty detail within the community.

During the four weeks of support details, the company prepared for the annual general inspection due the third week of January. Soldiers not performing the various battalion "gofer" assignments worked to get barracks, equipment, and themselves ready for the inspection. Although no one directly admitted it, I do not think an officer or NCO in the battalion thought we had a chance of passing. Mismanagement, neglect, and inadequate funding over a period of many years could not be corrected in a matter of weeks.

Despite the importance of the inspection, I was surprised that the battalion commander, Lt. Col. William King, did not seem overly concerned. He rarely checked on our progress, nor did he issue guidance for preparation. At times I thought he just did not care. Eventually, I decided that he knew as well as I the bad shape we were in. Perhaps he was also confident that his job was not in jeopardy since all the division's battalions which had been inspected in the last six months had failed. Futile or not, it seemed that we should at least make the best effort possible—and perhaps some of the work would benefit us after the inspection.

Christmas Eve found A Company as the guard unit for the community. We provided mounted guards in roving jeeps at the airfield, walking guards at the ammo holding area (which contained a small amount of training ammunition), and various other patrolling guards responsible for entranceways and storage areas. The missions required every man we could muster. For the forty-eight hour period of December 24–25, the soldiers' Christmas consisted of two hours on guard followed by four hours off. "Off" was a misnomer since, even while not actively on guard, each man had to be at the guardhouse as a ready-reaction force in case of emergency.

Due to the installation-support detail, no leaves were granted over the holidays. This was not a major issue because most of the men had neither accrued leave nor available money for the long expensive trip back to the States. Nonetheless, for many it was their first Christmas away from home. Despite their feelings of being grown-up, tough soldiers, most were, in fact, eighteen- or nineteen-year-old young men who were not quite comfortable being six thousand miles from loved ones during the holiday season. For those of us who had our families with us on the Germany tour, it was a little better. However, guard duty on

Christmas Eve a few miles from home seemed almost as far as the six thousand from our birth places.

The wives who were in-country did their best to help by baking cookies and sending decorations to the barracks and to the guardhouse. Carrasco pushed the mess hall to provide extra chow and a constant supply of hot soup and coffee. The names of those with families in-country were juggled on the duty roster to give them a few hours with their families on both days.

About 2200 hours on Christmas Eve, a fine snow began to fall. As I checked each guard post, I found the men in surprisingly good spirits. Most wished me a Merry Christmas and made no complaints about the plunging temperature. My most vivid memory of that Christmas on guard duty was of the swirling snow falling on the soldiers as they made their rounds. Snow accumulated on their helmets and parkas until they were almost invisible in the white darkness of Christmas Eve.

About midnight I managed to make a quick trip home with the intention of putting together Christmas toys for my daughters. While it was not my favorite job—in my mind, guard duty was preferable—it still had to be done before the girls jumped out of bed on Christmas morning. I arrived home to find Dick Earle and three other bachelor lieutenants busy at assembly. Earle explained that they knew I was working and that Linda might need some help. He did not need to explain that lieutenants also got lonesome on Christmas Eve, and they welcomed the opportunity to be a part of family—any family—preparations. Linda later told me that Dick and 2d Lt. Tony Milanti, dressed as Santa's elves, had made a tour of all the battalion officer's quarters about dinner time. In exchange for a drink, they had listened to the children's latest wish list.

My arrival home was well timed. The lieutenants were just about finished with getting everything put together—except for a doll's high chair that seemed to have too many pieces. Part of the problem appeared to be the massive amounts—and various kinds—of Christmas cheer that Linda had been pouring the help. With my sober assistance, we finally got the high chair together, with only a few parts left over. My liquor cabinet was just the opposite—nothing whatsoever was left over.

Christmas Day was much the same as the day before. Between guard-duty checks, I made brief trips home to see how the girls liked their presents. To the soldiers on duty, we delivered great amounts of turkey, dressing, and the various trimmings. Of the many faults of the army of the time, the ability of cooks to prepare holiday meals was not one.

Guard duty continued through New Year's. The only good thing about the arrangement was that it kept the troops out of town and generally out of trouble. Still, each guard mount (inspection before going on duty) included a search for hash, pills, and alcohol. Despite our efforts, one soldier became so stoned between guard tours that he could not get out of bed. Judging by his smell and actions, another had consumed enough booze while on guard to place him well beyond drunkenness.

Another incident was not quite as bad but nonetheless was an indicator of the level of discipline—or at least of the boredom imposed by guard duty. On a late-night inspection, I observed one of my jeep patrols speeding wildly across the airstrip, weaving in and out of parked helicopters. The sergeant in charge of the vehicle admitted that he was in pursuit of a rabbit.

No one was unhappy to see installation support completed after New Year's Day. What faced us, however, was not much better. For the next three weeks every effort of the company went into preparation for the AGI. The division regulations stated that one week was all that was allowed for such preparation, but no one said anything about our extended efforts. For five days a week we labored sixteen to eighteen hours a day. Saturday was good for a "short" workday of eight hours, and Sunday afternoon provided four more hours to attempt to be prepared.

The AGI for the battalion took three days. Each half day was devoted to inspecting either the troops and barracks or the vehicles and maintenance. Alpha Company was the first for the check of the billets, in-ranks inspection, and questioning of the soldiers on their knowledge of general military subjects. We failed that half of the battery miserably—flunking every area inspected. Fortunately, the only rating was pass or fail; if there had been degrees of failure, we could only have received the lowest possible mark.

As soon as the inspection was completed, I met with the other company commanders to pass along what the inspectors seemed to be looking for. Succeeding companies did a little better on the AGI, yet to no one's surprise, the result in each company was failure.

Alpha Company's vehicle and maintenance inspection did not occur until the third day. With the intel gathered from other companies' inspections, several of our scores almost reached the passing point—but none actually met the division's minimum standards.

On the completion of the inspection, the battalion's five companies tallied a total of zero passes against ten failures in the two-part inspection. I was tremendously disappointed, even though I realized that substantial progress had been made in six weeks. At the final outbrief, the division inspector general made no comments about progress as he informed us that of all the division's battalions that had been inspected in the preceding six months, the 2d of the 30th easily rated in the bottom half. I could only conclude that at least fifty percent of the division sure as hell must be in sad shape.

On the plus side, Lieutenant Colonel King seemed finally to have realized the battalion's poor state of readiness. In a company commanders' meeting following the AGI outbrief, he said that the IG had informed him that we would be reinspected in six months instead of the normal one-year interval. While he said our work was cut out for us and that he would be taking a more active role in supervising the next AGI preparation, he did not mention the widespread rumor that another failure would mean his relief from command. And no one mentioned that he would not be the only one to get the ax—company commanders would also fall.

CHAPTER 5

BEEN DOWN SO LONG, IT LOOKS LIKE UP TO ME

February 1975

Dear Sir:

I am writing this letter to try and explain to you the problems that are facing me and my peers in Europe.

I am a member of the United States Army stationed here in Germany. I am a High School graduate and when I finished school I wasn't sure what I wanted to do with my life, so instead of just bumming around I decided to join the Armed Forces. I was promised by the recruiters that I would get the chance to go to college classes and would have a rewarding future.

I enlisted for four years and after my Basic and Advanced Individual training I was sent to Germany for what the recruiters had promised me was only a 16 to 24 month tour. When I arrived I found out that the tour is a 36 month thing—and by that time it was too late to do anything about it. That really didn't bother me at first because I figured it would just give me more time to get more schooling and the rewarding future they promised.

Since that time I have found out that as an infantry soldier I spend around 70 percent of my time in the field or working late getting ready for AGIs or other inspections. Every time I have requested to attend college classes, it has been denied. There are men in the company who have been trying to just get enough schooling to finish high school and haven't yet been allowed to—and they have been here almost three years. As for the rewarding future I was promised—my main function here seems to be scrubbing floors and sweeping streets. What kind of job can I expect to get after my service with a background like this.

I have been trying to get someone to listen to my problems

for the last six months and nothing has been done. It seems as if the only way you can get any attention in the Army is to mess up—and that doesn't always work either. Even though I do not use drugs, I turned myself in as a drug abuser last month. It didn't do any good, a man like me doesn't have any chance of getting out.

The situation here in Germany is so bad that a large number of people are praying for a war just so they can have a chance to leave. Also, the condition of the buildings here are terrible. I live in one room with six other men. These buildings have been here since before the Second World War and they deny any sort of privacy. If it were possible to get permission to live off post the Army would pay me another $75.00 a month for rent. That means that the six of us in our room are paying $450.00 a month for one room. I would like to know just what the Army does with all that money if they don't use it to improve the living conditions.

At any time the Army can come into our rooms and have access to our personal belongings. They can rip through our wall lockers and through anything we own and take away whatever we have if they don't think we should have it. We live and are treated like animals, and yet we are expected to act and work like men. If it wasn't so tragic, it would almost be funny.

Although I might be harassed for writing this letter by my superiors I am praying that something can be done. If nothing else, hopefully it will warn others who may be thinking of joining the Army of just what they are getting in to.

Thank you for your time.

SP4 James J. Shockley
Company A 2nd Battalion 30th Infantry
APO New York 09033

Sp4 Shockley was no trouble maker. He had been selected by my predecessor as the company commander's driver and had stayed on in that job during my first weeks of command. His position was traditionally held by one of the company's most motivated and intelligent soldiers and was usually a stepping stone to earning sergeant stripes.

Because he was my driver, I had a little more personal relationship with Shockley than I did with most of the soldiers. We had already shared freezing jeep rides across the countryside during our brief field time and during late-night checks of the guard posts. There was nothing in Shockley's letter of which I was not already aware, and I was taking measures to improve the conditions he cited. Shockley explained that he had written the letter with the intention of sending it to his congressman back home but wanted to know from me how much trouble he would get in if he did so. I assured him that writing his congressmen was well within his rights, but I also explained that if he did, the letter would be forwarded through channels back to the company, and that within a month to six weeks, I would be the one charged to answer the letter.

With that explanation over, I invited Shockley to take a seat and to tell me what he saw as problems in the company. For the next half hour he restated the elements of the letter and expanded on its contents. It was obvious that he wanted a chance to just get it all off his chest, at least as much as he wanted solutions to the shortcomings he had listed.

I made no direct promises to Shockley, except to tell him that it was my priority to improve the living conditions in the barracks and to arrange for a number of the company to attend high-school completion courses as soon as possible. Those without diplomas would have the highest priority, but college courses would also be investigated. I also reminded my driver that our first job was to improve the company's ability to assume the combat role that we could easily be thrust into with little notice. When I completed my talk, I handed Shockley's letter back to him, with no questions about what he was going to do with it. He stood, saluted, and requested permission to be dismissed. As I returned his salute, he handed the letter back to me saying, "Here, you keep this, sir. Maybe you can do something about it."

Any commander who does not realize that his soldiers know what is right and what is wrong with a unit has little chance of making any major impact. Shockley understood what was wrong with A Company as well as with the rest of the army. Regardless of the quality, or lack thereof, of the soldiers entering the volunteer army, they shared a desire for what every young person entering military service has always sought—security, the opportunity to learn and improve themselves, and the feeling that they contribute to their unit and country. Soldiers share the common desire to be in the best company in the best battalion in the best army, and when they are not, they rarely place the blame on themselves but rather, and usually quite correctly, they lay the fault on their officers and on the massive, faceless, all encompassing "army" in general. The vast majority of soldiers realize that to accomplish their goals in the military, a certain amount of discipline is required. As long as that discipline is administered fairly, they accept it as a part of doing business in the army.

While there are many reasons for a young man to join the army, he must keep in mind that at some time during his enlistment, he may be called upon to do what soldiers are supposed to do—fight and, if necessary, die. In the 30th Infantry we had only to look at the campaign streamers on the battalion colors to be reminded of sacrifices measured in blood and lives in such well-known battles as the St. Mihiel and Meuse-Argonne in World War I and Tunisia, Sicily, and the Rhineland in World War II. On our dress uniforms, in addition to individual awards, each of us wore a Presidential Citation with three oak leaf clusters and a French Croix de Guerre with palm for the 30th's actions in the two world wars. (For a history of the 30th Infantry and a list of campaign participation, see Appendix D.)

Other streamers credited the battalion for earlier duty in such remote and unknown wars as the Mindoro Campaign of the Philippine Insurrection. While the 30th Infantry had not been committed to Vietnam, the battalion's current captains and senior NCOs wore on their uniforms' right shoulders combat patches representing nearly every division and separate brigade that fought in Southeast Asia. While many of the soldiers must have often felt that the closest they would ever get to combat was payday night in downtown Schweinfurt, deep in each man's mind was the knowledge that the men of the battalion might be called upon to do great deeds and add still more battle streamers to its colors.

In a good unit, a new commander can ease into his position while not making any major changes or decisions until he has an opportunity to thoroughly evaluate the company and to allow the soldiers to get the feel of the new Old Man. I had realized from my first moments in A Company that such a leisurely assumption of command was not possible. Immediate action was required, not only to meet the needs of the soldiers but also to meet the demands of the army.

None of the problems in A Company or in the rest of the battalion—or in the army as a whole for that matter—could be studied or solved in a vacuum. Each was interrelated to others and was often the result of actions apparently unrelated to the current challenge. Drug abuse was one such problem. Soldiers, as well as civilians, use drugs to ward off boredom, to feel better, or to escape their surroundings. Other factors adding to drug use are accessibility and acceptance. Taking little action to prevent their use or availability adds to their abuse.

With those factors in mind, many interrelated actions had to be taken to fight the drug problem. Repainting of the barracks and repairing facilities were immediate priorities. Meaningful, demanding training—not merely "scrubbing floors and sweeping streets," as Shockley had so aptly written—had to be undertaken. Offenders had to be punished quickly and severely—dealers jailed, users fined and reduced in rank, and repeated users eliminated from the army with a bad discharge.

Discipline problems were also related to other factors and circumstances. Soldiers who had no fear of punishment for their actions or who were so dissatisfied with their surroundings that punishment did not matter—the old "it don't mean nothing" philosophy left over from the Vietnam years—could be depended upon for little but trouble. Unhappiness with their jobs and displeasure with being in Germany mixed with readily available, cheap—and legal—alcohol kept even the nondrug users in turmoil.

In my first months of command, rarely did a night pass without my having to go the MP station to sign for a soldier who had been arrested for drunk-and-disorderly conduct, fighting, disrespect to MPs or duty personnel, or a combination of all of those charges. Calls by the company charge of quarters (a junior NCO who was responsible for the company area after duty hours) to help break up fights or to get the losers to the medical dispensary and the winners under restriction were as regular as the trips to the MP station.

Fights downtown were usually over the few local German women who dated GIs or were the result of a new soldier's attempting to visit a bar another unit had claimed as its own. Sometimes the trouble started with a soldier entering segregated establishments or those that were considered by the locals to be off-limits to GIs. Still other disputes were over drug deals gone bad, one man's brushing up against another, or simply one soldier's not liking another's looks. Except for the location, language, date, and kind of beer served, many of the Schweinfurt public houses closely resembled the movie versions of Western saloons—to the point of adopting names like the "Bonanza," "Long

Branch," and "OK Corral." Brawls did not really need a reason to break out—they were just a routine part of going to town.
While fights and drunkenness were obvious breaches of discipline and good indicators of low morale, drugs offered a different and more severe problem. Heroin addicts cared not how
they got the money to buy drugs but only about staying high, or
at least keeping the pangs of withdrawal at bay. The poppers,
shooters, and mainliners fed their habit by being barracks
thieves, holdup artists, and pushers. People foolish enough to
value their money more than their life when a junkie needed a
fix were likely to lose both.

Other drugs like LSD, speed, downers, and the craze-
inducing pills known as "mad dogs" at least were not as all-
consuming as heroin. However, the results of use—fights,
beatings, and robberies—were usually the same. I soon decided
that Top's original estimate that everyone used hash or marijuana
was almost conservative. Nickel ($5) and dime ($10) chunks of
hashish, capable of keeping a soldier stoned for a day or more,
were so common that it was a rare day that we did not find a
soldier in possession or find the foil-wrapped drug on the floor
or street, where it had been hurriedly disposed of at the approach
of an officer or senior NCO.

The only good thing about hash was that it produced mellow
reactions instead of aggressiveness. I never knew of a soldier
getting into a fight or causing any trouble whatsoever while under the influence of hashish. The problem was, however, that
the drug was illegal. While it was difficult to explain why alcohol
was legal and hash was not, my soldiers had to be depended
upon to do what they were told—often under extremely trying
conditions.*

Solving the problems of the company was similar to the nature of the difficulties themselves. No one item stood alone.
Each area of indiscipline and degree of low morale was interrelated to the rest of the problems. Solving part would help take
care of the whole, but concentration in a single area would
weaken the rest. *Everything* had to be a top priority for imme-

*As a company commander I certainly knew the rules—yet I must admit
that after a fourth or fifth consecutive night of getting my soldiers out of
the vomit- and urine-soaked MP drunk tank, or visiting soldiers in the
hospital who had fallen through a window while drunk or had been beaten
senseless by an inebriated "friend," I often thought how much simpler my
job would be if hashish were legal and alcohol were not.

diate action—which meant total dedication, concentration, and eighteen-hour-plus work days.

Discipline problems not related to drugs—such as insubordination to an NCO, failure to make formations on time, and slovenly appearance—were fairly easy to correct. Basically, all it took was letting the company know that such actions were not to be tolerated and that deficiencies would attract immediate punishment or corrective training. Much of this improved almost immediately when I made it apparent that VOLAR or not, the principles of rank and respect had not changed.

For any army to function, there must be a distinction between the ranks and no questioning of legal orders. The do-your-own-thing philosophy of the sixties and seventies generation might be a fine life-style on the streets back home. However, in the military, even the peacetime army, a simple designation of rank structure is required.*

To gain control and discipline in Alpha Company, punishment was administered quickly and severely through a system of administrative, nonjudicial, and judicial actions. Administrative punishment is a formal name for what first sergeants have done since armies began. Minor breaches of discipline are best taken care of by the NCOs, with the incident not ever coming to the attention of the company commander. While the time-honored technique of a soldier's "falling down the stairs as many times as it takes to get his attention" were pretty much a thing of the past by the midseventies, there were still ample "shit details" to keep troublemakers busy: oil sumps in the motor pool needed cleaning, grass had to be mowed, and paint had to be applied.

A more formal part of administrative actions ranged in severity from the pulling of a soldier's pass privileges to referring a man to various drug and/or alcohol abuse programs. The ultimate administrative action was throwing a soldier out of the army by taking advantage of army regulations which permitted "chapter" discharges.

The principal punishment option in my hands as a company commander was the nonjudicial Article 15. Under that provision

---

*Today it is still difficult to understand the permissiveness and lack of respect for authority of any kind that marked the years following the end of the Vietnam War. What is more difficult to understand is how the army let these ideas infiltrate and skew the basic tenets of leadership that have worked since the beginnings of military forces.

of the Uniformed Code of Military Justice (UCMJ), I could punish a soldier by reduction of one rank, forfeiture of seven days' pay, and assignment of extra duty and restriction for up to fourteen days. An additional part of the Article 15 permitted the assignment of a soldier for seven days to the local correctional confinement facility (CCF). The CCF resembled basic training more than jail, but it was in many ways more feared than actually being put behind bars. In the CCF a soldier had no privileges, spit shined everything, endured detailed inspections, and accounted for every waking minute. Long forced marches, extended PT sessions, and the requirement to double-time everywhere were methods of getting a soldier's attention in the CCF.

More severe nonjudicial punishment could be administered by the battalion commander in the way of a field grade Article 15. This process could result in the reduction of one rank including the busting of a buck sergeant from E-5 to Sp4 or corporal. Fines could go to the maximum of thirty days' pay, with an equal number of days of extra duty and restriction. Again, the latter thirty days could be served in the CCF at the discretion of the battalion commander.

At neither company nor battalion command level was an Article 15 an arbitrary process. Once an Article 15 was read to a soldier, he had the right to visit with a staff judge advocate lawyer for advice on whether to accept the action. It was strictly up to the soldier whether to accept or turn down the Article 15. However, if the soldier refused to accept the action, he made himself vulnerable to referral to summary court-martial where the punishment could go as high as three months' confinement in a military prison, with a concurrent loss of pay and rank. While this might seem threatening to a soldier, it also served as a check and balance against a commander who might want to administer an Article 15 without the proof that would be required for a conviction in summary court. My policy, as well as that of most commanders, was never to offer an Article 15 unless I was sure I could get a guilty verdict in a summary court.

For infractions deserving more severe punishment than that provided by an Article 15 or summary court, there were the intermediate special court-martial and the highest judicial board, a general court-martial. Each of those required approval before initiation by higher levels of command than the battalion. All we could do was to refer a case through the proper channels. While the special and general court-martial took much more work and preparation, they did offer advantages beyond the normal justice they administered. Both could, and usually did, include bad conduct or dishonorable discharges along with punishments that varied from six months to life in confinement at the military prison at Fort Leavenworth, Kansas.

This wide range of nonjudicial and judicial proceedings offered many courses of action to commanders at all levels. As with all punishment, it had to be administered quickly, equally, and fairly for it to do any good in building and maintaining discipline. Unfortunately, for some time in Europe, amid changes to the VOLAR system, RIFs, and a general not-give-a-shit attitude, only the most severe breaches of discipline had been dealt with.

My immediate announcement in word and action to soldier, NCO, and officer alike was that the lackadaisical enforcement of rules and regulations had ceased—while at the same time doing my best to be quick, fair, and impartial.

Most offenses occurred during off-duty hours, either downtown or in the barracks after returning to the company. A run-in with the MPs, a fistfight, or disrespect to the sergeant on CQ resulted in an Article 15 administered before the effects of the previous night's hangover were past. Paperwork, completed during the morning formation, was read, along with his rights, to an offender immediately afterward. An afternoon trip to the staff judge advocate allowed the soldier to receive legal advice. When the duty day was completed, the man was in front of my desk for the Article 15 proceedings. By my direction, Article 15s, formal counseling, and other "negative actions" always took place after duty hours. Formal training time was not to be interrupted by disciplinary action. Also, since off-time is a soldier's most valued possession, using it up during correctional actions was another means of gaining his attention.

If the man chose to accept the procedure—and most did because they were aware of the evidence against them—he had the option of remaining silent, speaking in his own behalf, or having another person speak for him. Once the soldier had his say, I would read the statements against him or have witnesses relate their observations. Rarely was anything revealed that was not already known.

Once everyone had been heard, I studied the evidence and statements and announced to the soldier what his punishment was to be. Unless a member of his chain of command asked for leniency and/or the crime was a first offense, the punishment was usually the maximum: a reduction of one rank, a fine of a week's pay, and either seven days in CCF or fourteen days of restriction and extra duty. Occasionally, one or more of these punishments was suspended for up to thirty days. However, I could set aside the suspension with no hearing and for any reason.

Upon completion of the administering of the Article 15, the soldier still had one last option. He could, in writing or verbally, request a review of the punishment by the battalion commander. In eighteen months of command at A Company—and during more than twenty years in uniform—I never saw a punishment under this procedure reduced or set aside. Soldiers knew the trend but, nonetheless, occasionally appealed, not in hope of a reduction, but to delay the punishment. If no appeal was requested, rank was immediately removed, and the CCF term or the restriction and extra duty began.

When a soldier reported for an Article 15 or any other counseling or action, he was accompanied by his team leader, squad leader, platoon sergeant, and platoon leader. Their presence was partially to offer observations on his performance but, more important, to teach them that they shared responsibility for any wrongs committed by their troops. Depending on the offense, I usually kept the chain of command in my office after the soldier was dismissed for counseling of various levels of intensity.

Chain of command involvement permeated every action of the company. One area in which I did not initially employ the technique was fixed quickly. On my first night in command I had received a call at two in the morning to sign for a soldier from the MP station in accordance with division policy that only a company commander could do so. When I departed the MP station with one still drunk and extremely sick soldier, I wondered what in the hell I was doing there alone. On all future calls to sign for a soldier—and there were many in the first months—I contacted Carrasco with instructions to call in the offender's entire chain of command. One call to Top was easier than my calling the chain myself—and it also guaranteed that Carrasco would be raising hell with all concerned.

While fair and timely punishment got the attention of a majority of the soldiers and produced an improvement in discipline and behavior, some either did not get the word or chose to ignore the fact they would have to be responsible for their actions. Along with keeping note of new offenders, Carrasco and the company clerk reviewed the unit records to establish a list of multiple offenders. Any soldier who appeared on the list with two or more offenses which resulted in an Article 15 or court-martial was immediately considered for elimination under the various "chapters" categories.

During my first weeks in command, I often gave third chances to multiple offenders if they had the positive recommendations of their chain of command. With *no* exception, that was a bad decision on my part. Every person on the list with two offenses—and the initial number was over fifteen—committed still another offense that resulted in a discharge.

My initial reluctance to institute an arbitrary two-and-out rule stemmed from my idea that with time and proper leadership, nearly any soldier could be motivated, taught, or forced to comply with proper soldierly requirements. While I am still not sure that this is not true, after a few weeks of testing my theory in the realities of the post-Vietnam, all-volunteer army of the mid-seventies, I concluded that there simply was not adequate time to dedicate to the conversion of the unmotivated, the ill-disciplined, or the out-and-out thugs. The old army rule of thumb that ten percent of the people take ninety percent of the time was all too accurate. With too little time available, all we could do was to get rid of the hoodlums and poor performers and spend more time with those who could do their assigned jobs. Again the reasoning was quite simple: if we could not depend on a man in garrison, then it was a safe bet that he would be worthless in combat.

Another discovery I soon made—again the hard way—was that soldiers waiting for a bad discharge could be depended upon only to get into more trouble unless closely watched. One soldier had received Article 15s for disrespect to an NCO and for possession of a dime bag of hash. His real trouble had begun, however, with his arrest downtown with a suitcase containing well over $10,000 worth of marijuana.

The German authorities held the soldier in jail for several weeks only to mysteriously release him just prior to trial. Official channels revealed no reason for the soldier's sudden release. It was only through Sergeant Liebrich's knowledge of the German language and a friend of his on the local police force that we found out that the normally efficient German *Polizei* had lost the evidence—or, more likely, had it stolen from their evidence room.

The inability of the German authorities to take legal action did not prevent us from processing paperwork to eliminate the soldier as an undesirable under Chapter 13. Even though the discharge was completed from our end, it still took several weeks to be processed through the various channels including division. In the meantime, we had a soldier on our hands who had virtually nothing to lose. Secure in the knowledge that we wanted to be rid of him as soon as possible, he knew that as long as he did not commit any major, jail-resulting offense, he had little to worry about. With this in mind the soldier ignored my orders restricting him to the company area until his discharge. After coming in several nights in a row to check the company and finding the soldier had fled the barracks for downtown, I had his bunk moved beside the CQ desk so he could be watched more closely. The first night of this new arrangement, he managed to disappear again. He was attempting to sneak back into the barracks a little after midnight when I happened to see him on one of my late-night checks.

Figuring that there must be some reason for his nocturnal visits downtown, I read him his rights under Article 31* of the UCMJ and conducted a body search. He seemed unconcerned when I found two "nickel bags" of hash and a used hash pipe in his pockets. He continued to be disinterested during the Article 15 proceeding the following day—and for good reason. Previous punishments had reduced his pay to zero, he had no more stripes to take, and he was already restricted to the barracks. Nonetheless, I followed through on the Article 15 for no other reason than it added something to his records in case he ever tried to appeal his bad discharge.

While an Article 15 and regular restriction to the barracks had little influence on the soldier, there were actions that I could take that would get his attention. After a quick trip to the arms room, I called the soldier before my desk. A few minutes later, at my request, S.Sgt. Randy Beal came into the office. Beal, a squad leader in Liebrich's platoon, was a Vietnam veteran with rows of hero and "I-was-there" ribbons and had the well-earned reputation of taking the responsibilities of a noncommissioned officer seriously. With no comment directly to the soldier, I reached into my desk and withdrew a .45-caliber pistol and a full magazine. Inserting the magazine into the pistol, I handed

---

*Article 31 of the UCMJ gives those in the military the basic "Miranda rights" of any U.S. citizen: the rights to remain silent and to a have access to legal counsel. While reading the rights was usually a formality, I always read them verbatim from a plasticized card I carried in my billfold.

it to Sergeant Beal saying, "This man is your responsibility until he gets on the plane to leave the country. If he attempts to break restriction again and flee the barracks, shoot him."

Needless to say, such an order would never be given to anyone who might seriously consider carrying it out. Beal knew and I knew that I was not serious. Of course the soldier certainly did not know of our lack of resolve to add a .45 slug to his inventory of body parts. A little less than a week later the soldier was on his way back to whatever block he had come from with a bad discharge in his pocket. He had never strayed from the barracks again, and according to Beal, the man was almost polite in his final days in uniform.

Other soldiers awaiting discharge did not require armed escorts. However, extraordinary means to keep them out of further trouble were at times required. Successive brawls in a Schweinfurt nightclub and with the MPs who attempted to arrest him brought another troop before my desk. I quickly processed the paperwork to discharge the troublemaking private. While I considered whether or not to assign Beal and his .45-escort duty one more time, Carrasco informed me that he thought that the escort should be from the man's platoon instead of from elsewhere in the company. Top added that he already had a volunteer.

Waiting outside my office was a buck sergeant, with sleeve-splitting biceps and a nose that had come in contact with more than a fist or two. To my question about why he sought the escort duty, the sergeant explained, "Sir, me and Jones* came to the company together a little over a year ago. We used to be drinking buddies before I got promoted. Except for a few breaks, everything could be the other way around, with me getting kicked out. He'll do what I say. There won't be any problems."

There was no hesitation in my decision to grant the sergeant's request, for I was sure he could handle the duty. I was much surprised the next morning to see the sergeant in formation with a deep cut above one eye and the other nearly swollen shut. Standing next to him—or doing his best to stand considering the cuts, bruises, and abrasions that covered his face and other areas not as obvious—was Jones.

After dismissing the formation, I grabbed Top, with the intention of gathering the chain of command to begin court-martial proceeding against Jones. Assault on an NCO would negate the

*Name changed to protect the guilty.

discharge—at least until after jail time had been served. Carrasco put a stop to my plans as he explained that no further action was required. It seemed that minutes after the sergeant began his escort duty, the soldier had balked at following the NCO's instructions. The sergeant looked the brawler in the eye and invited him behind the barracks saying, "If I whip your ass, you do as I say until we put you on a plane out of here. If you win, no sweat. I'll say I fell down the stairs and tell Top and the Old Man to get another escort."

One only had to look at the obvious damages to determine who had come out the best in the fight. Another indication was that the sergeant remained the escort, and to the best of my knowledge, the soldier gave him no more trouble.

Along with administering fines, extra duty, and rank reductions to those needing rehabilitation, there were other means of regaining discipline in a unit nearly out of control. At least once a month, and almost weekly in the early days, I conducted a complete "health and welfare inspection" of the company. The normal procedure was to have Carrasco hold the company outside the barracks following morning formation. The officers and senior NCOs then inspected every nook and cranny of the company area, including personal wall lockers, automobiles, and equipment of all types.

Legally, the purpose of the inspection was to eliminate any items that might threaten the health and physical welfare of the unit. Originally the H&W had been a means of disease prevention and control and a method for generally increasing the unit's comfort level. Our more current purpose did not follow the original intention but did allow us to find illegal drugs and weapons as well as to recover government tools, ammunition, and equipment. My initial inspection discovered two pistols, three switchblade knives, several grams of heroin, two drug-shooting kits, fifteen tabs of LSD, over eighty assorted upper or downer capsules, and almost a half pound of hashish along with a half dozen or so well-used pipes and bowls. We also found several smoke grenades, trip flares, and thousands of rounds of ammunition of various caliber. Enough U.S. Army small tools—screwdrivers, pliers, wrenches, and hammers—were confiscated to make up nearly a quarter of the shortages in the motor pool.

Most of the drugs were discovered in common-use areas such as the desk in each four- to five-man room, which prevented individual responsibility being fixed. In only two cases was hash found in a soldier's wall locker, and those resulted in Article 15s.

While health and welfare inspections were an excellent tool for cleaning out the barracks, they were also a serious detriment to what little morale remained in the company. A soldier's privacy did not amount to much, and the wholesale search of his belongings chipped away at whatever dignity remained. In many units, including some in which I had served but not commanded, a typical H&W threw personal belongings onto the floor, ripped bedding from bunks, and generally tore hell out of everything.

In an effort not to devastate what was left of morale with H&Ws, I carefully and forcefully briefed my inspectors to ensure that no damage was done during the inspection. At the same time, I demanded that every area and item, including the automobiles of the officers and senior NCOs, be checked with equal enthusiasm. With the exception of the drugs that could be directly attributed to individuals, all illegal items discovered in the first H&W were confiscated, and no individual actions were taken against the owners. At the following formation, I informed the company of this policy, while assuring the men that such leniency would not occur at future inspections—and that there surely would be more of the same.

Along with the H&Ws, I also conducted barracks inspections of a different type, with a much more specific purpose. German shepherd dogs trained as drug sniffers could be requested from the MPs to make a tour of the barracks and motor pool. Ruled as a legal search by the highest civilian and military courts, the only requirement was a prebriefing by the dog's handler on the canine's experience and actions when marijuana or hashish was detected.*

The usual procedure for a dog inspection was to keep the soldiers out of the barracks at the end of a morning inspection. Accompanied by the handler, Top and I would then tour the barracks. When the dog smelled hash or marijuana, it would alert us by scratching and barking. In a common-use area, we conducted an immediate search. For alerts on secured wall or footlockers, the owner was brought up from the formation, read his rights, and ordered to open his locker.

Dog inspections were quite effective, since the canines were

---

*While the military had other dogs trained to sniff out explosives, the only drugs the dogs could detect at the time were cannabis derivatives.

so proficient that they could detect the smallest trace of cannabis, including used pipes. While some alerts were false—and even then there was a pretty good chance that there were traces of pot smoke in the clothing—the dogs were extremely accurate. Regardless of their proficiency, however, there was a trade-off in morale. Even those soldiers who shared the command's interest in getting drugs out of the barracks resented the intrusion of a dog and an MP into their living areas.

Despite the seriousness of sniffer-dog inspections, they did occasionally offer a bit of comic relief. More than once—and on one occasion at the wall locker of my company drug and alcohol counselor—the dogs enthusiastically alerted on remains of food brought back from the mess hall.

Be it drugs or mess-hall chow discovered by the dogs, their presence never failed to get the attention of the troops. Late one evening, as I returned to the barracks for a final check, I ran into the company commander of another infantry unit down the street. Along with him was his family pet, a German shepherd. While we talked, the canine saw something in the shadows and barked several times. Before the last bark had stopped echoing across the quadrangle, shouts of "drug dog" and "narc in the area" were heard from every barracks within hearing distance. Sounds of commodes flushing and windows being raised to discard contraband followed.

I suppose that a disciplined unit can be created by absolute centralized power with threats and administration of punishment replacing any form of real leadership—in fact, I have had the unenviable duty of serving under several commanders, including three-star generals, who led by the fist and court-martial rather than by the head and heart. The primary problem with compassionless leadership is that it may create discipline in peace, but does little to build men who will fight in war. Soldiers with more fear of their own commanders than of the enemy cannot be depended upon on the modern battlefield.

While strong discipline had to be administered and demanded in the rebuilding of A Company, it would not lead to success on its own. Proper actions and correct behavior deserved reward. However, decent living conditions should be a standard rather than a reward. Review of the work orders submitted by the company revealed six-month-old requests on which no action had been taken. A call, followed by a personal visit, to the facilities engineer yielded nothing but frustration. According to the engineers, little money was available for repairs and none for improvements. Each person I questioned and demanded action from would only say that all the barracks were due to be renovated within a year and, therefore, any money spent would be a waste. That was the reasoning of people who did not have to live in the shanty quarters provided my soldiers.

Like the "little red hen" of children's stories—and practically every other soldier who had ever served in the infantry—I realized that the only way to get any results was to do it ourselves. With that in mind, I instructed each platoon to appoint a part-time handyman, who would be responsible for replacing window panes, light bulbs, lock hasps, and any other broken or worn-out item in the platoon areas. In addition I told Top to select a soldier in the company to work directly for him, full time, to improve the barracks' living conditions.

Staff Sergeant Cook did his part as well. Machine-gun barrels were excellent trading material for paint, brushes, shower heads, and latrine fixtures. When Cook showed up with a truckload of five-gallon paint cans, I never asked where he got them. My only question was how many .50-cal barrels had it cost.

Using the newly designated company handymen, supplemented generously with soldiers serving extra duty time by way of Article 15s or "first sergeant justice," we soon had the barracks livable, if not gleaming. Hallways, offices, and rooms were painted from top to bottom. The company dayroom was redecorated, the pool table recovered, and the television repaired. Extra cues and chalk were purchased as were subscriptions to popular magazines. Additional periodicals were added to the dayroom stock by placing a box outside the orderly room for books and magazines contributed by the soldiers themselves.

The final paint job was applied to the walls of the latrine that had been painted black to stop graffiti. Of course the bright, clean, white walls attracted the pencils and pens of a few poets who wanted to question the parentage and sex habits of Carrasco and myself or to bad-mouth the army in general. So I instructed Top to have the CQ runner paint over graffiti each morning. I was not surprised that the few markings which had appeared initially soon dwindled to nearly nothing. Although they would never have admitted it, the soldiers were as proud of their new living conditions as were Carrasco and I.

While I demanded adherence to use of the chain of command, I also provided the soldiers a direct avenue to the company commander. Each Thursday night from 1700 hours until as late as needed, I provided an "open door." During those hours any soldier, for any reason, could have direct access to me to seek advice, ask assistance for personal problems, and/or to generally express complaints or difficulties.

Although an open-door policy was certainly not new* to the army or even to the company, I did my best to ensure the spirit of the procedure was followed. Any problem or question was recorded and acted upon as quickly as possible. At times Top and I could immediately take care of whatever arose; other problems required involvement by additional members of the chain of command.

In addition to the open-door policy, I did my best to see that I had as much personal contact with the soldiers as possible. This began within minutes of a new soldier's reporting to the company. Interviews with the troops revealed that usually the first person they had met was a drug pusher or someone offering to share a bowl or a needle. By changing that trend, making Top and me the greeters, not only could we warn them about the consequences of drug use, but also we could begin their orientation to the company's mission.

Each night before I left the barracks, as well as on my frequent late-night checks, I went from room to room. If a soldier wanted to show me a picture of his girl back home or the car he was hoping to buy, I looked and made the appropriate comments. Of soldiers whom I knew were having personal problems or who had been ill, I inquired about their progress. Much like a small-town preacher visiting his congregation in their homes, I made the rounds—and found the informal moments with the company to be some of the best of times in command.

*During my entire time in command in Germany, as well as prior duty in combat and later assignments in the United States, I would be hard pressed to list a single innovative action of leadership on my part. There simply was no reason to think up new ways to command successfully. During two hundred years of experience by American soldiers and countless centuries by men in other armies, effective leadership techniques had already been discovered. All one had to do to be successful in the post-Vietnam army was to follow the basics and do them well and with enthusiasm, fairness, and good intentions. The same remains true today.

One problem that was revealed early in the sessions was the feeling on the part of the troops that the promotion, awards, leave, and pass systems were unfair. Some of their concerns were well founded, but the major deficiency was a failure by the chain of command to keep the soldiers informed about procedures and priorities. That was easily remedied by having each platoon maintain a bulletin-board list of the rank order of those to receive the next available stripe or other positive action.

While swift justice was administered for abuse of drugs—including alcohol—and for any incident remotely race related, assistance was also provided in those areas. Any soldier found guilty of a drug or alcohol offense was, in addition to the punishment, referred to the Ledward Barracks Community Alcohol and Drug Rehabilitation Center. Use of the facility was also open to soldiers who voluntarily sought assistance in the program, which varied from off-duty classes of two weeks' duration to commitment to a detox center for whatever period necessary. Volunteer participation also provided an assurance that no criminal or negative administrative personnel actions would be taken.

Racial tensions were constant, with one-on-one confrontations routine and out-and-out riots always a possibility. Along with my phase-progression of getting the predominantly black platoon integrated, I conducted monthly "race relation council" meetings, composed of representatives of each platoon. The principal accomplishment of the council was that it provided a forum for complaints and an outlet for frustrations. While it was rare for the meetings to result in any direct changes in company procedures or personnel actions, the meetings did seem to do some good in letting the men express themselves.

In February 1975, regardless of race, one of the dominant complaints of the soldiers of A Company was common to all soldiers of all ranks in Germany at the time. As a budget-cutting measure, the Department of the Army decided to arbitrarily extend the thirty-six-month European tour by three months. For those of us who had been promised a three-year tour and who were looking forward to a normal rotation away from the expenses of Germany and to the familiarity of the States, the extension was not well received. For the eighteen- and nineteen-year-old soldiers in the ranks, who had understood from their recruiters that they were volunteering for a maximum rather than a minimum of sixteen months, the decision was a blow to any morale gained.*

Oddly, the extension provided positive aspects despite the overall negative impact. While everyone, including the NCOs and officers, felt betrayed by the very elected and appointed leadership we had taken an oath to follow, the extension applied equally to everyone, regardless of rank or position. Difficulties and hardship, when shared equally by all, can—with proper leadership and a complete sharing of information—add to, rather than reduce, cohesiveness.

During my first three months in command, the condition of the company had required far more punishment than reward for the soldiers. Everyone—with the possible exception of those soldiers whom we were putting in jail or kicking out of the army with bad paper—realized that it was to his advantage to remove drugs from the barracks, reduce racial tensions, and regain a level of discipline that would lead to success on the battlefield. Yet, many wondered to themselves or questioned their chain of command about when the continual changes would affect them personally.

Beyond improving the quality of life in the barracks, Top and I began a sports program that included both on- and off-duty time in an effort to offer alternatives to drugs and boredom. In addition to intracompany competition between platoons, we entered competition with the other units. "Combat football," where each team attempted to push an inflated, six-foot ball across a line, was popular whether played on snow or frozen or muddied ground. Since the only rule was the team got a point for crossing the goal line with the ball, the games often produced so many injuries that we had to substitute "combat volleyball"

---

*In my more than twenty years in uniform, every budget cut I experienced had its first impact not on equipment, weapons, or other items produced by civilian companies back in the various congressional districts, but rather on the young men and women who had volunteered to serve their country. Change-of-station moves, pay raises, housing, and recreation facilities are the first to feel the budget knife. Regardless of rhetoric about requirements to maintain hardware readiness, the bottom line is that, in every case, the politically appointed civilian leadership in the office of the secretary of the army and the pork-barrel-riding members of Congress care more for their own interests and those of their profit-minded constituents than for the welfare of the soldier in the barracks.

until everyone healed. Actually volleyball was not much safer because, along with the normal rules, the troops added punching, kicking, and scratching across and under the net as much as they could manage.

My headquarters section, composed of clerks, mechanics, and supply types, fielded its own team. At their request I joined the squad in competition with the infantry platoons. In the initial minutes of my first combat football game, no one seemed to want to block, tackle, or use any other of the possible maiming tactics on the company commander. After the first shot was delivered, however, everyone including the platoon leader of our opposition took a lick at the Old Man. I did my best to return whatever was delivered—with a little extra. Maybe it was because of my five-inches-over-six-feet height and over two hundred pounds, or perhaps just the spirit of competition, but after everyone had at least one shot, the game calmed down to its usual mayhem where all participants were treated with equal aggression.

The battalion competition was a bit more sedate and much better organized, with regular officials hired by recreation services. While the battalion basketball league had a positive aspect in building unit morale, it had its downside. The A Company team, despite my expert coaching—or perhaps as a result thereof—did poorly in the initial games. Finally a team floor leader emerged as a great ball handler who was also a fair tracked-vehicle mechanic.

When the last game of the season arrived, we were only one win away from at least a tie for the battalion championship trophy. We held our own down to the last minutes due to the ball stealing and pin-point shooting by the mechanic. His performance was one of the greatest individual efforts I have ever seen on a basketball court at any level of competition. Unfortunately, a shot from near center court by our opponents at the final buzzer put us in the defeat column.

The loss was disappointing for coach, players, and remaining members of the company alike. It was not until some weeks later that I learned that my team-leading mechanic was hooked on junk and, in fact, had shot up with heroin shortly before the big game. With his fantastic performance in mind, I could only hope that he would report to a Veterans Administration detox hospital following the discharge that we hastily pushed through the channels.

By the end of February our hard work was beginning to show

a few results. Blotter entries and trips to the MP station slowed from nightly to "only" two or three a week. During one of the weekly command information classes in which I discussed current problems and outlined upcoming events, I promised the company that if we could go thirty consecutive days without a blotter entry, we would take a day off or training holiday.

Blotter entries included all types of transgressions—varying from traffic accidents and lost billfolds to murder and armed robbery. While we had reduced the daily and often multiple daily entries to two or three a week, the idea of thirty blotter-free days seemed all but impossible to everyone, including me. Still, it gave us something to shoot for. Outside the orderly room, I posted a large sign with the heading "Blotter-Free Days." Each day I added a number or, all too often, reduced the number back to zero.

Lieutenant Colonel King, the battalion commander, supported our efforts to reduce blotter incidents and made similar promises to the rest of the battalion: a day off for thirty blotter-free days. In addition, he combined such factors as reenlistment rate, inspection results, maintenance records, and his personal observations to designate a monthly battalion honor company. And A Company won the first award. At the battalion pay-day formation which concluded February, King presented a plaque for the orderly room and streamer with stitching spelling out "Honor Company" for the company guidon. Along with his congratulations, the battalion commander explained that the plaque and streamer were ours until the results of the next month's competition were announced.

The company seemed pleased with the honor and gave a loud cheer when it was announced. I was happy with the honor-company designation if for no other reason than for the positive morale it provided. At the same time I sincerely doubted that we deserved an honor of any type. King made some remarks during his presentation about cream rises to the top. All that I could think of was that if we were the cream, I would hate like hell to see the skimmed milk.

CHAPTER 6

SWEAT IN TRAINING SAVES BLOOD IN BATTLE—AND ALSO KEEPS YOU OFF THE STREET AT NIGHT
March–April 1975

Discipline is the foundation on which an infantry unit builds the expertise for combat and the spirit to achieve victory on the battlefield. In no occupation except the military service is the penalty for being untrained and ill-prepared as severe. For the athlete there is always another game and a new competition. For the businessman the loss of dollars or of sales territory can be bested by profits in another year. Even lost love is cured or replaced in time. For the soldier who goes down in defeat, the end can be death—and what more final result can there be?

All soldiers—even those of us who served in the confused post-Vietnam years—realize that, at any time, they may be called forth to kill or be killed. While death is a horrible end in itself, the warrior must realize that not only is his life in the balance but also the lives and freedom of those he professes to defend. Such responsibilities weigh heavily on any man who chooses the profession of arms. For the NCO and officer who choose to lead such men and be responsible for their welfare and lives, the burden is that much greater. Popularity would be nice. Fame, fortune, or the merest spark of recognition would make the days a bit easier to get through. Yet, the ultimate responsibility and the only acceptable reward of command at any level is the survival of the men entrusted to one's leadership and the successful defense of home and country.

Lives lost, blood shed, tears spilled, destinies denied— whatever the cost, only victory is acceptable for the professional soldier. One need but look at history to understand that a well-trained, highly motivated, and adequately equipped army is often a nation's only chance for survival.

Former victories also do not promise future successes. The city/state of Carthage on the North African coast had a magnificent war record after its founding in the ninth century B.C. Over the years it was victorious in battle after battle and war after war. Yet it took but one loss to end Carthage forever. In 146 B.C., Rome invaded and, after a long and difficult struggle, defeated the city/state. On the surrender of Carthage, the surviving men were immediately executed. The women were likewise killed, but only after being ravished by their captors. The children of Carthage were sold into slavery. All houses and public buildings were burned and their foundations razed. Wells were poisoned or filled in. Salt was applied to the fields so no crop would ever again grow.

No second chances were given the soldiers and citizens of Carthage.

On the plains of Europe during the mid-1970s, I doubt if many of the soldiers had heard of or cared about the demise of Carthage. Most were aware of the recent wars in the Mideast and the various brushfire revolutions in Africa, but with the negative opinion of military action of any kind brought on by the lengthy Vietnam War, few really believed that we would have to leave our warm barracks, cold beer, and plentiful drug supply for any real unpleasantries. The Cold War, then in its third decade, provided a real threat, but its long-term existence had diminished the thought that "cold" could become "hot."

Regardless of the prevailing opinion—apparently shared by the folks back home, many soldiers, and, unfortunately, some of the military's senior leadership—that we were experiencing a lasting peace, it would have been nothing less than criminal for me to approach my command time in any other manner except with the belief that combat could occur at any time. Any casualties sustained by A Company due to poor training or leadership would be blood on my hands that could never be removed. The Chinese proverb said, "the more you sweat in peace, the less you bleed in war"; I believed it and began preparing Alpha Company for battles I hoped we would never have to fight. With a fair level of discipline established, we could look to what our real mission was—to be prepared to repel the Warsaw Pact forces that were garrisoned just across the East German border.

All of the soldiers in the company were graduates of basic and advanced individual training amounting to at least sixteen weeks. Training in the army, however, is neverending. Company training is coordinated with battalion, battalion with brigade, brigade with division, division with corps, corps with the theater command, and the theater command with the Department of the Army. Expenditures of ammunition, use of training areas, and funds for replacement parts are all carefully budgeted.

At the company level, we prepared detailed training schedules, outlining formations, classes, maneuvers, and all other activities hour-by-hour. No minute was unaccounted for; even off-duty hours were listed as "commander's time." We prepared the schedules no less than two weeks in advance of specific training and developed long-range plans extending out as far as a year. The schedules had to be coordinated at all levels to insure that training assets were available and that we were following the training guidance published by each of our higher headquarters. We then posted approved schedules on each platoon's bulletin board.

Training was a constant, ongoing activity, with concurrent classes in such areas as first aid, use of protective masks and clothing, weapons, etc., taking place even during installation support and preparation for the AGI. Other time periods were scheduled for more in-depth training. March and April were to be the company's first intensive training time since my assumption of command. I hoped the past ninety days had instilled enough discipline and teamwork for us to take advantage of the opportunity.

Our "sweat in training" served purposes other than the prevention of "bleeding in war." I was certainly not the first commander to understand that physically challenging, difficult training paid off by also leaving the soldiers too exhausted to venture into town at day's end. One aspect of this train-with-pain philosophy that I had not thought of, however, was that the leaders, and in particular myself, would be just as tired as the soldiers.

Thinking that good training also keeps the soldiers off the streets at night, I planned a foot march to the company's "general defensive plan" (GDP) positions along the East German border, located a bit more than thirty miles from Ledward Barracks. We would march twenty miles the first day and then on to our defensive positions the second. After a day of reconnaissance and classes on the GDP, we would march homeward. The plan called for a field kitchen to meet us at each bivouac site to serve a hearty meal.

Our march was at a forced pace covering three to four miles per hour. We took ten-minute breaks every fifty minutes—rest was only the secondary purpose. At each stop the NCOs had to check their soldiers' feet for blisters and to supervise the frequent changing of socks and liberal application of foot powder. Inventories were also made to ensure each man had his assigned weapon and equipment.

With millions of dollars of tracked and wheeled vehicles sitting in the motor pool, it might have seemed a bit ridiculous for us to be wearing down the leather on the bottom of our boots. However, foot mobility is a basic soldiering skill regardless of unit of assignment. Armored personnel carriers, tanks, helicopters, airplanes, ships, and any other sophisticated weapons of war—past, present or future—are merely a means of delivery, support, or cover by which the foot soldier could reach and conquer his objective. No victory can be achieved without the foot soldier's occupying the space that was formerly held by his enemy—be it a dusty hilltop, a muddy rice paddy, or a marble-floor castle. Sailors, airmen, and rear-echelon soldiers can provide critical and most welcome assistance, but if an infantry grunt does not place his boots on it, no piece of territory can ever be considered taken or neutralized.

Our feet did not fail us on our march to the GDP. Although bitching and complaining accompanied us during the first few miles, not a single soldier fell out of the march. The officers and NCOs continually moved up and down the formation, giving words of encouragement, checking on the conditions of the men, and exchanging a few words. With rare exceptions, the soldiers seemed glad to be out of the barracks. They even appeared proud as we marched through the small, farm villages that dotted our path. The children flashing the two-finger *V* sign, which still meant victory near the Communist border, made everyone's step a little lighter.

One other training benefit of the march to the GDP was that each soldier could better grasp why he was in Europe and what would be expected of him if the proverbial balloon actually went up. The Alpha Company sector was on the forward slope of a thickly forested hill mass that paralleled the border along the battalion area of operations. Positioned about two hundred feet above the open plain, we had an unspoiled view and fields of fire all the way to the border. With the three-kilometer plus range of our wire-guided, antitank weapons (TOWs), we would be able to engage enemy targets within seconds after they crossed the international border only four kilometers to our front.

The A Company line stretched for a little more than three kilometers—nearly double what an infantry company would ideally be assigned. Our covering the distance would be assisted, however, by the attachment of a platoon composed of five M-60A1 tanks. A section of two TOW missile launchers from the battalion combat support company would round out our firepower. Our concentration of fire would be on the two passes with hard-surface roads that led from the border, through our sector, and on toward Schweinfurt and the German heartland.

Shortly after our arrival at the GDP, I gathered the company to explain to them how we fit into the big picture in the defense of Western Europe. Across the plain to our front, I pointed out the double fence, topped with rows of barbed wire and guarded by a watchtower every kilometer or so. With the binoculars we passed around, the soldiers could actually spot East German and Soviet border guards patrolling the fence on foot, in vehicles, and by helicopter. One patrol was accompanied by a German shepherd scout dog. Top and I also pointed out to the troops that despite the Communist claims that the fortifications were to keep us out, it was obvious from their designs that they were to keep their citizens from escaping.

I explained to the company that in our sector we could plan on being outnumbered by more than ten to one in men, tanks, and artillery pieces. Our advantage would hopefully be the time we would have to dig in and the support provided by preplanned artillery fire and close-in air support from A-10 tank-killer, ground-attack airplanes. Minefields and obstacles prepared by the division engineers would serve as barriers and guide the enemy into our kill zones. More mines would be delivered by air and artillery barrage.

I also informed the men about the corps and division cavalry covering forces and antitank helicopters that would attrit the enemy forces as they crossed the border and before they reached our positions. While I left no doubt that we would stand and fight—and account well for ourselves—I also noted that we would have prepared positions several kilometers to the rear in case we had to withdraw. I did not add that in virtually every scenario, war game, and field exercise, the only way our meager forces had been able to stop the enemy's advance was through the use of tactical nuclear weapons which were capable of being delivered by the smallest artillery in the division—the 155mm howitzer.

With each platoon leader and platoon sergeant, I walked the company defensive sector pointing out our areas of responsibility and overlapping fields of fire. The company mortar platoon, which threw rounds in a high arc, selected its firing position to the rear of the company and planned fires on dead space where direct-fire weapons could not reach because targets there would be hidden in valleys or out of sight and protected by hills and buildings.

After each platoon had had the chance to position its squads, two-man foxholes, and locations for crew-served weapons, I walked back down the line to question each soldier to be sure that he knew that he was occupying the exact position where he would be if World War III became a reality instead of just a threat.

Most of the soldiers seemed impressed with the mission and their possible part in history. At the same time, most recognized that if war really began, their personal well-being was likely to come to an abrupt and violent end. Many of the soldiers were not happy when I explained that our position was in a German national forest and for that reason we could not prepare defenses in advance.

The return to Ledward Barracks was by the same foot-mobile transportation which had taken us to the GDP. Despite our navigating a different route on the return, the distance was little different from that of the outbound track. We arrived back in the company area early enough on Friday afternoon for the soldiers to have time to clean, maintain, and store their weapons and gear by the end of the day.

I was happy to be able to add four days to our blotter-free sign outside the orderly room. The joy was short-lived, however. Several hours before midnight, I was back at the MP station, along with a young soldier's chain of command. Before the night was over, I made another visit to the military police and one to the barracks to break up a fight.

Despite the extracurricular activities, I was aware of some progress, albeit extremely slow and often painful, in the company's discipline and training levels. My next step was to show the company that I appreciated their efforts and that all training did not have to be twenty-five-mile forced marches across the countryside or boring lectures inside a classroom. With some extra training funds from brigade, we rented commercial buses to transport the company to the U.S. Armed Forces Recreation Center at Garmisch-Partenkirchen in southern Bavaria. Garmisch-Partenkirchen has long been a winter retreat for Germans, and Hitler had built a private lodge nearby prior to World War II. The village also had hosted a winter Olympics during the 1930s. Since the end of the Second World War, the town and the surrounding Bavarian Alps have served as an R&R area for American soldiers.

Before departing for Garmisch, I met with the company and told them that while there was a training mission to the trip, our main purpose was to have a good time. I also warned them that anything short of well-disciplined behavior would not be tolerated. Anyone getting in any kind of trouble whatsoever would be returned immediately to Schweinfurt. More formal disciplinary action would follow on the return of the rest of the company.

With the recreation center providing billeting and rations, as well as ski and ice-skating instructors, we were able to enjoy three days of winter-warfare training in resort conditions. Some of the training was practical, most was just plain fun. We allowed time for the soldiers to visit the nearby castle built by "Mad King" Ludwig, which was better known to my soldiers as the model used for the Fantasyworld castle at California's Disneyland. Nights were free so the soldiers could frequent the American movie theater, the enlisted and NCO clubs, and the downtown discos.

The three days passed quickly and with no trouble at all—or at least none that I knew of until the day after we returned to Ledward. Doug Musser stopped me after morning formation and said that we needed to talk about allegations that were being made about one of his NCOs. After Doug added that it included members of the third platoon, I told him to get Liebrich and Carrasco and report to my office.

Minutes later we were listening to Musser report that rumors were sweeping the company that one of his squad leaders was a homosexual and had performed various acts with one of the soldiers in the third platoon while we were in Garmisch. Musser added that it was common knowledge in the platoon that the sergeant had been transferred to us from another battalion because of similar accusations.

From my observations, the sergeant had done an absolutely outstanding job during the month since he had arrived in the company. I had been particularly pleased to see that he was an excellent role model for all the company: the sergeant was hard core, demanding discipline of his squad in training and appearance. The only complaints I had heard about him were that he was too demanding and often kept his squad after duty hours to repeat training until they got it right.

My conversation with Musser and the others quickly revealed that a soldier in the third platoon seemed to be the source of the rumors. Minutes later the soldier was in front of my desk. He seemed happy to tell me what he had seen and heard late one night in the Garmisch barracks. After his explanation, I had him repeat his observations in writing. According to the soldier, "I came back to my room a little after midnight to find Sergeant X sitting on the edge of Private Y's bed. No one else was in the room. When he saw me, Sergeant X asked 'what room is this?' When I told him, he said he must have walked into the wrong room and he left. He acted like he was drunk and messed up. I went to bed but about ten minutes later I heard the door open and Sergeant X came back in, took off his trousers and got in bed with Private Y. For about fifteen minutes I heard heavy breathing and slurping sounds before I fell asleep. I did not hear Sergeant X leave the room."

When I asked the soldier if he had anything else to add, he said, "Yes, sir. I also have heard that Sergeant X has been carrying on with Private First Class Z in his own platoon."

With their platoon leaders present, I then proceeded to question Private Y and Private First Class Z. Private Y, new to the company and—according to Liebrich—doing a good job, stated that on the night in question he had drunk a few beers in a downtown club where the accused sergeant and another NCO, Sergeant A, were also drinking. According to the written statement that I had the soldier prepare after our interview, "I did not see Sergeant X until the formation the next day. I have never participated in any homo act with Sergeant X, and he had never made any moves toward me. I'm from South Philly and know about queers and don't like them. I also don't think Sergeant X is one.''

Next in my office was Private First Class Z who seemed very surprised to be questioned about Sergeant X. In his statement Private First Class Z explained, "Sergeant X is a tough, no-nonsense NCO. My only association with him, other than in the platoon, was that I ran into him in a bar in Schweinfurt last month, and we shared a cab back to the barracks to save money. He did not say or do anything unusual that night or any other time.''

Sergeant A next reported that he and Sergeant X were good friends and had "drank beer and chased girls all over Garmisch every night of the trip." He added that the charges against X were "bullshit" and just a private's attempt to get back at a good NCO.

Liebrich was waiting outside my office with another NCO, Sergeant B, after my interview with Sergeant A. Sergeant B stated that due to a shortage of NCO rooms he had shared quarters with Private Y, the accuser. According to Sergeant B, he had been out drinking, returned to the room about midnight, and went to sleep. He added that he was a sound sleeper but hardly thought that the things rumored to have happened could have without awaking him.

Every commander has the responsibility of ensuring the rights and safety of his troops are protected—that includes making sure that the NCOs of the unit do not overstep their responsibilities and powers. At the same time, the sergeants of a company must be protected against efforts to jeopardize their authority. Often, finding the fair, accurate settlement to such disputes is one of a commander's most difficult tasks.

What I was faced with was not an atypical situation. Homosexuals have never been accepted by the American army and, according to official policy, are considered to be "detrimental to good order and discipline." On a more practical side, young men who often find the first test and proof of their manhood by becoming soldiers have a low tolerance for what they consider queers. Despite the more recent acceptance of homosexuality by the United States as a whole, in the military, officially and among the troops themselves, it continues to be unacceptable.

I concluded that I had a single person making accusations that could not be confirmed by any other source. That enough was sufficient evidence for me to make a decision. In every case where only two sides were known—a sergeant's and a private's—the word of the NCO was the one accepted as truth. With all other witnesses and interested parties also denying the charges, my determinations were made that much easier. The sergeant was returned to duty, where he continued to be an exemplary NCO in every manner. As for the private who had made the accusation, I arranged for his transfer to another battalion. Unfortunately for him, his departure was not quite soon enough. The night before he moved out, the CQ found him in the shower beaten nearly unconscious. Not surprising, no one had seen the assault. Even the private claimed that he had not seen any of his attackers.

I made an honest attempt to find the men who assaulted the private. My major concern was that the beating might have been administered by NCOs, but no one seemed to have seen anything at all. Knowing that Carrasco could often get information that I could not, I told him I wanted to get to the bottom of the incident. A few days later Top told me that no sergeants were involved. Top added that while he did not know who—and he had really not made a great effort to find out—the beating had come from only one man, and he was a private in Sergeant X's platoon.

My only further action was to discuss the incident with the company at my weekly command-information session. I explained that I took accusations against NCOs seriously and would not tolerate any abuse of the soldiers. My summary of the investigation and the facts that there was nothing to substantiate the rumors begun by the private seemed to satisfy the company. I never heard the incident mentioned again.

While the investigation had taken much of my time the first few days after our return from Garmisch, the major focus of the company was preparation for our coming three-week maneuvers at the Hohenfels training area. In addition to working with the battalion S-3 on the plan for the training period—coordinating the availability of ranges, ammunition, fuel, and other needed supplies—emphasis was also on a more immediate matter. Stories circulated all over the battalion and Ledward Barracks that the last time the 2d of the 30th had gone to Hohenfels, it had hardly been able to keep enough tracks and vehicles operational to conduct the planned maneuvers. According to Top and Dick Earle, Alpha Company's poorly maintained vehicles had littered the road from the motor pool to the railhead as well as all across the training area.

Maintenance, like discipline and combat readiness, is not an area where problems are solved quickly. We had made some progress before the IG, and we had continued to concentrate on maintenance since then. The key to our improvement had been following the simple, detailed instructions outlined in the "dash 10" operators manual that was now an integral part of each vehicle. These instructions provided checklists for pre- and post-operations as well as procedures for quarterly and annual maintenance.

Pre- and postoperation checks focused on areas that would prevent excessive wear or damage to the vehicle itself and to safety items which protected the driver and occupants. Included were such things as checking the oil and fluid levels—not a simple matter in an M-113 because there were eleven to be checked. The checklists were similar to the ones used by aircraft pilots, but unlike aviators, drivers paid little heed to the proper procedures. Some of this lack of attention to detail was just poor discipline. However, the major reason was that an M-113 or jeep driver rarely had his vehicle fall ten thousand feet if he failed to check each item on his list.

With improved maintenance in the forefront and discipline a continuing consideration, I instituted measures to insure the proper procedures were followed. We began with the basics— each driver and assistant driver, along with his vehicle NCO or officer commander, attended a class on the purpose of daily pre- and postoperational maintenance and the necessity for more thorough quarterly and annual shakedowns. After the class, each person reported to his vehicle. Dick Earle, bullhorn in hand, then went through each of the checklist points. We did not proceed to the next item until a platoon leader or sergeant confirmed the check had been made and the results recorded on Form 2404, the Daily Inspection Sheet.

This by-the-numbers approach was continued until each driver, assistant and leader knew it by rote. Quarterly thereafter, we repeated the procedure for several days to train new drivers and refresh the old. While this process seems most basic— because it is—it more than justified itself. When parts broke on Alpha Company vehicles, it began to be due to fair wear and tear rather than negligence.

Quarterly and annual maintenance were different matters. While the vehicle crew was responsible to assist, these procedures were the responsibility of the company motor pool personnel. During quarterly maintenance, filters were changed, and a more detailed inspection of all parts was conducted. The annual inspection required the removal of the power pack, transfer case, and transmission.

While the maintenance records showed these inspections had been conducted in the past, a quick look into the engine compartment revealed enough dirt, oil, and diesel to make it obvious that the packs had not been removed in far more than a year. Staff Sergeant Thomas made no attempt to persuade me that the inspections had been conducted. According to Thomas, in the two years he had been in the company, none of the previous commanders required the maintenance to take place, and he readily admitted that the previous quarterlies and annuals had been conducted with "an M-1 pencil" rather than wrenches and screwdrivers.

Thomas enthusiastically followed my orders to maintain with tools rather than pencils. During the months between the IG and our departure for Hohenfels, every vehicle in the company was pushed through the maintenance bays. Many weeks we operated on a flex schedule so that every vehicle could be serviced. If it was 2200 hours before a vehicle could be moved into the bay, then that is when its crew reported. If it was daylight before they finished, then off time was provided the next morning.

Our efforts were made more difficult by a lack of spare parts. Frequently parts we ordered took 60, 90, or even more than 120 days to be delivered. Constant checks of the supply system and complaints through the chain of command only revealed that much of the in-country repair stocks had been sent to Israel during the 1973 war and had yet to be replenished; parts which should have been available from in-country depots had to be ordered from the States.

To remedy the parts shortage, Dick Earle and a mechanic made trips to salvage yards across Germany where worn-out and wrecked vehicles were scrapped or transferred to repair facilities. Fifths of Jim Beam bourbon to German contract workers in charge of the salvage facilities usually gained Earle and his "wrench turner" entry to the yards. For the small sum of ten or twenty dollars out of our own pockets, Dick frequently returned with a truckful of critically needed items.

Still other parts were secured from units across Europe. Cooke and his .50-caliber barrels seemed to be able to produce almost anything requested. By the time the company was scheduled to move to the Hohenfels training area, all of the M-113s were operational except one—the "dog" track I had finally found in the ammo dump during my first week in command. After repeated attempts to fix that 113, Thomas had determined that only a new engine would solve the problem. With a few phone calls, Earle discovered that power packs were available at Hohenfels and training units received priority. We would tow the broken 113 to Hohenfels and exchange the old engine for new on arrival.

The only vehicle we would leave behind at Ledward would be the famous Gamma Goat. Despite our best efforts at tweaking the supply system, trading, and downright stealing, we had been unable to keep the Goat operational for more than a few days.

Movement from Ledward over the six kilometers to the railhead for transport to Hohenfels showed that our maintenance efforts were paying off. Only one APC dropped out of our convoy, and Thomas had it repaired and at the loading point in time to make our train.

Like all U.S. Army operations, our convoy to the railhead began several hours before daylight. Under the leadership of Dick Earle the company's two jeeps and two trucks joined the battalion road convoy to Hohenfels. Wheeled vehicles could easily make the 140-kilometer trip within three or four hours without disturbing German motorists on the autobahn. It was much more economical—and safer for our soldiers and the German motorists—to send the 113s by rail. Another advantage— one that no one cared to mention—was that the old, worn-out, poorly maintained APCs would be unlikely to endure the journey to the training area.

Since this was my first rail out-load, I paid particular attention to the proceedings. I soon understood why Top and Earle had scheduled inspections to be sure each 113 had the proper steel cables with turnbuckles for tie-down and heavy triangular blocks cut from twelve- by twelve-inch timbers to brace each track front and back.

The railcars stretched from the marshaling yard beyond our sight into the darkness. In shifts, the battalion began the load plan. Each vehicle approached the rear rail car from a ramp on a concrete loading dock. With a ground guide leading, the APCs proceeded from car to car down the length of the train. For safety reasons, the guide and the APC never moved at the same time. The guide marched to the front of each car, checked to be sure the steel connecting ramps between cars were in place, and then turned to signal the APC forward, using arm-and-hand signals to keep the driver centered. When the 113 reached the guide, it stopped. The guide then moved to the front of the next car to repeat the process.

While this procedure was slow, it prevented guides from falling between cars since they did not have to walk backward. Also, the guide could pay close attention to prevent the driver from going too close to the edge of the rail cars, which were barely wider than the tracks themselves. This was critical since the railcars were prone to flip if the load was not centered. Close in this case, like in hand grenades, could have deadly results.

Despite the darkness and a freezing temperature, the battalion was loaded and tied down by daybreak. Minutes after we finished, Top appeared with a hot breakfast, huge urns of coffee and juice, and C rations to carry for lunch. To no one's surprise—at least to no one who had been in the army for more than a day or two—we had hurried only now to wait. We sat beside our tracks for more than two hours before a connecting locomotive finally brought the passenger cars in which we would ride behind the chain of APC railcars.

What should have been only a three-hour train ride took a little more than twice that amount of time. Our troop train came at the bottom of every priority list. Every half hour or so we pulled over to an alternate track to allow passenger and freight cars to pass. No one, including me, was unhappy with the delays. Ample space in the passenger cars allowed everyone to catch up on sleep.

At Parsberg we unloaded at a railhead similar to the one at Schweinfurt from which we had begun our journey. The offloading was uneventful except for the "Merchant Lady of Parsberg." Dressed in a traditional German dirndl and head scarf, the middle-aged woman sold wurst sandwiches, fruit, and sodas to the soldiers at the railhead. Working from a Volkswagen van stacked high with goods, she wore a huge apron with pockets—one for dollars, one for D-marks—which grew heavier and heavier as the van emptied.

The German stationmaster told me with some disdain that the merchant lady bought a new Mercedes each year, lived in a nice home, and took annual vacations across Europe on her profits. With a battalion of soldiers arriving and departing by train weekly, it was easy to believe the stationmaster's story. It made little difference to us. Her prices were reasonable, and after all, was not the pursuit of capitalistic economy one of the things we were stationed in Germany to guarantee?

After another road march of ten kilometers, we arrived at the cantonment area of the Hohenfels training center. Billets for the troops, and maintenance areas for the vehicles, were available for the brief times we were not in the maneuver areas or on the firing ranges. While the noon meal would be C rations so we could maximize training time, mess halls were available for preparation of breakfasts and dinners. Of all morale factors in training—and in combat, for that matter—the only influence more positive than good leadership and fair treatment is hot chow. C rations are adequate, and even tasty when eaten in limited amounts, but well-prepared food reminds the soldiers that someone does care about their comfort and welfare.

The schedule guidance for the three weeks at Hohenfels included mounted maneuver training and a limited live-fire exercise. That directed training took up less than a week of the allotted time, so it was up to each company to plan the remainder of the exercise period. My plans were simple. We would start with the basics of individual marksmanship and work our way up to live fire and maneuver. My rationale was that our sole purpose was like that of any infantryman in any conflict at any time—to close with and kill or capture the enemy.

To accomplish that mission, every man had to be able to fire his weapon and hit where he aimed. In a concentrated, eighteen-hour training day, we began with the basics of sighting the M-16 rifle and dry fire. The next step was to use a twenty-five-meter zero range so that each soldier could set the sights on his weapon until the bullet strike corresponded with the sight alignment. With the senior NCOs as shooting coaches, each soldier stayed on the zero range until he could fire a three-round shot group into the one-inch center of the target. Each soldier then committed his zero elevation and windage adjustments to memory as well as writing them on a small piece of paper and taping it into the hollow handgrip of his M-16.

The final test of marksmanship was on a qualification range consisting of pop-up targets at fifty, one hundred, two hundred, and three hundred meters. At alternate distances with no pattern, upper-body silhouettes popped up for three to five seconds. In that time, the shooter had to find his target, aim, fire, and strike the silhouette. Scorers on each firing lane recorded the hits and misses.

As added incentive, we prominently displayed an eight-inch bronze infantryman trophy at the entrance to the firing line. The trophy had a brass plate reading, TOP MARKSMAN, A COMPANY 2/30 INFANTRY, 1975. That—and a three-day pass to the best shooter upon our return to Schweinfurt—encouraged competition among the soldiers. At the completion of the firing, two soldiers had seventy hits out of seventy-two opportunities. A shoot-off, accompanied by cheers from the two finalists' platoons, lasted twenty-six targets before one of the soldiers finally missed.

During the M-16 qualification and the shoot-off, we were visited by the division commander, Maj. Gen. E. C. "Shy" Meyer. We had been warned of the visit, and I had carefully briefed the company on the importance of presenting a positive attitude and being careful of what was said to the general. Meyer, over six feet tall and rail thin, had a friendly outgoing manner that was a hit with the soldiers and me. The division commander liked our marksmanship trophy and even borrowed a rifle to fire a few rounds which, mostly, hit the targets.*

Dick Earle had performed as officer in charge of the range; all the E-6s acted as safety NCOs. Procedures for properly running firing ranges have changed little since the fielding of long-range, accurate rifles prior to World War I. Nonetheless, I had Earle review the manuals so that we followed the correct procedures. By the end of the day, I was happy with the range results and satisfied that if the enemy attacked in lanes, popped up at preset intervals, and did not shoot back, then if the balloon ever went up, perhaps we could actually send a few godless Communists to their just reward.

After the M-16 qualification, I turned the company over to the platoon leaders. Each platoon was assigned a sector in the maneuver area. The only instruction they got from me was to be gone two days and to coordinate delivery of hot chow with Top. When I had included this mission on the training schedule,

---

*Meyer proved to be an excellent leader during his command of the 3d Infantry Division. Unlike many senior officers, he knew what was going on in the trenches and understood the problems of company-grade officers and NCOs. For those of us who served under Shy Meyer in the 3dID, it was no surprise when President Jimmy Carter jumped the general over many higher ranking officers in 1977 to make him the chief of staff of the army.

weeks before our arrival at Hohenfels, several of the platoon leaders asked for additional guidance. I gave them none, telling them that they could do anything they thought their platoon needed. Whatever they did was up to them.

During the two days, I neither checked on the platoons nor did I require any reports beyond maintaining radio contact with my command post (CP). My reason for this rather unorthodox training period was to give the platoon leaders the chance to establish themselves with their units and to learn to think and act independently. An additional benefit would be the cohesion and camaraderie developed in the platoons. Weeks later, stories got back to me that each platoon had trained long and hard. According to some of the soldiers and NCOs, the two days had been tougher and more demanding than that on the official company schedule.

When the platoons returned from the field, we concentrated on the firing of crew-served weapons. The mortar platoon had its own firing point and had received clearance for firing into the impact area located in the center of the Hohenfels training center. Beginning with occupation of the firing point and the laying in of the track-mounted 81mm tubes, the platoon worked through day firing and into night actions.

From my observations, the mortar platoon was extremely slow, both in calculating and in firing each mission. Partly this was due to the double and triple safety checks demanded by peacetime regulations; nonetheless, the platoon obviously needed extensive practice. With a little extra coordination and lots of talk, I was able to secure a two-day extension for use of the firing point and extra ammunition to make it worth their while. By the end of the four days of live fire, the platoon's accuracy had improved greatly, and its speed had increased to respectability. With every visit to the mortars, I emphasized that speed and accuracy were critical ingredients to the survival of the rest of the company, which depended on the organic firepower of the platoon.

While the mortars did their firing, the remainder of the company rotated through ranges to fire the M-60 machine gun; the M-203, 40mm grenade launcher; the 66mm light antitank weapon (LAW), and the heavier antitank 90mm recoilless rifle. Many of the soldiers had not fired the weapons since basic training, and some had never fired the 90mm at all.

Unfortunately, the only weapon we were unable to fire at Hohenfels was the one most critical to our mission (to repulse or at least slow a Warsaw Pack tank-heavy attack). Our two TOW missile launchers and carriers represented our most effective tank killers as well as our maximum range. While the LAW and 90mm could stop a tank only within four hundred meters—a distance at which a tank with eight-inch steel armor looks incredibly large to an infantryman protected by only one-sixteenth-of-an-inch-thick cotton fatigues—the TOW was accurate to more than three thousand meters. The problem with the TOW was not its accuracy or range but its expense. As the cost of a TOW was $10,000 per training missile, practice had to be done with simulators instead of the real thing. To maintain the soldiers' interest, the simulator training was evaluated, scored, and recorded with the consolidated battalion TOW training. The incentive was that during our next scheduled training at Hohenfels, the battalion's annual allotment of two live TOW rounds would be fired by the two crews who produced the best scores in training.

The final day on the ranges was devoted to firing the .50-caliber M-2 machine guns. These heavy weapons, little changed since their invention during the First World War, were still the most lethal weapons the company could bring to bear against personnel and lightly armored vehicles. Firing from the mount on each M-113, as well as from the ground-mount tripod, every man in the company had the opportunity to fire 150–200 rounds. The .50-caliber rounds, as well as whatever ammunition we needed on the other ranges, seemed to be in adequate stock and available on request. When we agreed to accept much of the ammunition in loose lots, which had been turned in as excess by other units, we were able to secure even more than we had originally requisitioned.

The major surprise about the ammunition we received was not its quantity but its age. Each container and crate of military ammunition is marked with a lot number and date of manufacture. The base of each round is similarly marked but with less detail. In Vietnam, I had become accustomed to receiving ammunition often less than three months from the arsenal of its manufacturer. In Europe, where ammunition had been stored since the end of World War II and was replaced by new only when depleted, we were issued ammunition manufactured as early as 1951—older than many of the soldiers who expended it. Fortunately, properly stored ammo, unlike infantrymen, does not show its age nor lose its lethality with the passing of the years.

Extra ammunition was of great assistance in raising troop morale. Practically every soldier, regardless of his overall dedication, enjoys "popping caps" on the range. Another advantage of the extra ammo was that I was able to invite the Hohenfels range control NCOs to join us in the shoot. These sergeants were notorious for being chicken, i.e., demanding additional police calls on the ranges or for just shutting down ranges if they disapproved of how they were being run.

Called "black hats" because of their distinctive baseball caps, range control NCOs had authority over any member, regardless of rank, of a visiting unit to ensure that safety rules were enforced and the areas preserved. During our visit to Hohenfels, A Company did not receive a single negative report from the black hats. The other company commanders in the battalion received from two to a dozen. In response to their questions about how we were staying out of trouble, I only smiled and replied that my men were disciplined and professional. I made no comment about the several times I had been called to a range by one of our shooting-companion black hats, who politely explained what we needed to do to prevent being officially written up for some transgression.

The weeks at Hohenfels concluded with company maneuvers, using various movement techniques and defensive plans. After that was a twenty-four-hour exercise, evaluated by members of the battalion staff, which culminated in a live-fire shoot at targets representing infantry, motorized forces, and tanks. The safety requirements for the live-fire were so stringent that little good was derived from the exercise beyond the troops' continued enjoyment of using their weapons for something other than ceremonial sticks.

The greatest feat of the final week was not the training itself but survival of the weather. Snow, a brief thaw, a refreeze, and then a driving rain turned the maneuver area into thick mud. Being cold, wet, and miserable is something which one does not really need to practice—no improvement comes by repeating the process. Nonetheless, it was good for the company to see that we could continue to move, shoot, and communicate, regardless—or in spite—of the weather conditions.

At the end of our training period at Hohenfels, I felt for the first time since assuming command that, if needed, the company could fight. I was not sure for how long or how well, but now at least the tax payers would get a little return on their dollars.

Beyond increased readiness, Hohenfels had produced a positive side effect. Training had been so vigorous and sustained that there had been little opportunity for the troops to get into trouble. Only one minor incident—a soldier caught shoplifting from the Hohenfels garrison PX—and one major breach of discipline had occurred. The latter had the potential of being much more severe, but quick action by several of the NCOs had stopped the beginnings of a race riot before it really got started.

At about the midpoint of the training period, we had returned to the cantonment area to maintain vehicles, weapons, and bodies. After all the maintenance was completed, the soldiers were permitted to purchase beer. The good local brew, bottled with old-fashioned porcelain, "flip-top" stoppers, proved too much for a couple of the troops. An argument over something no one could recall resulted in fists being thrown. That should have ended it, but the problem was that one soldier was white, the other black. Friends of each soon joined in the fracas, and it was about to escalate from fists to steel bunk adapters (connectors used to stack bunk beds) and beer bottles. Just before things really got rocking, two buck sergeants, one white and one black, waded into the mass of soldiers and broke up the fights.

Other than putting an end to beer in the barracks for the remainder of the night, at Top's advice, I took no further action. Carrasco said the NCOs had stopped the fight before it got out of hand and would prevent such further outbreaks. Top concluded, "Sir, if we are ever to get complete control of the company, the young NCOs are the ones who are going to have to take their responsibility in hand and do their job. Six months ago, we would have had one hell of a riot tonight. The buck sergeants would have ignored the fight, or maybe even joined in. We're making progress. Just leave this as NCO business."

As usual, Carrasco was right. No further talk or consequences of the night reached me.

Although I had only been through one rail loading, it seemed to be fairly old hat by the time we convoyed to Parsberg for the return to Schweinfurt. After an additional safety warning about the increased danger of fatigue, we began the loading. Soon everything was secure, and we were aboard the troop cars—and almost instantly asleep for the rail trip home.

Despite the fact that we had been away from families and/or sweethearts for three weeks, homecoming did not mean going immediately home. No one was dismissed until every item of equipment—especially weapons—was cleaned, inventoried, and secured. This meant that despite our arrival at about 1700, it was almost midnight before anyone was allowed to leave. No time off was allowed the next day or the following one, either. Everything had to be thoroughly cleaned and repaired before any off-time could be granted. If the enemy decided to come across the border, he would not be so gallant as to allow us time to recover from Hohenfels.

Finally, after three weeks of days averaging eighteen hours each of training time and three days averaging twelve hours each of maintenance, we got our time off—one day added to the weekend for a three-day holiday. The holiday proved to be even less fun than most of the training. Three weeks of pent-up hell-raising let go all over Schweinfurt and Ledward Barracks. I spent about as much time in the MP station and the company area as at home during the three-day break.

It was almost good to see Tuesday arrive and be on the way back out to the field. For the remainder of the week we worked in the local training area to evaluate each of the company's nine infantry squads in mounted and dismounted patrolling and offensive and defensive operations. Squads from Liebrich's platoon had been evaluated the best in the company for the previous two years, and everyone expected a repeat. Speculation on their victory ended up being premature. While the squads of the third platoon did very well, the top squad in the company proved to be from the second platoon.

The winning squad was led by a staff sergeant who had joined the company at about the same time as I had. He was Southern born and extremely quiet, and I had already noticed the personal care he took of each of the ten men in his squad. On weekends he frequently had the entire squad to the small off-post apartment he shared with his wife and baby. His reasoning was simple, he later told me. If they were at his home, they were not out getting into trouble. The sergeant took the same care of his men in training. If he was not satisfied with their performance during the day, he had a squad meeting after evening chow to review once more the day's training objectives.*

No sooner had we recovered from the squad tests than we moved out to the Hammelburg area to support the Ranger School of the Federal Republic of Germany. For a week we were to

---

*After my departure from Germany, I was not to see the sergeant again until I ran into him on a live-fire range at Fort Lewis, Washington, in 1986. He had just completed a tour as a first sergeant with the elite 2d Battalion, 75th Rangers and was going on to be an infantry battalion sergeant major.

serve as aggressors for the German Ranger student patrols. All of our support was dismounted, which made for some long marches.

Despite the lengthy hours and physically demanding details, it was an excellent week. The soldiers enjoyed competing and usually winning in the war games with the Germans. For me, the assignment's best attribute was that we were sixty kilometers from the "flagpole." Completely on our own except to coordinate with the German school cadre, not a single battalion, brigade, or division staff officer visited us to look over our shoulders and do whatever it is that staff officers do. On one occasion, a UH-1 helicopter did circle the training area, trying to get a response on our radio frequency. I instructed the men to remain hidden in the foliage and for the RTOs to maintain radio silence. The best visitors were no visitors at all, and I intended to keep it that way.

The final week of April 1975 was devoted to training designed to increase the soldiers' confidence in their equipment and themselves. We began with an exercise to demonstrate the effectiveness of the protective masks against chemical attacks. Each soldier rotated through an airtight unit built in the training area to serve as a gas chamber. Tablets of CS gas were burned in a special container which emitted a heavy fog of tear gas.

Wearing his protective mask, a soldier entered the chamber and found that he could breath comfortably. His platoon leader or sergeant, also masked, then ordered the soldier to remove his mask and answer a question, such as the serial number of his rifle or one of the general orders. This allowed ample opportunity for the tear gas to take effect, causing tears and choking. If the soldier responded calmly, he was ordered to place the mask back on, clear it by blowing outward to get rid of the gas in the mask, and then exit the chamber. If a soldier became panicky, he was allowed to exit the chamber without replacing his mask. Outside, in the fresh air, he was reinstructed in the proper techniques of masking while surrounded by gas. He then repeated the process until he performed all aspects properly.

To the former or current street-protester who might have encountered tear-gas clouds in the open, our repeated practice with a high concentration of gas might seem a bit cruel. Perhaps it was, but with the Warsaw Bloc sporting at least a half-dozen types of gases which killed rather than just irritated, the exercise seemed worthwhile.

Our next confidence training was to practice "swimming"

the M-113 armored personnel carriers. The thirteen-ton tracked, steel-and-aluminum, box-shaped carriers in no way resemble water craft, yet the manuals say they not only float but that they also "swim" forward and backward, with the rotation of the tracks. There were good reasons for this training beyond adding confidence. Spread behind—and beyond—our GDP positions were rivers at intervals of every fifty kilometers or so, which could not be forded. If World War III began, bridges over those waterways would be downed early. Whether we were going forward, or more likely, backward, crossing these waterways would be key to our survival or ultimate victory.

To swim an M-113 takes less than a half hour of preparation: drain plugs have to be closed; skirts must be lowered to extend down over most of the track and road wheels; a board at the front of the vehicle must be extended to prevent waves from washing over the front and into the engine and troop compartments. Finally, a sump pump, located under the floor panels, must be checked.

On the day before our swim, our confidence training took on new meaning when a 113 from another company entered the Main River training site too fast and at an improper angle. Almost without a ripple, the track sank to the bottom of the ten-meter-deep river. The driver and commander popped to the surface as did the marking float which was tied to the track for just such occasions. Safety boats swept in to pick up the two on the surface and to drop a diver in an attempt to rescue the crew member who had yet to surface. Unfortunately, the rope holding the float was cut by the propeller of the boat's outboard. It took nearly a half hour for the safety divers to find the 113 and to attach a cable. When the track was winched onto the bank, the missing soldier's body was recovered. We had hoped that an airpocket had formed and that he might still be alive. Apparently a pocket had formed, but it did not last until the rescue. That the soldier attempted to save himself was apparent by his bloody fingertips and the scratches around the hatch that he had been unable to open.

By the time it was A Company's turn, we had replaced the rope holding the float with a steel cable. I commanded the first 113 into the river. I had selected as driver the soldier who had most recently passed the heavy-vehicle driver's test. Our passenger was Carrasco. Conflicting emotions must have swept through the company assembled on the bank to watch their commander and first sergeant enter the river. No doubt some—

perhaps many—would have liked to see the track imitate a rock. At the same time, however, all must have hoped for our success since they were to follow.

Whatever their thoughts, the 113 swam just the way the manual said it would, and Top, our driver, and I crossed the river and returned as dry as when we departed. The rest of the company was just as successful. By the end of the day, the Alpha Company navy was ready for another aspect of a conflict we hoped would never occur.

CHAPTER 7

WHAT CAN BE ACCOMPLISHED IN ONE MONTH IN COMBAT TAKES SIX MONTHS IN PEACE—OR MORE
May–June 1975

Alpha Company of the 2d Battalion, 30th Infantry, was not my first command. Neither was it the first unit I had joined that was having problems. Five years earlier I had assumed command of an infantry company in Vietnam* which recently had been badly mauled in an assault of a North Vietnamese Army bunker complex. Nearly a quarter of the company had been killed or wounded. When I arrived by flying into a jungle clearing aboard a helicopter, I found a company with poor morale, little confidence in its leaders or itself, and a general attitude that the Viet Cong and NVA were forces greater than the company could handle. The situation in Vietnam was similar to the problems confronting Alpha Company in Germany a half decade later: discipline had to be reinstilled, a confidence in the chain of command—including myself—had to be developed, and lastly, a sense of being able to accomplish the assigned task of closing with and destroying the enemy had to be built.

In Vietnam, time to accomplish these objectives worked for and against us concurrently. In the positive column was the fact that we had twenty-four hours a day, seven days a week, for a 365-day tour to make an effective fighting unit out of an undisciplined, unmotivated rabble. On the negative side was that, unlike a classroom or the peacetime army in Germany, mistakes were paid for in blood and lives. While that was certainly a negative, it provided positive motivation for survival as well.

*See VIETNAM 1969–1970: *A Company Commander's Journal*, Ivy Books, 1988.

Using the same principles of leadership in Vietnam that worked later in the peacetime army in Europe—exercising the chain of command, ensuring fair treatment of all, taking personal interest in the well-being of every individual, and leading by example—my command showed nearly immediate improvement. By the end of a month, we were an extremely effective fighting force. At the conclusion of six weeks, the company led the battalion in enemy body count and after two months led the brigade. More importantly, the body counts were achieved with minimal friendly casualties. In a kill-or-be-killed situation, the company quickly demonstrated that it preferred the former to the latter. Pride in accomplishment went hand in hand with the joy of survival.

By May of 1975 I was in my sixth month of peacetime command. Admittedly, the twenty-four hours of duty every day in combat were reduced to fourteen-to-eighteen-hour days "only" six days or so a week. Still, I was disappointed. In thirty days of combat I had turned an extremely poor company into one of the best; after 180 days of peacetime command, I was just beginning to see improvements, and we had a long way to go before "good" or "combat ready" would go in the same sentence with "Alpha Company." I was beginning to wonder if General Sherman's pronouncement of "war is hell" might not be amended to include "but peacetime can be even more of a bitch."

Another difference between combat command and peacetime command was the relationship with my family. Serving in Vietnam had been a part of what I felt was a responsibility. Family separation was as much a given as was the possibility of not coming back at all. Command in peace is different. Many wives had problems with husbands going off to war and leaving them for a year or longer—but most understood, waited, and began anew on their husbands' return. For many wives who had already been separated from husbands for more than half their marriages, it was difficult to understand the long hours and absences to Hohenfels and other training areas. It was a common conclusion in Schweinfurt at the time that if a soldier returned home to have his dog bite him, his children not recognize him, and his wife missing, then perhaps he had been spending too much time at the company.

The army has long considered married officers a two-for-one system. In addition to getting an officer, the army gets a free "add on" in the way of a wife. Volunteer work is expected, and the rank system mirrors that of the husband—the "colonel's wife" and the "general's wife" receive the same respect and deference accorded the husband.* A "good army wife" is usually one who is willing to live her life through her husband and show no outward trace of her own personality. Rather than pursuing her own career, the "good army wife" attends coffees and teas and occasionally enrolls in a class at the officer's club on some challenging subject such as tole painting or silk-flower arrangement. For the truly motivated, there is Red Cross assistance to lend at the local clinic or various jobs at the post thrift shop—again all volunteer.

Of course, not all spouses fit into the mold of "good army wives." Some did their best to find work—either on U.S. military reservations or on the economy. Despite the low pay usually afforded wives by employers who realized that they, too, could take advantage of the two-for-one attitude, some wives took whatever job was available to have an excuse to miss the monthly teas and coffees. Their own self-esteem and sense of self-worth also played an important role in their job search.

Other wives, unfortunately, fought the boredom and lack of an allowance for their individuality at the bottom of a bottle, at the point of a syringe's needle, or in the arms of other men or women. Some wives just said to hell with it and went back to the States to file for divorce or to hope for a better tour with the next set of orders.

From my observations in Schweinfurt in the midseventies and the decade after, perhaps the most important characteristic of a "good army wife" is a reasonable low level of intelligence and a lack of ambition for anything other than to become the "colonel's lady." Low intelligence helps in not having a mind of one's own and being able to get excited about arranging flowers and attending parades and ceremonies. Ambition to be a colonel's lady is critical for the "good wife" because it means she will be subservient to current "ladies" and will do the proper things to ensure her husband stays in good graces with the colonel's lady's husband. While it had been repeated often enough

---

*In twenty years of service I did meet a few—the key word here is *few*—exceptions to wives who wore their husbands' rank. Even the second or third wives, acquired later in careers, when rank already had been attained, quickly adjust to being the "boss's lady."

to become a trite military maxim, the phrase "the wife cannot help a career, she can only hurt it" is true. She can definitely hurt it. Anyone who does not believe that an army wife's failure to develop a good relationship with the colonel's wife will not hurt the husband's career is either naive, ignorant, or has not spent long among uniforms.

Linda and I had married shortly before I entered the army. The fact that she is bright and ambitious meant that she was not totally adept at becoming an army wife. In Stuttgart and Schweinfurt she tried but, fortunately, was too independent to be able to add "good" to army wife. Since "fair," "moderately okay," or even "satisfactory" were prefixes not allowed with "successful army wife," we had to make some decisions.

While the results admittedly were not easily arrived at, we eventually reached a consensus that would serve us well as an "army couple" for the next twelve to fourteen years. "Two-for-one" would not work for us. Linda agreed to "one-and-a-half-for-one" and did her best to lead her own life as well—and has done a pretty good job at it I might add. While attending the wives' meetings and doing the volunteer work that were the most important, she continued her formal and personal education and development.* Oddly, Linda's less than 100 percent dedication to being an army wife did not decrease the company's, battalion's, or division's level of readiness. Hordes of communists did not immediately cross the border nor did the freedom of Western Europe seem to diminish.

While the first six months in command had been taxing on family life and on my confidence in the length of time required to turn a unit around, significant progress had been made. Troublemakers, drug addicts, and those unable to adjust to a disciplined life-style had been eliminated from the service. Those who could be retrained, disciplined, or even punished into becoming adequate soldiers had been given the opportunity to do so.

---

*By the time of my retirement in 1988—at a rank not particularly helped nor hindered by my wife—our agreement had worked well for us both, for she was making more money than the "colonel and his lady" and was in a position to make hiring decisions about retiring colonels' attempting to make the transition to nonuniformed life.

Soldiers and leaders alike were beginning to show pride in being members of Alpha Company and displayed confidence in being able to accomplish their assigned duties. This status was not achieved easily or without immediate and long-term impact on the participants. Soldiers eliminated from the army carry bad discharges on their record the rest of their lives. For those "merely" disciplined by reduction in grade, fines, and restriction, the monetary loss alone often affected wives and children who were already having great difficulty in living on a soldier's meager salary in Germany.

In my twenty years of service, I did observe a few commanders who were ruthless and seemingly without compassion, but they were very much the exception. Most commanders accept the responsibility of leading American soldiers as a calling more closely akin to a religious vocation than a professional business. I was not the only commander to lose a night's sleep in consternation over whether to eliminate a soldier or give him another chance—and then lose more sleep in wondering if the decision made was the best one.

The bottom line of decision making differs little in peace or in battle. Commanders get paid to make decisions—right or wrong. In combat, a commander cannot be hesitant. Casualties may have to be taken to protect the unit as a whole and to accomplish the mission. Decisions are based on all the facts available and with the unit's welfare and mission in mind. Once made, the only room for constructive second guessing is in learning from mistakes and profiting from successes.

With no regrets, but with a sincere sense of compassion, I eliminated sixteen soldiers from A Company and the United States Army in my first six months of command. This amounted to more than 12 percent of the total company strength and would exceed the casualty figures of many infantry units in actual combat. Perhaps a better commander could have turned around those men and made them into good soldiers. Maybe their shortcomings were the result of my ineptness and that of my predecessors. However, I doubted that then and still do so today. Most of the sixteen should never have been allowed in uniform; some did not have the basic intelligence to be soldiers, a few were out-and-out criminals, and others were so hooked on drugs that their minds were no longer their own.

In retrospect, I suppose that a few of the sixteen men I presented with bad discharges and tickets back to civilian society might have been salvageable. If resources and time had been available, perhaps a couple of the sixteen might have become constructive rather than destructive members of the company. But resources were not available and more important, neither was time. A very real mission was assigned the company which would be difficult enough to accomplish with a well-trained and disciplined unit—and perhaps not even then. My responsibility was the accomplishment of that mission and the protection of the lives of the entire company. If I had to eliminate some with bad discharges to better our ability to accomplish our mission— and, more important, save the lives of the many—then so be it. I had learned in Vietnam that apologies were not a part of a commander properly doing his business. By the end of my sixth month of command in Germany, I had determined that apologies were no more a part of peacetime leadership than combat command.

Of the sixteen discharges, six were as a part of courts-martial sentences—time in jail followed by bad paper. Those six had committed offenses ranging from assault on an NCO to possession of drugs for sale. The most serious of the cases was the result of a long-term military police investigation to determine the source of distribution of an LSD-type drug known as "purple haze." The MPs finally made their arrest at the enlisted club. A late-night phone call informed me that the primary pusher of "purple haze" in Schweinfurt was a proud member of A Company.

The nineteen-year-old soldier was in possession of $2,000 cash and well over $10,000 worth of drugs when apprehended. When I signed for him from the MPs, I had a jeep and two armed guards waiting. The soldier's next stop was the European central confinement facility for U.S. Forces at Mannheim, where he waited in pretrail confinement prior to his time in court. At the next morning's formation, I announced the arrest of the soldier and his present location. Top cut the lock on the man's wall locker to inventory and mail his personal effects to his home address. Except for a brief return to Schweinfurt for his trial, which resulted in a one-way trip to the U.S. Military Disciplinary Barracks at Fort Leavenworth, Kansas, we never saw him again.

The remaining ten of the sixteen early discharges were the

results of various "chapter" proceedings and a new procedure called the expeditious discharge program (EDP). Designed as a part of the VOLAR system, to allow commanders to eliminate new soldiers who could not adjust to the military, the EDP virtually allowed commanders to fire troops who were doing poorly. The program's main restrictions were that the soldier could not have been in the service for more than six months, had to agree to the action, and could not receive less than a general discharge.

Top and I kept a "five-and-one-half-month roster" that allowed us to review the progress of each soldier nearing the end of that period of service. Since basic and advanced training had usually consumed nearly four months of the allowed six, we were forced to make our decision on whom we would offer discharges after only six to eight weeks of observation. Despite the short period, it was more than adequate. In practically every case where we took action, we were amazed that the chain of command in basic and advanced training had not already eliminated the candidates we selected for EDP.

For soldiers failing to meet minimum standards after being in the army for more than six months, the process was a bit more complex. Much more paperwork was involved, including detailed records of formal (written) and informal (verbal) counseling sessions. Usually a history of discipline problems and/or drug abuse had to be proven. Unlike the EDP, a soldier had no choice of agreeing to a chapter discharge, but he did have the right to appear before a review board of officers and NCOs to plead his case if he desired to remain in uniform.

One of the chapter cases was a six-foot-four-inch, 250-pound Samoan. A well-disciplined, intelligent soldier when sober, the man became a terror who fought anyone—including groups of MPs—who got in his way when he was drunk. Once, when he was unable to find someone to fight, he stood outside the barracks of another battalion shouting racial epithets until his challenge was answered.

On two occasions we enrolled the soldier in alcohol-abuse counseling with no noticeable improvement. The Chapter 13 hearing, conducted at the request of the soldier in his attempt to stay in the army, was fairly brief. I presented the list of alcohol-related offenses and the evidence that formal counseling at the local rehab facility had been unsuccessful. When asked by the board president to summarize why I felt the man should be eliminated from the army, I responded, "Sir, this soldier likes to drink, and he likes to fight. Some day he will beat someone to death. I don't want that to happen to a member of my company or to anyone else. Maybe a discharge is only passing our problem on to the civilians, but hopefully back in the States or on his home island of Samoa, the pressures will not be as great, and he can whip his alcohol problems. Within the parameters of the general discharge I've requested for him, he will retain the right to use VA facilities and their alcohol-rehab programs."

It did not take long for the board to reach a decision. Within a few hours, the soldier was on a plane out of Germany and out of the army. I have no idea if he ever beat anyone to death or if he overcame his dependence on alcohol, and I must admit that I had few thoughts or concerns about him after his departure. What I did think was that I was glad to be rid of a problem soldier who took much time away from properly training and caring for the well-being of the men who were performing.

Another soldier eliminated under the chapter system was the "PX hero" who had worn the unauthorized valor medals to my assumption-of-command ceremony. Not surprisingly, he had been unable to provide any proof that the medals had ever been awarded. By the time I decided he had had ample time to produce verification, other factors influenced me to decide against court-martial or Article 15.

The first factor was the pregnant wife and two children who had accompanied the soldier to Germany. Along with a family, he had a two-inch-thick file of letters of indebtedness for various loans for cars, furniture, and stereo equipment. One of his unpaid debts was for a man's pinkie ring ordered from an advertisement on the back of a comic book. In an attempt to show compassion—if not for the soldier, at least for his wife and family—I shelved the judicial matter and had Dick Earle sit down with the soldier and respond to each of the letters. The ring, more likely worth fifty dollars rather than its five hundred purchase price, was easy to take care of. In a registered package, it went back to the seller.

The car, furniture, and stereo loans were a bit more difficult. They had been purchased from legitimate businesses, located just outside the gate of his last Stateside post—at the usual high price and nearly 20 percent interest rate typical of stores that specialize in marketing to enlisted soldiers. From experience,

Earle and I knew such businesses would take almost any amount if the soldier would just show good faith by resuming payments. After all, there was not much chance of repossessing goods from Germany. Earle and I were not naive enough to trust that the soldier would send the money to his creditors as he promised in the letters we helped him compose. On our demand he produced mail order receipts for each payment.*

Three things ultimately resulted in the elimination of the "PX hero" from the service—none of which had anything to do with his originally coming to my attention by wearing the unauthorized medals. First, more letters of indebtedness arrived for items he had ordered from catalogs and not paid for *after* Earle and I had attempted to help him take care of his debts. Second, the soldier validated his supervisor's evaluation that he could not perform his assigned duties as a mechanic by incorrectly installing wheel bearings in the Gamma Goat and ruining them. The destruction of spare parts was bad—worse was the fact that we had waited four months for the hard-to-secure parts, and it would take that long to get another set. In the meantime the Goat would continue to be a mere ornament in the motor pool rather than a vehicle of transportation.

These two incidents were more than ample reason for me to begin elimination proceedings, but there was more. The third and final error on the part of the soldier occurred the weekend before I began his Chapter 13 paperwork. On a Sunday afternoon I walked the mile or so from my quarters to the barracks area to check on the company. Things were unusually quiet, so I began my walk home after a brief visit. On the way out of the main gate, I passed the Ledward bowling alley. Out the door walked my problem soldier carrying what appeared to be a new bowling ball bag. He then hailed a German cab—a Mercedes—to transport him to the enlisted quarters which were about a half mile away.

*As a commander of U.S. Army soldiers, I had certain responsibilities to ensure they met their financial obligations. At the same time I was much more interested in the welfare of my troops than in the money-making of some shopkeeper back in the States. The only letters of indebtedness I responded to were those that included a copy of a valid signed contract in which the soldier had acknowledged his payment responsibility. Even when that information was available, I often added a letter in return, stating that "if you had gone to as much trouble to investigate the ability of this soldier to pay his debts as you have gone to collect, none of this difficulty would exist."

Although the soldier seemed to have enough money for bowling and taxis, he was either unable or unwilling to pay his lawful debts. Since he could not perform his assigned duties with any proficiency, it was time for him to rejoin the ranks of the civilians. He brought his pregnant wife and two children to the discharge board. After reviewing the soldier's file, the board's only vote of sympathy was to grant my recommendation that the soldier receive an honorable discharge because of his length of service and tour in Vietnam.

Along with the sixteen discharges, my first six months in command produced twenty-four Article 15s—eighteen company grade and six field grade. With the exception of my first month in command, when eight Article 15s were administered, the rate slowed to two to four a month. These numbers were less than half those of the other companies in the battalion and much less than the twenty-five to thirty given in some companies in the division.

My philosophy was that Article 15s should be administered to get a soldier's attention—as I had done in my first month of command—and for serious offenses that merited punishment as well as for demonstration to the rest of the soldiers that such actions would not be tolerated. To ensure the latter purpose was served, Top and I assisted by posting a copy of each Article 15 on the company bulletin board.

Once I felt that I had the discipline of the company fairly well in hand, I looked at Article 15s as a last resort. When a soldier made a mistake, proper punishment or retraining could best be taken care of unofficially by the soldier's chain of command. While physical abuse of the soldiers was not tolerated, I saw no problem with a soldier who had committed a minor offense, such as being late for formation or failing to take proper care of his personal appearance, being kept after duty hours to wash and wax the floor of his platoon's storage room or given a very dirty job, such as cleaning out the grease pits in the motor pool. My only requirement was that a member of the soldier's chain of command be present to supervise. By the time I had been in command for six months, I trusted the sergeants enough to feel confident that such extra training would not be abused. As for the soldiers themselves, they usually much preferred action taken within their platoon or by First Sergeant Carrasco than official punishment which would go into their personnel files.

Courts-martial and Article 15s were not reserved only for the lower ranking soldiers. NCOs who failed to perform or who conducted themselves improperly also faced disciplinary action. One buck sergeant had repeated difficulties in leaving his German girlfriend's bed early enough to make our morning formation. The first two times Top found extra duties for him to perform. When that failed to do any good, I referred him to the battalion commander for a field grade Article 15 which cost the man a stripe and a couple of week's pay.

Another NCO's troubles proved to be much worse. Previously reduced from E-7 to E-5 for drunkenness and several days' AWOL, the man had not responded to the punishment or to time in the detox center. He departed the ranks of the NCOs and became an E-4 after becoming so drunk on duty that he could hardly stand. I would have preferred to find assistance for his drinking problem rather than reduce him again. However, he left me little choice by being drunk on duty in front of the men he was supposed to lead. Not to bust the sergeant and take his stripes would have set an inconsistent example for the soldiers under him, who knew that they would be severely punished for the same offense. If punishment is not fairly and equally administered to all ranks for similar offenses, it is not only useless but also detrimental to good discipline.

An opportunity to validate our progress was provided in May 1975 during the company's second rotation to installation-support-battalion duty. While we had not attained the level of discipline and basic proficiency that I desired and demanded, progress since my first experiences with ISB was evident.

The drudgery of ISB concluded with an even more unpopular duty of soldiers. To celebrate the 200th anniversary of the formation of the Revolutionary Militia, which eventually became the United States Army, a parade was scheduled for all American forces stationed at Schweinfurt. From the sidelines, military parades appear to be patriotic, colorful affairs; in the ranks they are tiresome and boring. Except for the pride and showmanship that go with the pass in review, few marching soldiers have ever been known to enjoy a parade.

However, I was well aware that reviews were important for one reason. Parades would bring out ranking officers—both on the reviewing stand and in the bleachers—as well as the soldiers' families and residents of the local community. Even though the results of the parade would not stop, or even slow, one Commie tank on the GDP, I intended to wow the hometown fans.

My pursuit of excellence on the parade field was not undertaken just to impress ranking officers and civilians—and then again in a way it was. Some would judge us by how impressive we were in the spotlight of a review, not by how well we performed at Hohenfels, during ISB, or on the daily MP blotter. For others an impressive showing would go far toward downplaying our less than stellar performances in the areas of major drug busts, fights, and poor IG results. A good appearance on the parade field might earn us a bit of slack in other areas on other days.

A week prior to the parade I conducted inspections for fresh uniforms—starched to rigidity with knifelike creases—and boots with shines so mirrorlike that gaps in the inspector's teeth would reflect. Each uniform was laid out on the soldier's bunk for inspection, and when it was considered satisfactory, it was secured until parade time in a plastic bag in a wall locker. Haircuts, both with helmet on and helmet off, were inspected at the same time.

Twice a day, at morning and noon formation, I practiced the company in marching and making the turns which would be a part of the parade. We sized the company with tallest left to right and front to rear and ensured that the right rank, which would be next to the bleachers and reviewing stand, was made up of NCOs who had the most marching experience.

When parade day arrived, I conducted a final inspection. Soldiers who wore prescription glasses were ordered to wear the black-rim, army-issue specks. All jewelry, including wrist watches, was removed to prevent any eye-catching glint or glimmer. Helmet covers, which had already been checked to ensure they carried no graffiti, were adjusted for tightness and appearance. During the last minutes before we marched out onto the parade field, each member of the chain of command checked his men and each other. Top even gave me a final once over and ran a stocking over my boots to remove dust without scratching the spit shine.

Our preparation was certainly not enough to make the parade fun or the unusually hot day any more comfortable. However, any task is much easier when you know you are prepared. All the soldiers had to do was to look at the other companies to realize that we stood out as the best by far. These observations were not ours alone. In the following days, letters came to the company from the community, brigade and battalion commanders praising the appearance and performance of A Company. Comments included, "I would like to express my personal and official appreciation for your truly outstanding performance," from community commander Brig. Gen. Hugh F. T. Hoffman. Col. Neal Creighton, the brigade commander added, "Fine job and a first-rate performance" while King, the battalion commander, wrote that we "looked proud, performed well, and epitomized the American soldier." All of the letters went on the company bulletin board. It was nice for a change to post something beside Article 15s and the results of court-martial.

As soon as the parade was over, our thoughts of celebration of a two hundred-year anniversary were quickly put behind us, as we again focused on the present and the future. The last three weeks of June 1975 were dedicated to training and testing for the Expert Infantryman Badge (EIB), a decoration bearing a silver rifle on a blue background. The EIB was awarded infantrymen who satisfactorily completed a series of skill and physical tests. This included disassembling and reassembling all the basic infantry weapons and mines, applying proper camouflage, adjustment of artillery, gathering and reporting intelligence, and displaying mastery of map reading and use of a lensatic compass. Adding to the difficulty of the exam was that each process had to follow the procedures as outlined in the various manuals.

Before being allowed to undergo the twelve different stations, each candidate had to qualify with his individual weapon and pass the army physical fitness test which included tests of agility, upper-body strength, and a two-mile run, that had to be completed in less than sixteen minutes. The final test was a twelve-mile forced march with full pack, helmet, and M-16 rifle to be completed within three hours.

Most of the captains in the 2d of the 30th had been in the army a few years longer than I and had already received their EIBs during previous troop assignments. Once the EIB is awarded, it is valid for the rest of one's time in uniform. While I did not have an EIB, I did have the Combat Infantryman Badge (CIB) which looked just like the EIB except it has a wreath around the rifle. It is far more coveted than the EIB since it is awarded for actual combat service with the infantry.

Soldiers who had a previous award of the EIB or the CIB were not required to test during current EIB training. Most of the NCOs in the company who already had one or both were selected as trainers or testers. While I had the option to merely observe and/or assist the testing, I decided that the best way to ensure that the maximum number of my soldiers received the EIB was to join the competition myself. Negotiating the PT test and twelve-mile road march with soldiers eighteen to twenty years old was not easy on my twenty-eight-year-old body, but I tried not to show my fatigue as I encouraged and pushed my troops along.

Surprisingly, the most difficult part of the test for me was the disassembly and assembly of infantry weapons. The actual mechanics were no problem. In fact, I could tear apart an M-16 rifle or M-60 machine gun in the dark and on occasion had accomplished a quick fieldstripping under fire in combat to fix a stoppage. The difficulty was in breaking habits instilled by years of practice, as I had to relearn the procedures by the book and in proper sequence.

Other than my own personal example, I added other factors to help A Company soldiers to get their EIBs. The competition was set up so that only the most accomplished soldiers would pass the various tests. Many of the soldiers, including some NCOs, had taken the EIB training and test for several years without result. Top and I added after-duty, volunteer training and kept weapons out of the arms room with the CQ for late-night practice.

A little over two-thirds of the company passed the physical tests and moved on to the skills examinations. Using the platoon sergeants and other NCOs who had their EIBs, I established one final review before each individual test station, which was manned by soldiers from division and other infantry battalions. Each man had a dry run under company supervision within minutes before he faced the official evaluators.

After I finished my tour of the afternoon round-robin of tests, I waited in the control tent with my fellow company commanders while tests results were posted. With both Ledward infantry battalions going through the testing, results were slow to be posted. Above the results boards was a notice declaring that, with over two-thirds of the division's thirty infantry companies tested, the top company thus far had received twelve EIBs. It was after dark before the final results were posted. Our battalion had produced from four to twelve EIBs per company. Alpha

Company had the twelve, tying the division record. While I was personally proud that one of the twelve was me, my main feeling was that the company was continuing its forward progress.

CHAPTER 8

COME FORTH LAZARUS, AND A RETURN TO THE OTHER SIDE OF THE MOON

July–August 1975

The continuing efforts to make Alpha Company into a combat-ready unit were not taking place in isolation. Other companies in the battalion, as well as in the brigade, division and the army, were struggling to rebuild a fighting force reduced to ineptitude and lack of enthusiasm by the results of the Vietnam War, the all-volunteer system, and a nation that, if not openly hostile, did not seem to care for its men and women in uniform.

Proficiency of any military unit rises and falls with the passage of time. Regardless of the level to which it has sunk, it is unusual for an organization not to show some improvement; rarer still for an outstanding unit to maintain a fine edge of constant readiness.* Since there are never sufficient assets to keep all units completely combat ready—particularly in the lean years following a war—units with the most apparent need receive the maximum help in resources, manpower, and leadership.

When I assumed command, I did not doubt that A Company and the rest of the 2d of the 30th Infantry were in need of maximum help. No unit in the division was good or even satisfactory—some were just better than others—and we were quite apparently the "others." My observations must have been shared because about the time I arrived, the worst began receiving the best—or at least the best that were available.

_____

*The only exceptions to this up-and-down trend in the U.S. Armed Forces units are in elite units such as the Army Rangers, Marine Force Recon, and Navy SEALs. Even those exceptions contribute to the roller coaster of overall readiness, however, because the very best are siphoned off from the regular units to fill the slots in the elites.

Al Todd assumed command of C Company and John Mackey took over headquarters company during the same ceremony in which I had received the guidon of A Company. Ron Glancy had joined the battalion a few months before that time and was in command of B Company. Kurt Pierce assumed command of the battalion's combat support company (CSC) during the weeks in preparation for the previous IG. With the exception of Pierce, all of us were combat veterans and had led at least one company previously. Todd, Glancy, and Mackey were all within a year of making major, and I was only two years out of the selection zone.

The five of us 2d of the 30th company commanders worked well together and made every effort to help each other. There was still keen competition among all of us, but there was also a sense of being together in competition against the rest of the division. While all of us made some strides during that first six months, much more common were the failures and problems. Todd, for example, had a soldier murder a German civilian in an attempted robbery. Glancy had a soldier mysteriously fall down a barracks stairwell to his death.

One of the more comical incidents—at least it seemed that way to those of us with an infantry sense of humor—occurred one morning prior to a battalion formation on the company streets between the the barracks. Seeing Mackey, Pierce, and Glancy huddled in discussion across the quadrangle, I walked over to join in the conversation while we waited the few minutes for the troops to assemble.

Shortly after I joined the others, an explosion ripped the morning air, throwing bits of glass and plaster that sent us ducking for cover. Then with the other three commanders, I looked up at their barracks where smoke was pouring from a gaping hole. I could see all three company commanders mentally counting the floors to fix the source of the explosion. As Mackey and Glancy confirmed it was not from their company areas, I could hear an audible sigh of relief. About the same time, Pierce swore, "Oh, shit," and plunged into the building on the way to the second-floor billets with the newly formed hole in the wall.

Fortunately, no one was injured in the blast, which had been caused by a booby-trapped artillery simulator in a latrine. The lack of injuries added to the humor of the "floor-counting commanders." By day's end—and after a wholesale restriction of his company to the barracks—Pierce had found his bomber and had most of the glass replaced in the latrine windows. The soldier, on his way home with an early bad-paper discharge, would eventually explain that he was bored and was just trying to create a little excitement. As for the soldier who tripped the booby trap on his way to the toilet, he certainly must have developed some apprehensions regarding future visits.

While there had been many other challenges in training, discipline, and maintenance since the IG debacle the previous January, the failure of the inspection and the impending reinspection were never far from my mind or those of the other company commanders. In addition to gaining our attention, the poor results had also seemingly motivated Lieutenant Colonel King to become more involved in his battalion's activities.

Leadership and charisma were still not among the assets of the battalion commander, but he had learned a few things in his more than fifteen years of service. King certainly understood that results that could not be accomplished by personality alone could be attained through force, threat, and downright ruthlessness. While King never became a "popular" commander with troops or officers, he did gain our respect—from the soldiers as a boss who demanded superior results, from the officers because he still allowed us the latitude to imprint our own personalities on our commands.

As a part of the overall battalion preparation for the IG reinspection, King scheduled frequent inspections of the billets, soldiers, and equipment. Each succeeding inspection had tougher requirements and standards. During regular training time and even during off-duty hours, King was on the constant lookout for soldiers wearing incorrect items of uniform, needing haircuts, or abusing their vehicles, weapons, or equipment. Those who did not meet the battalion commander's standards were referred to what he called the "school of the soldier," four hours of additional training—drill and ceremony, basic soldier skills, military courtesy, and in-ranks inspections—all conducted on Saturday morning. An interesting part of the school, and one that made it more effective, was that the immediate supervisor of each attendee had to be present to oversee and/or supervise the training. Since each company had fifteen to twenty "students" in the school each Saturday, it meant that virtually the entire chain of command

The author at his desk at Alpha.

Building 209, Leward Barracks, Schweinfurt, Germany. A Company billets on 2nd floor.

Tent City, Leward Barracks. Temporary home of Alpha Company. Spring, 1976.

Alpha Company's protective mask storage area.

SP4 Peterson in the A Company Arms Room.

Alpha Company M-113 Armored Personnel Carriers in the track park.

Company Motor Pool maintenance bays.

Company visit to East Berlin. In uniform, left to right: SFC Leiberich, SSG Hornbeck, SSG Thomas, and SSG Cook.

En route through Schweinfurt to **REFORGER**.

East German border near the Company **GDP**.

Left to right: Meridith, Linda, and Reveilee Lanning with East German border in the background.

had to be present. Although I did spend some Saturday mornings in my office catching up on paperwork, I, too, spent several hours observing the training.

As the weeks passed, more and more soldiers improved their conduct—or learned to avoid the battalion commander. King steadily raised his standards to the point of referring soldiers to the school for an unbuttoned pocket or a name tag hand-sewn on a uniform rather than machine stitched according to regulations. Another item that we all soon learned was dear to the battalion commander's heart was the condition of a soldier's combat boots. During each inspection of the barracks and personal gear, King closely checked all boots. Although he never explained why, it took little thought to figure out that, despite the fact that we were mechanized, feet and boots were still the primary means of transportation for infantrymen.

Beyond the normal desire to improve the battalion, King, myself, and the other company commanders had good reason to be concerned. Failure of one IG was bad, failure of two meant that we would be looking for new jobs with relief-for-cause, career-ending efficiency reports in our files. Rumors from credible sources abounded that a new battalion commander had already been selected to replace King. The new lieutenant colonel was reportedly interviewing candidates for company command and gathering his favorites—"pet frogs" as they were commonly known—from previous assignments. Most common of the rumors was that a new battalion commander was a certainty. The only variable to the stories was in how many of the five companies would have new captains after the inspection.

Any unit which is at a satisfactory state of readiness and has an average amount of discipline should be able to pass an IG with a couple of weeks' concentrated preparation. As we had so aptly demonstrated in January, a unit below standards in readiness and discipline could not hope to complete the inspection with satisfactory results. While A Company had made great progress in the intervening six months, I had little confidence that we were at a point where a normal preparation period would produce passing scores. We were much better but still far from good. As with any challenge, if we were to pass the reinspection we needed an edge—and I had several ideas in mind.

First, the preparation which would enable us to successfully fight the Warsaw Bloc might not be enough to win an encounter with our "friends" from the office of the inspector general. Knowing that any military victory is greatly dependent on up-to-date intelligence, I began our formal preparation for the IG by gathering information on the enemy.

Typically, the IG team conducted two to three inspections a month. Beginning a little more than two months before our scheduled IG, I dispatched an officer or senior NCO to each inspected battalion immediately following their IG. Along with copies of inspection sheets, we gathered a list of every question asked by the team members. Each of these items was compiled into a master list from which we planned our own preparation. At every formation, Top asked a soldier at random one or more of the questions—such as general orders, effective range of various weapons, division history, and characteristics of enemy vehicles and units. If a soldier responded incorrectly, he did pushups while the company repeated the correct answer. Before the end of each formation, Top repeated questions from that day or those of previous days as the company responded in unison. As more and more questions came in from our recon of other units, I had my operations sergeant put together a mimeographed pamphlet of IG-team queries.

Questions and lists of inspection points were not the only focus of our intelligence efforts. As early as a month before our inspection, we had assembled a file on every member of the twelve-man IG team. We knew their names, hometowns, previous assignments, and a general summary of their demeanor and style of inspection. Our survey produced some interesting results. Two members of the team were veterans of the same combat units in Vietnam as two of my platoon sergeants. One of the junior inspection officers was a college classmate of one of my platoon leaders. I thought that with little effort I should be able to pair the inspector with a guide from the company who shared a common background. As the weeks passed, our efforts increased to the point of pairing inspectors from the same state or region with as many of his "homies" as possible.

None of these efforts were against regulations. The inspectors were selected for their proficiency and integrity. Acquaintances, commonalities, or hometowns would not influence their opinions—except maybe, just maybe, if an area or person was on the edge of pass or fail, it might make the difference.

Of course, all of those intelligence efforts would be useless if the company was not reasonably prepared for the inspection itself. Although division allowed only one week on the formal training schedule for IG prep, I had focused all training since our return from Hohenfels in March with the inspection in mind. Repeated preinspections were held, each following the procedures used by the IG. Like preparation for the army birthday parade, I conducted inspections of uniforms and head and footgear until they were well above standard.

Readiness for the inspection was not occurring in a vacuum. We helped the other companies in the battalion, and they assisted us. It was not unusual to find all five company armorers moving through each company's arms rooms, inspecting, cleaning, and mending weapons and updating paperwork. We secured additional help wherever available. The last of the "magic" excess .50-caliber barrels went to get members of the USAREUR trainers in weapons and tracked-vehicle maintenance at Vilseck to visit for a few days to assist. It also helped that one of the team members was an old friend of one of the Alpha NCOs. Similar help came from brigade and division staff NCOs and soldiers—with no exchange of machine-gun barrels or spare parts.

During the final weeks before the inspection, days stretched to eighteen hours, and seven seemed an inadequate number of days for a workweek. While the soldier bitched about the long hours and sparse off-time, I noticed that unlike the days of preparation before the January inspection, this time they seemed motivated to do well rather than just to get by. Late one Saturday evening, I was in the motor pool, checking the progress of a soldier who was working under a dim droplight as he replaced the worn track pads on an M-113. His team leader was working side-by-side with him, just as dirty and tired. After a few words of encouragement, I turned to move on to the next vehicle. As I did so, I heard the soldier remark, "Say, Sarge, what a bitch. This is a great way to spend a Saturday night. Only one more workday until Monday."

The battalion plan called for A Company to be first in line for the maintenance portion and last for the in-ranks and billets inspection. Mechanics, armorers, communications specialists, and supply personnel from the other companies and headquarters of the 2d of the 30th joined us the last night for one final check of vehicles, weapons, radios, files, and records. The most experienced were organized into a team that, using the checklists we had gathered from other inspections, would conduct a mock inspection during the hours before the real thing. Except for brief returns to the barracks for quick showers and changes of uniforms, the crews worked all night. Sandwiches, soup, and coffee were delivered to the motor pool because no one had time for trips to the mess hall.

As the time for inspection grew nearer, the apprehension elevated. Jobs and careers on the line were important, but just as critical were the investments of time and energy expended in preparing for the inspection. We had come a long way, but beyond actually undergoing the IG, there was no way to accurately measure the results.

Despite the bone weariness felt by all, the final hours rushed by. Knowing that nothing is ever completely prepared or finished in an infantry company, I decided we had to quit sometime and declared us ready an hour before the IG team arrived. In a final meeting of the company, I told the men that I was proud of their hard work and determination and would accept the results as the best we could have done with the time and circumstances available. We were all so tired that the words had little impact. Almost as an afterthought, I offered a few last remarks saying, "We've come a long way. Our efforts will speak for themselves, but there is one final item that may make the difference. The inspectors are soldiers just like us. Regardless of what they see, our attitude will make a difference. One thing in which I pride myself is something I had also found true in you as well. None of us kisses anybody's ass. I had much rather kick the IG's behind, and I'll damn sure not kiss it, but in a few hours I'm going to be on my best behavior. I'm actually going to make them believe that I'm glad to see the sons of bitches."

The last comment brought on a good laugh and the first spontaneous company cheer I had heard. I was not the only one ready for the inspection. Bring the bastards on.

Top and I offered a short in-brief for the IG team before turning them over to the company guides we had so carefully selected. Top and the mess hall had added one last touch. Coffee, juice, and a variety of pastries were available for the team. An urn of hot water with a pile of tea bags was also on the table. Strange drink for men in a U.S. infantry division, but our intel said that one of the IG team members was a "tea sipper."

During the maintenance inspection, the IG requested that only the guides accompany them on their rounds. Members of the chain of command were to stay out of their way. During the early hours I remained in my office and read the first newspaper I had had time to leaf through in weeks. As was his habit when nervous, Carrasco began cleaning his desk and everything else in reach. He spent an hour taking apart his telephone, carefully cleaning and polishing each piece, and then reassembling the device.

By midmorning the guides and other observers were passing along information on how things were going. Most of the information was either very bad or very good, and there was little reason to believe the accuracy of either. Every half hour or so, Top would run out the gang of NCOs and lieutenants who gathered in the orderly room to find out how the inspection was progressing. By late afternoon the tension hung like cigarette smoke over a poker game, and Top had the cleanest telephone and desk in all of Europe.

The IG finally sent word that they were ready to present their results. I quickly assembled the platoon leaders and sergeants and the section chiefs for maintenance, commo, supply, and arms. Lieutenant Colonel King was the only attendee from outside the company. In a manner which seemed quite appropriate, the IG team announced its results like the jury in a courtroom trial. Areas included in the inspection fell into three categories— those that were inspected basically for courtesy and had nothing to do with the final results, areas which were graded but only an average passing score was required, and finally, the "big four," tracked-vehicle maintenance, weapons, supply, and communications. Each of the big four had to be rated satisfactory or the entire inspection was graded a failure. Averages did not count.

The IG spoke slowly as he turned large pages on an easel, which displayed the inspection results area by area. He seemed to dwell on the courtesy items and commended us for doing well in areas that had nothing to do with the results of the inspection. I remember thinking that satisfactory scores in meaningless areas would not be much solace after being relieved of command.

As the IG turned the page on the easel for the items that had to average to a passing score, I immediately noted that all the numbers were in blue—there were no reds denoting "unsats." With no need to average the total for a satisfactory rating, I paid little attention to the remarks as I waited for the big four. The first of the must-pass categories briefed was supply. Staff Sergeant Cook had come through with a nearly perfect score. Communications followed with a 75 percent. Weapons squeaked through with a 71. One more item—the most important—to go. Everything rested on the evaluations of the tracked vehicles. The IG turned the master page for the category. Blue and red were about equal, but at the bottom was a big 73 in the bluest blue I had ever seen.

Throughout the out-brief, my officers and NCOs had remained quiet. Except for an occasional sigh of relief or a smile, there had been no reactions. Not until the IG concluded by stating, "Congratulations, you have passed the maintenance portion of the retest of your annual general inspection," did we realize and accept the results. Still, there was no celebration or cheering. A few handshakes and "well dones" were exchanged, but we all knew it was not yet over. An unsatisfactory on the billets and in-ranks inspection would still put us on the negative side of the IG ledger, and more than one of us would be jobless.

I kept my chain of command in the classroom after the IG and Lieutenant Colonel King departed. Plans for the second part of the inspection were reviewed. Guides and section chiefs were told to report to Captain Todd in C Company immediately after our meeting to brief him on what to expect for his maintenance inspection the next day.

Soldiers of the 2d of the 30th were not the only ones to be aware of the importance of the inspection. Schweinfurt was a large community, but the grapevine was short, swift, and generally accurate. Within minutes after the IG announced his results, I doubt if any NCO and officer on Ledward did not know the outcome. By evening the word spread to the troops and families. Soldiers and their family members with whom I had only a nodding acquaintance—and some I did not know at all—stopped me on the street with congratulations. It was a great feeling—even if my time in command might not last but for two more days.

While we did not celebrate the maintenance results, I could sense the pride in the leaders and the men. Several of the soldiers stopped me in the company area and told me if the IG thought we had done well on the first part, he was going to be amazed by the way we kicked ass on the second. We did not let up. New questions and areas of inspection used on our sister companies were added to the edge list. An almost constant chatter of questions and answers rang through the barracks. At 2000 hours the evening before the second phase of the inspection, I called a meeting of the chain of command and told them to cease preparations. A good night's sleep would be a welcome change and the rest might provide the final needed "edge on the edge."

The next morning, I accompanied the IG while Top went with his deputy on the tour of the barracks, layouts of individual equipment, and personal inspection of each soldier. At our first stop, the IG went straight to a trooper who had been in the company only a few weeks. The IG's first question was "How do you check the track tension on an M-113?" My heart felt like it was going to stop, and thoughts of the months of preparation swept through my mind as I concluded that the inspection had begun poorly and would go downhill. The question was one I had never heard Top ask nor was it in our crib book. Suddenly, I realized that the soldier was responding—and giving the correct answer. Standing next to him was his smiling team leader, who, I later learned, had added a few questions of his own in preparation.

After the soldier's lengthy explanation, the IG, a look of amazement on his face rivaled only by my own, turned to his recorder and said, "Give this man a commendable." After questioning the other six men in the room and asking questions that were covered in our preparation, the IG closely inspected their gear, bunks, and equipment. The more he looked, the less he said. As he moved to the hall, he turned to the recorder one more time saying, "Give them all a commendable."

While satisfactory and unsatisfactory were the only ratings in the maintenance inspection, the individual portion allowed a rarely awarded commendable rating. I was aware of the commendable evaluation but never expected to receive anything above satisfactory. As we moved down the hallway to other rooms, the rating was repeated on more than one-half of our stops. In the rooms not achieving commendables, the IG did not reveal his evaluation, but things were looking good. On occasion, when I spotted Top and his group, he smiled—a truly rare occurrence for the first sergeant.

By the time the IG and his deputy had completed their rounds, I felt confident that we had done well. Still, I knew nothing was definite or official in the army until the paperwork is posted. While results of the maintenance inspection were announced as each company was completed, the troop inspection results were not announced until the entire battalion had been checked. Overall, the battalion was looking fairly good. Three of the five companies had passed the maintenance portion and everyone seemed fairly confident that the overall rating would be satisfactory.

Late that afternoon, my fellow company commanders and I, accompanied by first sergeants and platoon leaders, joined Lieutenant Colonel King and his staff in the Ledward theater for our official out-brief. With the IG team were the brigade commander, his staff, and several members of the division staff. As we entered the theater, John Mackey pointed out a lieutenant colonel from division who was rumored to be ready to take over the battalion if the final results were unsatisfactory.

Again the IG assumed the role of foreman of the jury. He began his briefing with a summation of the maintenance results of which all of us were already well aware. One bit of news that I did note when the results from all five companies flashed on the screen was that A Company, despite having gone first, had the best scores in the battalion.

Beginning with a long speech on the improvements of the battalion over the past six months, the IG finally got around to the troop inspection. He summarized overall scores, noted common deficiencies, and finally concluded, "Colonel King, I am pleased to announce to you and the members of the 2d Battalion, 30th Infantry, that the overall rating for your annual general inspection is satisfactory."

A brief moment of silence followed the announcement. Suddenly a group of lieutenants let out a whoop, which was quickly drowned out by a cheer from the leadership of the entire battalion. King turned to shake hands with each of his company commanders. Out of the corner of my eye I saw the lieutenant colonel from division make a hasty exit. For a half hour or so, we remained in the theater slapping each other on the back and exchanging congratulations.

As Top and I finally began walking back to the company, the IG stopped us just outside the theater. From my intel gathering about the team, I was aware that he had already successfully commanded a battalion and had an excellent combat record in Vietnam as well. I was also aware that he was the one who had failed us on the original inspection and still had held the red pencil if he had wanted to do so again. Regardless of the good feeling about the announced results, I felt no affection whatsoever for the IG. Not knowing what to expect, I accepted his handshake and expression of congratulations as he said, "Captain Lanning, I want to tell you that in over two years as the division IG, I've seen no company make the improvements that you have in A Company. In fact, I don't think I've seen better. Well done."

The IG's remarks added to the satisfaction of the afternoon, yet I thought at the time that if we were the best, things must be awfully bad elsewhere. Still, exhaustion aside, I felt absolutely wonderful.

As soon as we got back to the company, I saw that the troops had already gotten the word of their success. Before we released the men for a well-deserved, three-day weekend, Top called a quick formation. I repeated the remarks of the IG to the troops. While I pointed out that we still had far to go, I told them I appreciated their hard work and enthusiasm. As a conclusion, I forcefully added that anyone that got in trouble over the weekend and blemished the new reputation of Alpha Company would be in one hell of a lot of trouble.

While Top had been gathering the troops for my talk, I telephoned home to let Linda know the results. It was no news to her. Within minutes after the "sat" was announced, the news had swept troop barracks and housing area alike. About all that was left to tell her was what time to meet me and the rest of the battalion officers at the club for the victory celebration.

It was nearly dark before I got out of the barracks and on my way to the club. As I walked across the company street to my car, a soldier I could not recognize because of the darkness shouted to me from a barrack's window. "Sir, sir," he hollered, "Like Lazarus from the grave, like Lazarus from the fucking grave, sir." I could not have said it better.

One thing that is great—or perhaps not so great—about the army is that there is never much lag time between major challenges. Although the old maxim of "hurry up and wait" is still often all too appropriate for the individual, there is seldom excess time for units or leaders in the constant cycle of inspections, training, and maintenance. Reputations of leaders and units are gained through long-term efforts, but what is achieved in months can be lost in hours. Traditions and esprit aside, the army allows no resting on the successes of the past. Rather than what happened yesterday, the question is, "What are you going to do today—and tomorrow?"

Our most immediate "tomorrow" following the IG was a return to Hohenfels for three weeks of live-fire and maneuver training. While the two weeks between the IG and Hohenfels were primarily focused on the future, we also labored to consolidate gains already made. By the first of August, our objective of going thirty days without a blotter entry had been successfully reached, and we were nearing the goal for the second time.

In a fashion similar to what we did for the AGI, (Army General Inspection, official name for the IG inspection), I also worked an edge to assist going blotterless. Top, myself, and the rest of the chain of command developed a relationship with the MPs—especially the NCOs who worked as night and weekend desk sergeants. Several of us went on "ride-alongs" with MP patrols on the post and downtown. While I closely questioned any action they took against my soldiers, I supported them when they were right. Eventually, the efforts did provide some payback. Several times when A Company soldiers were involved in minor incidents, desk sergeants called Top or me to pick up the soldier immediately so they could forego a blotter entry. In each case, either Top or myself stopped by the MP station at a later time to thank the desk sergeant and let him know what action had been taken against the offender.

Loading the train and moving by rail across Germany was routine to me by the time of our second rotation to the major training area. As for Hohenfels in August, it was not cold and muddy as it had been on our last visit. This time it was as hot, dry, and dusty as my West Texas birthplace. Thousands of wheeled and tracked vehicles had churned the training area into a fine dust that fogged the air and blocked vision as it settled into every crack and crevice. I was beginning to understand why the German soldiers who had trained in the same area prior to World War II had called the area the "other side of the moon."

As with our previous visit, we focused part of our training period on the use of the many live-fire ranges. Again we had great amounts of ammo for small arms and for the mortar platoon. Our advancement was not in what we did but when we did it. Rather than firing mostly during the day, we concentrated on firing during darkness, using night-vision devices, and firing under artificial light provided by illumination rounds from the mortar platoon.

I again allowed the platoon leaders two days in the training area to do anything they liked. Upon completion of their own training, I brought the platoons together to practice cross-country movement in both daylight and at night. The movements included crossing open areas, traversing heavily wooded forests, securing stream crossings, selecting fording sites, and responding to enemy contact. We conducted the drills both mounted and on foot.

At the end of nearly a week, the company pulled into an assembly area. After a day of instruction on escape and evasion, just after dark the soldiers were issued crude strip maps and told to reassemble at a rally point separated from the start point by twelve kilometers of forest and streams. Patrols, both mounted and dismounted, from the mortar and headquarters platoons were made along the route to capture the line-platoon infantrymen. Anyone caught was returned to the start to begin their escape and evasion all over again.

For safety's sake, the soldiers were paired in buddy teams. The only hard-surface road in the area was on the eastern border of the training area. Anyone not making it to the rally point by dawn or in need of emergency assistance was instructed to head to the road by following the rising sun.

While the purpose of the exercise was primarily to instill in the soldiers the confidence that they could perform even when tired and when their leaders were not present, the E&E exercise also presented a "fun break." The adult game of hide-and-seek was played to the enjoyment of all. It was weeks before the dozen or so men who'd been captured heard the last of the harassment from the mortar and headquarters aggressors. For a long time barbs were thrown back by soldiers who bragged about sneaking through the net of soldiers attempting to catch them.

At the assembly point, Top and I waited for the finishers. The first made it a little after midnight and most came in about three in the morning. No one went to the highway for pickup, but Top and I thought a couple of times that we'd spotted pairs of soldiers near the hardtop. Apparently, everyone preferred to walk to the rally point rather than face the embarrassment of being picked up by the first sergeant and company commander.

After a brief stand-down for maintenance, we were back in the field for battalion maneuver training, which progressed to a brigade cross-country exercise. This three-day movement took us from Hohenfels to the large armor training area of Grafenwöhr. During this time I had my first good look at the new brigade commander, Col. Neal Creighton. Formerly the commander of the Combined Arms Training Center at Vilseck,

Creighton looked and acted the part of the consummate professional soldier. Tall, lean, confident, and good-natured, he had a natural aura around him that immediately identified him as the commander.* Creighton communicated well with the soldiers and the junior officers, and he was excellent in teaching and leading his battalion and company commanders.

My initial reaction to Creighton had not been so positive. Upon our arrival at Hohenfels, brigade dispatched a directive stating that clean windshields and headlights would be an item of concern to the commander. Several stories soon followed about the ass chewing that Creighton had delivered to company commanders and first sergeants whose vehicles did not meet his clean-glass standard. While it seemed like a silly area on which to concentrate, I had approached it with the attitude "What the hell? He's the brigade commander, and what he wants, he'll get." I followed this by securing yards and yards of target cloth and bottles of glass cleaner for each vehicle—and supplemented it by raising hell not with drivers, but with the vehicle commander whenever I found dirty glass. As a result, we never had any trouble with Creighton's frequent glass inspections.

It took a while for the brigade commander's real purpose to sink in. While clean glass and headlights were important to safety, they also provided a quick way for Creighton to see if his orders were being followed in other ways. If a company commander and his driver did not follow a printed directive known to have the commander's personal interest, then other less obvious procedures were just as likely not being properly conducted.

One of the best parts of the brigade maneuver exercise was that a platoon of tanks was cross-attached to A Company in exchange for an infantry platoon that went to the armor company. The platoon attached to us was from the 1st Brigade's C Company, 2d Battalion, 60th Armor, which was quartered a few kilometers from Ledward at Conn Barracks. Their company commander, Captain Gary Eldridge, was an old friend and classmate from the advanced course at Fort Knox. In exchange for Eldridge's company, Lieutenant Colonel King had to send

---

*As time passed, I began to admire Creighton so much that I overlooked that he was an armor rather than an infantry officer—a pretty big concession for a grunt of any rank.

Al Todd's Charlie Company to the 2d of the 60th. During the attachment, King had the option of moving the tank company's platoons any way he wanted, but the usual configuration, which best suited our actual war plans, was for Ron Glancy's B Company to remain infantry-pure, with my company consisting of two platoons of infantry and one of armor, with Eldridge having two armor and one infantry platoons. Each company kept its organic mortar platoon regardless of the rest of the cross-attachment.

This arrangement formed the combined-arms team, which was the organization in which we would fight in combat. On Creighton's insistence, the cross-attachments would be the same during all field exercises and along the border defensive line if we ever had to earn our paychecks for real.

The basic premise of the combined-arms team of the time, and of current U.S. Army doctrine, is that neither pure infantry nor armor can survive on the modern battlefield. Tanks need infantry support to protect them from hand-held antitank weapons, and infantry requires tanks to assist in defending against enemy armor. Regardless of the sophistication of infantry antitank weapons, the best weapon against a tank remains another tank.

Actual maneuver as well as offensive and defensive actions remained fairly similar, the major difference being the tanks' placements where they would have the best fields of fire for their 1,500-meter-range 105mm main gun. One major consideration was that the M-60 tanks weighed sixty tons and were much wider than our M-113 personnel carriers. Extra care had to be taken in selecting bridge crossings and routes through the villages. After a week of rolling across the German countryside with the tanks, combined with the limited knowledge I had picked up in the advanced course, I felt comfortable with the combined-arms team that now made up Alpha Company, or Team Alpha as we were called in our go-to-war posture.

At the end of the exercise we moved to the railhead at Grafenwöhr for our out-load back to Schweinfurt. As we waited for the trainmaster to get the cars arranged correctly, Lieutenant Colonel King called me to one side and informed me that a special officer efficiency report with a maximum rating was being prepared for his and Creighton's signatures to recognize the performance of A Company in the IG. I knew well that such reports are extremely rare and are put on the top of an officer's file for future promotions.* It was a recognition that I welcomed but was not sure I deserved. Regardless, I was happy as hell, and the train ride back from the "other side of the moon" to the barracks where "Lazarus had risen from the grave" was almost enjoyable.

*The Army promotion system requires specific amounts of time in each grade before consideration for promotion. For two years prior to the designated time in grade required for advancement, each officer is considered in the secondary zone from which two to five percent are selected for early promotion by the centralized board. Nearly a year after I received the special report, I was selected during my first year in the secondary zone for promotion to major. Without a doubt, the key to that selection was the special efficiency report.

CHAPTER 9

I'D RATHER BE A DOGFACE SOLDIER THAN ON THE OTHER SIDE OF THE WALL

September 1975

By the arrival of September 1975, I was reasonably satisfied with the level of discipline and readiness in the company. We did not cut back on the long hours, and everything we did still was top priority. Yet a certain relaxation was in the air. All of us felt pride in the company's progress and confident that we could give a good account for ourselves in battle.

Still, the company remained the focus of my waking and nonwaking thought and action. There were, however, other professional responsibilities outside of Schweinfurt that may not have taken much time in actual work, but did call for much thought as well as consultation with Linda. After eight years in the infantry, I would soon be in the promotion zone for major. Recent decisions at the Department of the Army called for all senior captains to select an alternate area of service such as logistics, finance, personnel administration, foreign area specialist, operations, or a host of other skill-specific areas.

The alternate specialty of choice of most infantry and other combat-arms officers was operations, personnel management running a close second. Both specialities were considered excellent career moves for assisting in future promotions and in selection for command assignments. The problem with personnel management was that it was a specialty in which integrity was a negative rather than a positive attribute. I doubt if there is a former, serving, or future officer who has not been or will not be lied to by his personnel manager.

As for operations, I had found in my experience that ops types were among the most boring and often the least intelligent of any in the army. Working with plans which are seldom executed and playing with the the x's and o's of war games instead of

139

reality, the guys in operations are usually those who choose whitewall haircuts, wear camouflage undershirts when off duty, own four-wheel-drive trucks, and marry subservient, non-English-speaking, third-world nationals.

Even those negatives were not sufficient for me not to at least consider the two specialties, but the peacetime army, when not in command, was boring enough without deliberately seeking a sleepy job. When I had pursued assignment to the Armor Advanced Course and mech infantry in Germany, I had sought what I thought was the future of the army. Ultimately, however, in selecting my alternate specialty, I looked not forward but backward.

During the Vietnam War, I had watched and seen the results of army spokesmen, in the guise of "public information officers," alienate reporters and finally the American public through their ineptness, ignorance, and, often, dishonesty. The war had not been lost on the battlefield but in the newspapers, on the televisions, and across the campuses of the United States. As soldiers we had done as well as any men ever put on the battlefield; as information and public relations practitioners we had lost our country's first war.

Considering the information officer specialty brought on advice from near and far—and in every case a recommendation to seek another alternate service area. I heard comments that ranged from "Do it and you'll never make major" to "Are you fucking crazy?" Regardless, public information looked challenging. Working with the post-Vietnam press would be mental if not physical combat. More important, the image of the army was at an all-time low,* and I wanted to do something about it. We had good raw material—the youth of the country—and an excellent service to sell, the preservation of the greatest way of life known to mankind throughout history. It was time that someone did it who knew and loved the army from the battlefield to the barracks and from the soldier to the sergeant.

Despite all advice to the contrary, I was near making the decision to ask for public information, when the army, as it is prone to do, dangled a carrot to help me make the decision. A letter from the public information specialty assignment officer

*A Louis Harris poll in December, 1973, revealed that the American public had more confidence in their local police, television news, and garbage collectors than in the military.

arrived stating that the field was no longer accepting officers relieved from other duties or unable to find jobs in other fields. Combat arms officers with "distinguished" war records were being recruited to fill the ranks of the public information field. This alone did not influence my decision—I had finally learned not to trust everything the personnel manglers claimed. The prevailing carrot was the last paragraph promising alternate public information and infantry assignments as well as advanced education at a civilian university for a master's degree in journalism and/or public relations.*

Filling in a half-dozen blanks on a printed form and signing at the bottom was all it took for me to request public information as my alternate field. A few weeks later, in near record time for correspondence to make the round trip between Schweinfurt and Washington, DC, I received another form letter with two parts and five paragraphs quoting regulations and policies. Hand written in Part I, paragraph 2, was that public information had been approved as my alternate specialty, and that code 46 would be added to my infantry code 11 to designate my new official specialty area.

Shortly after our August return from Hohenfels, Lieutenant Colonel King approached me with an offer to take the company to West Berlin for a week of combat-in-the-cities training. The opportunity came as a result of our AGI performance but was more than just a reward. Division had been authorized to send one company to Berlin each quarter but had not filled the obligation for well over a year. The last two companies had caused trouble in the training area, in the Berlin Brigade barracks, and at the checkpoint between the divided cities. Division's last company representative in Berlin was ordered home before it had completed training.

King was up front with the offer and the division history. According to the battalion commander, if I was not confident

---

*The army kept its promises of education and alternate assignments. Over the next twelve years I would serve as the public information officer (renamed public affairs officer, shortly after my entry) at division, corps, and Department of Defense levels. During that time I was fortunate to see information officers become trusted advisors of commanders, who had also learned the lesson of the importance of public affairs during their combat tours in Vietnam.

the company could stay out of trouble, I could turn down the trip with nothing else said. Of course, such an offer was more a challenge than an honest alternate. With no hesitation, I responded, "Sir, in battle there would be no option on whether to take the company or not. Besides, Berlin sounds like fun and a good training opportunity. There will be no problems from Alpha Company."

In addition to extensive briefings of the company by Top and myself over the next few weeks about the consequences of any improper actions during our visit to Berlin, we worked on acquiring our edge. Urban combat was the area of expertise of the Berlin Brigade, but there was no reason for us to arrive unprepared. Using the army's field manuals as guides to combat in built-up areas, and two NCOs who had experience with the Berlin Brigade, we trained so that we would be ready for the "experts."

Our transportation to Berlin was by a U.S. Air Force C-130, which would have to make two shuttles on the two-hour flight. We trucked south from Ledward to Kitzingen, where there was an airfield with sufficient runway length for the aircraft. We were up, and driving by deuce-and-a-half, before dawn only to wait, at no surprise to anyone, four hours for the C-130. A typical German, fall-morning fog kept the aircraft circling for another hour before it attempted to land. The airfield was not instrument equipped so the 130 had to land using only the vision of the pilots.

The plane made several passes trying to penetrate the fog and its one- to two-hundred-foot ceiling by following the instructions from a ground-control party. We could clearly hear the four-engine C-130 above the fog, but the pilots were having trouble lining up on the runway. On the fifth pass the huge aircraft suddenly punched through the mist to find itself about fifty meters to one side of the concrete strip. With a lurch, the pilots made a radical turn, causing the aircraft to whip from horizontal to vertical, wings extending from ground straight upward to the sky. Just as quickly the plane went back to the horizontal, with the maneuver placing it squarely over the runway. It touched down for a picture-book landing, with the sergeant in charge of the ground party exclaiming "Jesus Christ!"

The C-130 taxied up to our runway-apron assembly area and dropped its rear loading ramp. An air force senior master sergeant, whose identification tag stated that he was the loadmaster, walked a bit unsteadily down the ramp. From his name and the Spanish he was muttering, I surmised that he was of Hispanic origins. All I could understand was "crazy motherfuckers" and something about being six months from retirement. I do not really think that the rest of his remarks were praise of the officers in the cockpit.

As we loaded, I went up to the flight deck, expecting to see old battle-hardened colonels wearing fifty-mission-crush hats; a landing like that had to be executed by men with thousands of hours of flying time. What I found were two gum-chewing first lieutenants, who were barely old enough to vote. The Berlin training mission was looking more dangerous all the time.

With little time to contemplate the youth of the pilots, we were soon loaded and bound for our destination, Templehof Airport. Templehof had been the pride of Hitler and the planned location of memorials to the Thousand-Year Reich. By 1975 Hitler was, of course, gone, and Templehof had achieved more fame as the terminus of the Berlin Airlift than as a monument to the Nazis. Serving both as the military and civilian airfield for the western portion of the divided city, Templehof was one of Europe's busiest airports—at least it had been before the arrival of Alpha Company of the 2d of the 30th Infantry.

We taxied to the front of the main terminal then off-loaded to buses parked on the apron. There was not another plane or person in sight. The airport was like a ghost town. As I was staring around in amazement, an air force NCO approached and welcomed us to Templehof and Berlin and almost as an afterthought said, "I guess I should also congratulate you and your men. You just made the first landing at Templehof since its closure to civilian flights. They, and most of the military traffic, are going into the new airport which just opened yesterday."

With the riddle of the vacant airfield answered, we met the members of our hosting unit, B Company, 4th Battalion, 6th Infantry of the Berlin Brigade, and their commander, Capt. Bob Codney. Bob explained that our troops would be billeted in a barracks that was adequate but not really up to the standards of its namesake, the "Holiday Inn." He added that BOQ space was available for myself and my officers but seemed pleased when I told him that we would stay with the troops at the inn.

By the time Codney had briefed me on our training schedule for the remainder of the week and had given the soldiers a tour of the area, the second planeload arrived. After extensive briefings on the dangers and pleasures—at times difficult to distinguish between—and even more detailed explanations of the repercussions of getting into trouble with the MPs or local police, we turned the troops loose on Berlin.

While there were many bleary eyes and more than a hangover or two, the troops were all present at the next morning's formation. Since Monday and Friday were travel days, our week in Berlin was actually limited to three days—two of which would be devoted to actual training and one for a guided tour of the city on both sides of the wall.

The Berlin Brigade's six thousand soldiers shared the defense of the free portion of the city with even smaller units of British and French soldiers. At the end of World War II the city had been divided into four sectors, one each for the major Allied Powers. By the mid-1970s Berlin had essentially only two parts—East and West—separated by the wall which encircled the entire Western Zone. An island of freedom surrounded by communist East Germany, Berlin's main protectors, the NATO forces, were one hundred kilometers away should the East Germans and Soviets decide to overrun it. Though the brigade's survival, much less victory, was obviously in doubt, the troops in West Berlin did not intend to be just pawns or the cause of a rallying cry of "Remember Berlin" if World War III became a reality. The brigade had elaborate plans of fighting a delaying action which ranged from defense of major intersections to snipers and tank-killer teams perched in the surrounding highrises. Additional plans included using the city's underground drainage system as means of moving forces and as lines of communications and supply.

In addition to being the defense of West Berlin, the brigade was the representative of the free world to the comrades on the other side of the wall. Spit and polish were a way of life to the Berlin brigadiers and exhaustive inspections were conducted prior to each patrol along the wall. One benefit of the brigade's being in the spotlight was that U.S. commanders could transfer drug abusers and other troublemakers out of the city to units in West Germany—or "send them to the Zone" in Berlin Brigade language.

Our host unit offered training in the defense and attack of built-up areas. The training area was a pre–World War II park which had been converted into a mock city, complete with masonry and wooden houses, shops with appropriate signs, and automobiles parked in the streets. Closer inspection revealed that the cars were inoperative hulks and the buildings were empty, but the mock city provided everything necessary to learn how to fight and survive in an urban environment.

The wall dividing Berlin provided the park's boundaries on two sides. An East German guard tower loomed just on the other side of the concrete and barbed-wire barrier, and uniformed guards observed and photographed many of our activities. Early in the first training day my soldiers frequently made obscene gestures toward the tower, but by day's end everyone was accustomed to our uninvited guests and ignored them.

Although it is much easier to clear a building by fighting from the top down instead of from the bottom up, we practiced scaling walls with makeshift ladders and with the assistance of ropes and grappling hooks. When we had those methods perfected, we worked "top to bottom" after being delivered to the roofs of buildings by helicopter. We then either fought down the stairways or rappelled down the sides of the buildings to enter through windows. Even though combat in the cities is primarily a function of leg infantry, we were able to integrate M-113s (borrowed from our host unit) into providing covering fires and in the extraction of wounded personnel.

Knowing that the soldiers of the Berlin Brigade considered themselves the elite of U.S. Forces in Europe, I especially wanted—and demanded—that the company be sharp and competitive in training and well disciplined during and after duty hours. The soldiers understood this unofficial competition and responded well. Although the detailed attention and supervision by Top and the senior NCOs certainly added to their performance, the attitude lingered from the AGI that we were the best in the 3d Infantry Division and no one, even the pampered Berlin Brigade, was any better.

The competition between Codney's soldiers and mine came to a boiling point on several occasions—especially during the attacks against, and clearing of, buildings. A few fists were thrown amid shoving matches, but cooler-headed NCOs separated the soldiers before any real damage could be done. Despite the conflicts, the soldiers of the two companies got along reasonably well and, as the week progressed, seemed to develop a mutual respect.

Only one night was scheduled for training, so that left three evenings—and early mornings—for the soldiers to enjoy the sights, bars, and women of Berlin. Although the war was more than three decades in the past, our German hosts back in Schweinfurt still kept the multiple bombing attacks against their city in mind; while our presence was tolerated, we were never made to feel welcome at our home station. West Berlin was different. Americans had won the hearts of the city during the airlift, and Berliners were aware that the Allied forces in the occupied city were all that stood between them and the Communists, who had looted and raped the city at the close of the war. Americans in Berlin had long been forgotten as conquerors and were treated as liberators and preservers of a tenuous peace and freedom.

Knowing that the only sights my soldiers would see without it being a part of the training schedule were the inside of bars and discos and perhaps a bedroom or two, we set an entire day aside for a formal tour of the city. We began with the Western Zone and a visit to Spandau Prison, where the elite of the Nazis—those who had not been hung—were imprisoned after the Nuremberg trials. Guards for the prison rotated every month among the British, French, Americans, and the Soviets. This presence every three months by Soviet guards in the Western Zone was felt by many to be the reason the Russians had not allowed Spandau's last prisoner, Rudolf Hess, to be released.

Our next stop was the Soviet War Memorial, which was in West and not East Berlin. According to our guides, the Soviets built the monument before the city was formally divided, but with the knowledge that it was not in what would become their sector. As for our observation of the monument and its Soviet guards, we had to watch from our buses. A few weeks before, a West Berliner had shot and seriously injured one of the guards in protest of the treatment of his fellow Germans in the East. Since that time, visitors had been kept at a distance.

After a quick sack lunch, provided by our host company mess hall and eaten in one of the many lush Berlin parks, we headed for Checkpoint Charlie. Since Berlin was legally still an occupied city, each of the four powers supposedly maintained access to each of the sectors despite the wall and barbed wire that separated German from German. To show that the access remained in effect, American soldiers were encouraged to cross the boundary and tour the Eastern Sector. Though there was little danger on the other side, we received detailed briefings about staying on the main thoroughfares and not getting into any confrontations with the East Germans or their Soviet occupiers.

Even though our tour of East Berlin was supposed to be for fun, as in everything else we undertook, it still seemed reasonable for A Company to have an edge. Top finally came through by letting me know that Liebrich had learned that the exchange rate of East German marks for dollars was much better on our side of the wall. Officially the rate was supposed to be the same for both East and West German currencies, but, in fact, the dollar bought nearly four times as many of the Communist marks as those of West Germany—if exchanged on our side of the wall. Once we crossed into East Berlin our dollars would be worth only the exchange rate of the West German money. By the time we approached Checkpoint Charlie, the men of A Company were carrying a little over $4,000 in East German marks, representing quadruple the buying power we would have had if we had waited to make the exchange after the crossing. According to our hosts, our edge had been duplicated by other visiting units but never to the degree accomplished by Alpha soldiers. Another well-deserved record was chalked up to A Company.

We snaked across the border between the city sectors by weaving back and forth between heavy concrete barricades intended to stop a speeding car or truck bent on escape to the West. Guard towers, manned by East Germans and Soviets equipped with heavy machine guns and individual weapons, overlooked the fifty meters between Checkpoint Charlie and the gate at the other end of the barricades. This play, performed by cold-war warriors of both sides, had been running for more than fourteen years, but it was still quite evident that it was a drama rather than a comedy. Not a smile greeted us from a single guard, and each of the East Germans and Soviets seemed to grip his weapon a little more tightly when he saw our olive drab U.S. Army buses.

Knowing that crossing the border was routine did not prevent an inward sigh of relief once we were past the towers and barriers. Commonplace or not, it still seemed odd as hell to be entering the camp of our enemies, with us in dress-green uniforms with no weapons of any kind, while our Communist adversaries looked down on us through the sights of automatic weapons.

From the checkpoint to the center plaza of East Berlin, we passed closely packed, recently constructed apartment com-

plexes. According to our guides the housing had been built—
and poorly at that—by the Soviets to showcase how well
Germans on their side of the wall were privileged to live. The
buildings surrounding the East Berlin plaza were also new or
rebuilt in tribute to the Communist way of life.* This facade
evaporated quickly, however, for any visitor who wandered
more than a block from the city center. There we saw buildings
still displaying bomb damage from World War II and complete
blocks that were still vacant.

Outside the city center, the best kept parts of East Berlin
appeared to be those areas maintained by the Soviets. At the
Soviet Military Headquarters, we stopped to observe a change
of the guard, which rivaled the pomp and circumstance of the
ceremony at the Tomb of the Unknown at Arlington National
Cemetery. It was also interesting to note that the Soviet soldiers
were every bit as young as the teenagers who made up the majority of A Company.

Another short bus ride took us to the Soviet Cemetery where
the soldiers who died in the attack on Berlin at the close of World
War II lay buried. Of course, no crosses marked the graves, but
what was surprising was that the cemetery did not contain individual graves. Casualties had been so severe that the dead were
buried in mass graves approximately fifty meters square. Overlooking the plots were two enormous statues at least thirty feet
in height. One was of an elderly veteran soldier, while the other
was of a woman representing Mother Russia. Sympathy for one's
enemies, despite their former role as allies, is not easily felt.
Still, I must admit to feeling an overpowering sense of being
among men who had shared the profession of arms as I looked
over the seemingly endless plots of the dead.

Our final destination was the city center, where the soldiers
were allowed time for individual sightseeing and shopping. As
the buses unloaded and the men quickly disappeared in all di-
rections into the sides streets of East Berlin, I again questioned
my own judgment in bringing over one hundred GIs into the

---

*To the chagrin of the East Germans and the Soviets, the recently com-
pleted observation and television tower which overlooked the plaza had a
"flaw." When sunlight struck the convex surface of the platform near the
top of the tower, it reflected what was undisputably a cross. A change of
surface had not stopped the phenomenon, which by the time of our visit,
was hailed as a message of God against Communism by some, and as just
irony by many.

Communist Zone. Top and Liebrich offered an alternative to worrying about it by inviting me to join them in shopping for gifts to take back home. As we walked along the streets, we encountered a group of school children about six or seven years of age, all dressed alike in gray wool jumpers and white shirts. With a teacher at each end of their column, the kids were holding hands to prevent getting separated on the crowded sidewalk. We were quickly reminded that we were visitors in an unfriendly land, as all of the children stuck out their tongues or made faces as they passed. In heavily accented English, the last child in the line even managed to declare an understandable "Yankee go home." The boy must have been a little disappointed by our reaction. All three of us laughed so hard that even several of the children changed their expressions to smiles.

Although many of the shelves in the shops around the East Berlin city plaza were bare, we did manage to quickly spend our "highly converted" marks on such things as Russian dolls-within-dolls and Soviet-made perfume and pocket watches.* Top, Liebrich, and I were back at the plaza more than an hour before the deadline we had given the company. While none of the three of us said anything, I am sure we shared an apprehension about getting everyone back from their personal tours of the city.

During our wait, we walked around the plaza and stopped briefly to observe a troop of Soviet men and women performing what appeared to be folk dances while wearing dress military uniforms. The young women smiled at me and my senior NCOs, but I supposed there was no significance to their action as the men did likewise. After observing for a few minutes, I noticed several booths selling photos. Closer inspection revealed that the pictures were of North Vietnamese manning Soviet tanks on the streets of Saigon. Another colorful photo showed the Republic of South Vietnam's yellow and red striped flag on the ground while that of North Vietnam was being raised over the fallen country's seat of government.

Although Saigon had fallen more than five months earlier,

---

*Despite the low prices we paid for the items because of our money conversion in the West rather than the East, the comrades may have had the last laugh. At this writing, more than fifteen years after the purchase, Linda still has not managed to use all of the peculiar perfume. As for the pocket watch, it looks great and shines. However, except for a week or two after its purchase, it has not worked for a single second.

the Communist victory was still being celebrated in East Berlin—at least during visits by soldiers of the United States Army. Carrasco, Liebrich, and I had a joint total of more than six years in the combat zones of Vietnam. As we continued to watch the celebration, Liebrich finally broke the silence by asking no one in particular, "Was it worth it?"

After a long pause I replied as much to myself as to my NCO, "It really doesn't make any difference. We did our best. After all, it was the only war we had."*

Top, Liebrich, and I completed our wait for the rest of the company at a street-side bar, where we drank mugs of decent Communist beer for about a nickel a liter. Most of the men returned a good half hour early, and all were accounted for by ten minutes before the deadline. We were soon back on our buses and headed back for Checkpoint Charlie and the Western Zone.

One more night on the town and a C-130 ride, and we were back in Schweinfurt. That night I wrote in my journal about the visit to the two Berlins: "After seeing the Wall and the East, I am left wondering why there has not been a man great enough to bring it all back together." If anyone had suggested that in 1989 such a man would come forward, I would not have believed it. The fact that he would be a Soviet would have made the deed even more incomprehensible.

At the top of the company's agenda upon return to Ledward was not training or preparation for the next exercise or inspection, but rather a simple slow-pitch softball tournament. This single elimination match fought by the battalion's five companies was officially for a foot-high trophy, but mostly it was a recreational alternative to downtown and drugs. Far more important than either of those noteworthy goals, however, the tournament was fought for bragging rights. Though all of us certainly compared our scores in the Annual General Inspection (AGI), the number of blotter incidents, and the daily operational-vehicle rate, every battalion effort was made in concert and cooperation among the companies. Whether lending mechanics before an inspection, donating a spare part, or conducting joint training, the five companies worked together for our common good—in

---

*That conversation with Carrasco and Liebrich would later provide the title for my first book about the Vietnam War—*The Only War We Had,* Ivy Books, New York, 1987.

everything but softball and any other organized athletics which could be conducted with a minimum amount of casualties.

With the company's best ball players on the field and the rest of the unit in the stands cheering as if the games were the World Series, it was obvious that the outcome of the tournament was not to be taken lightly. Although I had desperately sought an edge in the competition, I had been unsuccessful. The tournament was taken so seriously by everyone that the battalion adjutant had had to confirm the company assignment of each player. No ringers were allowed nor could they be slipped into a lineup. Ultimately our edge was someone who had been in the company for well over a year and who was also one of our best NCOs. SSgt. Hazrat Ali came forward during our last practice game and said he thought he might be able to help in the outfield. I was more than a bit skeptical. Ali had immigrated to the United States from India and joined the U.S. Army for a job as a step toward citizenship. While he had learned soldiering well, softball was new to him. Cricket, however, was not, and Ali soon proved to be the best outfielder in the company—despite the fact that he refused a glove and caught the ball barehanded.

Since we had been in Berlin when the other companies had practiced, we were given a bye in the first round. We then had to win two games for the championship. The first was easy even though our opponents had won their initial match. While there were a few fights in the stands and a couple of shoving matches on the base paths, everything was fairly calm.

Our final game was held on a Friday afternoon with the entire battalion lining the field. Our opponents, Al Todd's Charlie Company, were confident and already telling us how they were going to enjoy the keg of beer that Al and I had wagered. By the end of the second inning, Alpha Company had clawed to a lead of 2 to 1. In slow pitch softball, a strike-out is a rarity, many-run innings the norm. Not so that afternoon at Ledward Barracks. While balls were hit with authority, each team's soldiers ran them down for an out. Sergeant Ali, playing short field, made catches one-handed, with both hands, and seemingly with no hands. Five innings later the score of 2 to 1 stood. A Company was the battalion softball champion.

The beer, provided by Charlie Company—and shared with them—tasted wonderful. All we had done, of course, was win a simple softball match; in the bigger picture the victory was much more important than that. Winning was becoming commonplace in A Company. Winners are winners and generally remain winners. Whether it be the AGI, softball, or fighting for real on the border, if we established a tradition of winning, it would carry over to things more important than "just" a softball tournament.

CHAPTER 10

DON'T MESS WITH THE HOME TEAM: REFORGER

October 1975

The secret of getting along in the Army, and life in general for that matter, is figuring out who you can fuck with and who you can't.

Personal Journal
October 12, 1975

While fall back in the States meant the reopening of schools, the beginning of football season, and the anticipation of colorful changes in trees, in the U.S. Army assigned to Germany it meant but one thing—the Return of Forces to Europe, REFORGER as it was more commonly known. This joint service exercise had originated in the late 1960s as a means of displaying the continuing commitment of the United States to the defense of Europe. Such a show of force had been necessary to placate European leaders who rightly were concerned about the cutback in support for Europe during the buildup in Southeast Asia.

After the conclusion of the Vietnam War, REFORGER continued. It had proved to be an excellent exercise in developing and testing methods of rapid deployment of heavy armor and mechanized forces, which would be needed to reinforce the thin line of NATO units spread across Western Europe. REFORGER also provided an outstanding training opportunity to those of us already stationed in Germany because it was the only annual free-maneuver exercise which allowed off-road movement over distances that were realistic in mechanized warfare.

Each year, one-half of the units permanently assigned in Europe provided the aggressor force, which represented the attacking Warsaw Pact Army. The other one-half of the units provided controllers and administrative support for the exercise. Being the aggressor force was much more beneficial to training and a lot more fun than the latter. This was the 3d Infantry Division's year for fun.

Although the nucleus of the REFORGER soldiers from the States was from the 1st Mechanized Infantry Division at Fort Riley, Kansas, which made the trip annually, their turnover rate was so large that it was unusual for any of their soldiers to participate in more than one or two REFORGERS. As a result, each year the 1st Division arrived with little knowledge of the terrain and style of combat necessary for success on the European Plain. Our preparation for the exercise made the experience no easier for them.

Being stationed near the exercise maneuver area definitely gave us a home-field advantage. Once exact boundaries of the exercise area, or "maneuver box," were designated, we began a concentrated effort to get to know it even better. Three weeks before the maneuver portion of REFORGER began, we in the 2d of the 30th and other 3d Infantry Division units held a two-day command post exercise (CPX) followed by five days of a tactical exercise without troops (TEWT, pronounced "toot").

The CPX was a mock battle conducted over the communications system which tied together each of the company CPs to the battalion and battalion on to brigade and division. Except to move symbols representing each of the platoons on the CP map board, no actual maneuver took place. In addition to testing the battalion communications net, the CPX also provided practice in selecting routes of advance, positions for defense, and a better understanding of the contested terrain. The five-day TEWT allowed us to actually traverse the land on which we would be facing our opponents during REFORGER. Each of the platoon leaders reconed his area by jeep, while maintaining communications with my CP, which was also jeep mounted, and checking out the maneuver box. With no troops to move, the pace of the TEWT was fairly slow, allowing long lunch and dinner breaks at country gasthauses that dotted the area.

The most interesting discovery doing our TEWT reconnaissance was the remains of campaigns in the same area during World War II. Late one afternoon, while attempting to find a trail through a dense forest that would keep our attack out of the easily observable valleys and main road networks, we came across five graves. Each was marked with a German military headstone noting name, birth date, and date of death. Each soldier had died on the same day less than two weeks before the end of the war. Not one of the five was more than seventeen years old, the youngest barely fifteen. In the final days, the Nazi supermen had had to rely on superboys—and they, like their elder brothers, had suddenly been frozen in time through death from American bullets.

Besides the youth of the five dead soldiers, there was another unusual aspect about the graves. On top of each rested a rusted Kraut helmet—one with a bullet hole. The undisturbed relics attested to the remoteness of the site. However, with more than twenty thousand American, German, and Canadian soldiers soon to be conducting war games in the forest, I knew the helmets would not remain much longer. In a nearby village, I stopped at what appeared to be a constable's office and, with a teenage boy—who was about the same age as the dead soldiers— serving as a volunteer interpreter, managed to get the constable to summon the local forest master. Eventually, we were able to explain the forthcoming exercise and recommend that the forest master remove the helmets before they became the souvenir of some GI's REFORGER. The old forest master must have taken me seriously because a few days later as we headed back to Schweinfurt, I detoured past the graves and found that the helmets had been removed.

Of course, advance reconnaissance of the maneuver area gave us an advantage in the exercise. Although we practiced every option and course of action we thought that the "enemy" might take, they could still do the unexpected. While our pre-REFORGER CPX and TEWT might seem a little unfair, especially to units arriving fresh from the States, our familiarity with the terrain actually added realism. As previously noted, we knew our General Defensive Positions (GDP) intimately, and every soldier in the company knew the exact position from which he would fire his first shots of World War III. Being equally prepared for something as simple as REFORGER seemed to fit the pattern of what we were trying to accomplish.

REFORGER was held in the late fall for two reasons—neither of which were of any benefit to the participants. First of all, the exercise could not be conducted until the German farmers had been able to gather their crops from the fields. Secondly, the late date also usually guaranteed that the ground of the maneuver box would be frozen for at least part of the exercise. Both of these precautions were designed to reduce maneuver-damage claims filed by the landowners and the German government. Even though each unit had maneuver-damage control elements and repair teams to supplement an entire engineer battalion dedicated to returning the countryside to its pre-exercise state, claims, nonetheless, mounted into the millions of dollars each year.

We departed Schweinfurt over twenty-four hours before the beginning of REFORGER and moved in highway convoys to our assembly area. The seventy-plus kilometer move was a good test of our maintenance, and I was more than pleased that the Alpha Company vehicles continued to run as we passed broken down M-113s, tanks, and trucks of various descriptions along the roadside. Under clear skies and Indian summer weather, the move to the assembly area was almost pleasant. Within hours of the start of the exercise, however, a cold front moved across Central Europe, dropping the temperatures to the teens and producing a drizzling rain that soon turned to sleet and snow. While the inclement weather might make the maneuver-damage controllers happy, it was not good news to infantrymen.

In the assembly area, we were joined by the same platoon of tanks that had been attached during the maneuver between Hohenfels and Grafenwöhr. Their platoon leader, Lt. George Spencer, and the crews of his five tanks were becoming an accepted part of the company. An artillery forward observer team, an engineer squad, and a section composed of two TOW crews from the battalion combat support company rounded out what was now Team Alpha. A final addition to our team was a captain who commanded an infantry company in one of the divisions that was providing support personnel and controllers for the exercise. Complete with his own jeep, driver, and multiple radios, the captain—called a controller—would be the one to sort out engagements and designate casualties and vehicle losses. Using formulas and calculating each side's strength in weapons, artillery, and manpower, combined with "luck" (which was determined by a throw of the dice), the controller/umpire would ultimately be the one to designate life or death and victory or defeat.

For identification we were labeled the Orange Force, or the "bad guys," while the interlopers from the States were the Blue Force or the "good guys." With elements of the battalion scout platoon reconning our front, we crossed the official line of departure and entered the maneuver box at 0100 hours. If the opposing forces reacted in the way we anticipated, it would be nearly dawn before we had moved far enough to reach their main defensive lines. In the meantime, we would be confronted with their cavalry screen, artillery attacks, and mine-field obstacles.

Except for a couple of minor delays caused by simulated mine fields—which slowed us only for the length of time that it would take our engineers to clear a path—we moved quickly and with little opposition. Even the snow, sleet, and cold were not all that bad. Drivers and track commanders had insulated face masks, fur-lined parkas, and cold-weather mittens. Although our cold-weather gear was bulky and none too pretty, it was more than adequate to protect against cold injury, while providing a degree of comfort as well.

Despite the good gear, I had the platoons change drivers every hour or so in order to keep them alert. Off-line drivers and the rifle squads rode in the warmth of the cargo bay of the M-113s. While conditions were cramped with bodies, weapons, and assorted gear, inside was warmer than outside, and riding was in every way superior to the infantry's typical transport—walking.

The warm interiors of the 113s were another result of detailed preparation for the exercise. Heaters for the 113s ran from the diesel system that supplied the engines and were great when they worked—the problem was that they rarely worked and spare parts were difficult to find. The importance of having heated tracks for at least an occasional warm-up and the difficulties in keeping the heaters operational had not been overlooked by the division safety office. Directives before REFORGER stated that each platoon had to have at least one of its four 113s equipped with an operational heater. For prevention of cold-weather injuries as well as for morale purposes, I had insisted that every heater in the company be operational before the start of the exercise. When told of the shortage of parts, I had informed the platoon leaders and maintenance section that the heaters in *their* vehicles could not be repaired until all other vehicles belonging to them had operational heaters. I have no idea where they scrounged, what they traded for, or if they stole heater parts, but as we crossed the line of departure, every heater in the company worked—including the ones in my jeep and M-113 command track, which were, by my order, the last to be repaired.

I alternated my command post between my 113 and my jeep. While the 113 would be my permanent post in actual combat, the jeep allowed more mobility, with less damage to the terrain, for trips back and forth to battalion headquarters and for quick recons or to check on the platoons. The only problem with that arrangement was the new division commander's policy that all canvas on jeeps had to be removed. With the issued top, side curtains, and doors, a jeep could be kept fairly warm with an operational heater. Regardless of how good the heater was, it did little good with the canvas removed—especially in the freezing temperatures of REFORGER.

My jeep driver, Sp4 Robert H. Bain, was a former NCO who had gotten into some trouble in another battalion and had been reassigned to us on a rehabilitative transfer. A Vietnam veteran with a Combat Infantryman Badge, Bain had filled in as my driver on a temporary basis several months before and had performed so well that I had kept him in the position despite his previous record. I never asked Bain what he had done to get in trouble nor did I check his official records. His present and future were much more important to me than his past. Besides, he was an excellent driver—which by my definition was one whom I could trust to drive safely and be able to read a map well enough to get us to our destination while I took a nap. His good war stories and his loyalty to me and his new company were also important.

Bain knew the tricks of the trade of being a jeep driver and wedged a poncho at the base of the windshield so that it formed a lap robe which held the warmth from the heater around our lower bodies. My driver said nothing about the no-canvas rule until several hours into the exercise, when he ran off the road and nearly turned us over due to the moisture on both sides of the windshield and the icicles which were forming on his eye lashes and mustache. With a look of resignation, Bain's question was short and to the point as he asked, "Why?"

I responded that the word from division was that no canvas allowed better vision. Bain looked at me in disbelief, as we struggled to see through the water-covered interior of the windshield. I then asked my driver if he remembered Lieutenant Colonel King's near fetish about boots and Colonel Creighton's emphasis on clean windshields and headlights and how those were indicators that readily showed a unit's compliance to orders. With a look of understanding mixed with bewilderment, Bain responded "Yes, sir" and kept silent about the things we were both thinking. The general had an indicator he could observe. Who cared that we froze our asses off or that it made transport more hazardous as long as he could have his indicator?

From the time we crossed the line of departure until dawn the next morning, we had little contact with the enemy. A couple of brushes with reconnaissance vehicles went in our favor because of our superior firepower. By following narrow trails through thick forests and avoiding the main roads and open plains, we stayed out of sight from their artillery forward observers. Other bad-guy units were not so fortunate, as we listened on the radio to reports of casualties and lost vehicles being assessed by the controllers.

With the sun still a few minutes from rising over the horizon, we made our first major contact with a mechanized infantry platoon. Although they were well positioned and camouflaged, our recon elements had spotted them. Masking our attack with simulated artillery-delivered smoke, we quickly overran the position with a minimum of casualties. We had also gained an advantage by concentrating our attack against one platoon rather than on the broad front.

With our breach of the enemy's front lines, we were now free to push on and attack artillery, command, and support units that had previously been far behind the lines in relative safety. Our penetration, combined with a similar success by Al Todd's Charlie Company, also caused the enemy to abandon his front line and withdraw to alternate defensive positions. The deeper we penetrated into the enemy's rear area, the less resistance we met.

Many of the support units from the States were U.S. Army Reserve and National Guard. Participation in REFORGER and generous time to tour Germany before and after the exercise were a prime recruiting tool for the Guard and the Reserve. We found many of the Guard and Reserve units asleep and with no security posted either day or night. Their positions were poorly selected and prepared. Even worse was the frequency with which we found cases of beer (both empty and full) in their perimeters. Every exercise directive and safety lecture had emphasized there was to be no alcohol used during the exercise. Apparently the part-time soldiers did not take the full-time rules of the Regular Army very seriously.*

---

*At the time, most of the Regular Army thought that the Guard and the Reserve were full of long-haired, poorly trained, undisciplined troops led by officers with more political clout than ability or experience. During the decade or so of the Vietnam War, the Guard and the Reserve had been a haven for those without the guts to refuse the draft or flee to Canada. When President Johnson made it clear that the vast majority of the Reserve forces would not be called to active duty as they had in previous conflicts, the waiting list for enlistments became so long that it took powerful connec-

By noon we had progressed so far into the opposing forces' rear that a two-hour cease-fire was called by the controllers to allow the enemy to sort itself out and to reorganize. We used the time to bring our tankers forward to refuel and resupply so that we would be ready to push on when given the go-ahead. The brief halt also provided the first opportunity in more than forty-eight hours for many of us to have a quick nap.

Along with the fuel tankers was a two-and-a-half-ton truck that provided the final edge that we had developed for REFORGER. While it was of little assistance in actual maneuver or in fighting the enemy, it was a classic producer of morale for the troops of Team Alpha. Bolted to the floorboards in the cargo bay were a gas-fired oven and grill, a large ice cooler, and all the necessary supplies to prepare chow and feed an infantry/armor team of more than one hundred men. Instead of having food delivered from the battalion trains in the far rear, our mess staff was able to follow the company only a few kilometers to the rear. Capable of cooking on the move and turning out meals during the briefest halts, the mess truck provided us at least two hot meals daily even during the height of the REFORGER exercise. Other companies on both sides of the "war" relied on C rations for most meals with a Class A ration only rarely being delivered—and then it was usually cold by the time it reached the troops. Our mess truck did not add to the combat multipliers the controllers used to access casualties, but the positive effect on Team Alpha was immense.

The mess truck, maintenance section, recovery vehicle, and fuel tanker which made up the "team trains" were under control of the company executive officer. When Dick Earle rotated in late summer back to the States at the end of his tour, I had appointed Gary Gaal as the acting executive officer pending the arrival of a more senior lieutenant. A few days before REFORGER began, 1st Lt. Jim Jones, a tall, black, former NCO who was a graduate of Officer Candidate School reported to the company. Although Jones immediately proved to be an outstanding leader with the troops, his entire career had been with Special Forces

---

tions to get in. While the Guard and the Reserve had made some progress by the mid-1970s, it was the mid-1980s before they reached even the minimum of readiness to perform their mission. Since that time much has been made about the "Total Army" and the important role of the Guard and the Reserve. I doubt, however, if any Regular veteran will ever develop more than minimal respect for the weekend warriors.

and Airborne units. Armored personnel carriers and mechanized warfare were strangers to him—so we began the exercise with two XOs: Gary as the acting executive officer and Jim looking over his shoulder, watching and learning.

During REFORGER, Gaal and Jones did not disappoint me. Dick Earle's combat boots were difficult to fill, but the two lieutenants were up to the challenge. For the duration of the exercise, we ate well and never had to halt because of low fuel in the vehicles. Several other companies in the brigade, including those from the 2/30, had upon occasion come to a stop because their XOs could not procure fuel or find their companies to deliver to. Gaal and Jones were so proficient that on one occasion I noticed that we were being refueled from a tanker with markings of our opposing force. Gary explained that while bringing chow forward he had found a lost truck and driver and had "captured them single-handedly."

Halfway through REFORGER I decided that I could not afford the luxury of two XOs and that Jones was ready for the task. In the middle of a cold, rainy night, I transfered Gaal to the leadership of the company's weapons platoon. Neither lieutenant missed a beat in continuing the mission in an exemplary fashion.*

According to army doctrine, the XO would be assisted by the company first sergeant, who would work out of the battalion trains to get supplies, ammo, and replacements forward to the company trains. That had been too boring a job for Carrasco, and with my permission, he had given the mission to S.Sgt. Cook. Top had outfitted my command track with the company's best mechanic, a tool box, a small locker of spare parts, and a tow bar. If needed, I could transfer the CP to the jeep while Top recovered downed vehicles or delivered the mechanic to a platoon where he was needed.

This system worked well in preventing the delays. In fact, the system worked so well that on one occasion, while I was in my

---

*Unfortunately, Jones's stay with the company would be short. Two months later he was promoted to captain and moved to the battalion staff. His replacement proved to be equally good, however. First Lt. Jim Silva, well over six feet tall and a solid two hundred pounds, was a West Point graduate whose hobby was playing rugby with an amateur team composed of Schweinfurt locals and a few GIs. Silva was a bit aloof and, at times, a wiseass—neither characteristic of which I found detrimental in an XO. Besides that, anyone crazy and tough enough to play rugby had to possess some positive characteristics.

jeep, I received a call from Carrasco asking for a brief halt. After I sent out a recon forward from Liebrich's platoon, I checked on Top to find him on the side of a road next to a German refuse dump, with a broken-down 113. Top pointed out to me that all that was the matter with the track was a broken aluminum fuel hose. He said that the broken line presented a problem because we were carrying no spare hoses. While we talked, the mechanic wandered up from the trash dump with a discarded bicycle. A few minutes later he had removed a part of the cowling for the bike's brake system and transformed it into a fuel hose. It held without leaking until Jones could bring an "official fuel line" forward.

By dawn of the third day of the exercise, our major opposition was not the enemy but exhaustion and lack of sleep. While physical conditioning and the ability to run long distances have long been admired in the army, the ability to function with little or no sleep for extended periods is a much more practical skill—and one to which the army pays little attention. Drivers were rotated as often as possible, but few of our vehicles had more than two qualified drivers assigned. Late one night I was surprised to find Sergeant Arford not in the TC's hatch but rather in his 113's driver's compartment. He explained that at each halt his driver was dropping off to sleep, so for safety's sake he had been forced to take the controls.

Spending much of my time in my jeep, I had worked out a schedule with Bain. Any time we halted for a recon, a map check, or for any other reason, I got out of the vehicle so he could stretch out across the seats and get a few minutes of sleep. On the move, when I felt confident that everything was in order, I napped as Bain drove. As did most of the soldiers in the company, both of us developed the ability to doze off within a minute or two and awake after a five- or ten-minute nap fairly refreshed. Regardless of that ability, however, by the third day of the exercise, leaders and drivers were operating on less than two hours of sleep a day.

By midmorning, our need for rest was overruled by orders from battalion to push on with all speed in an attempt to secure a bridge crossing over the major natural obstacle in the maneuver box, the Tauber River. The opposing forces must have anticipated our objective because they began pouring out reserve forces to block our advance. With orders to move quickly compounded by an increasing number of enemy, our casualties began to mount. On two occasions, we would not have had the firepower to break through enemy concentrations if battalion had not coordinated air force A-10 tank killers to lend support.*

By monitoring the radio I could hear other units attempting to be "first to the Tauber." Casualties across our front were mounting, but to the generals and colonels in their safe command posts far to the rear, destruction of men and machines were the natural cost of victory. Those of us in the midst of the fight knew that the men simulating killed and wounded in our mock war were just a part of the "game." Still, the realization was sobering that what we practiced today might be a reality tomorrow and that currently simulated casualties would, in fact, be very dead or seriously maimed in actual combat.

"Killed" and "wounded" soldiers as well as "destroyed" vehicles remained with the company but followed at the rear of the formation so they would not be counted in our combat power ratio. This allowed a fair evaluation of the conflict while also permitting everyone to participate in the training. It also made for one other great advantage—every member of the team was present to witness Team Alpha's being the first of the REFORGER Orange Forces to reach the Tauber River.

Our final objective was an ancient stone bridge over the Tauber, which, despite its age, was strong enough for sixty-ton tank crossings. The last few kilometers before the bridge were surprisingly void of enemy contact. Apparently we had slipped into a seam between defending units. When we reached a hillside overlooking the bridge, I realized that there was nothing between us and the river except a few sentries on the bridge itself. By radio I ordered the Team on line and instructed to the engineers to prepare to defuse any charges on the bridge that might be set to destroy it. Without a halt, the Team swung from a column to a line. Disregarding the order that Orange Forces were not to display U.S. flags, I signaled my 113 gunner to let fly a three-by-five-foot Stars and Stripes from the vehicle's long

---

*The A-10, known affectionately and otherwise by its pilots as the "warthog" because it was "ugly as hell and did its business in the dirt" (low level attacks) had never been proved in actual combat. Its detractors claimed it would never survive on a real battlefield because of its limited airspeed and low-level operations. Whatever its real capabilities, we grunts liked the warthog because it worked in peacetime war games and, more important, represented the first aircraft designed and fielded by the air force with a specific mission of ground support. (Desert Storm in 1991 would display the merits of the A-10.)

antenna. Within what seemed like seconds the antenna of every vehicle in the Team sported the national colors.

We arrived at the Tauber with flags flying and yells of "first to Tauber." The engineers did their job, and we gained the first foothold in crossing the river. As we were consolidating our defense of the bridge for any counterattack, a call came from battalion requesting our position. In the spirit of the occasion based in a giddiness of success and enormous fatigue, I responded, "Patton may have pissed in the Rhine in 1945, but let it be known that I just did the same in the Tauber at the lead of Team 'first to the Tauber' Alpha."

Soon after our capture of the Tauber River bridge, another administrative halt in the exercise was called to allow the Blue Forces to reorganize. By direction of the umpires, several cutoff Blue Force mechanized infantry and tank units were allowed to withdraw across the Tauber using "our" bridge. The break in the action lasted most of the afternoon and again allowed us to refuel and to bring the mess truck forward for a hot meal. Although the skies were still overcast, the rain had ceased. Temperatures warming into the the midthirties seemed almost balmy after the continual freeze of the past three days.

While drinking a cup of mess-truck coffee, I began to feel a little light-headed and initially attributed it to a lack of sleep. A bit later I thought back over the past few days and realized that I had drunk little water or other liquids. The cold had stifled my thirst to the point where I was nearly dehydrated. Several one-quart canteens later, I began to feel better. I then called the platoon leaders for a meeting and told them to make sure their soldiers were drinking at least two canteens of water daily.

Shortly before dusk, the halt was lifted and the war games resumed. A visit to our positions by Lieutenant Colonel King put the rest of the exercise in perspective. King was pleased with our "first to the Tauber" and other successes during the maneuver and related that according to the exercise scenario, the Blue Forces were being reinforced with more units from the States and NATO allies. The Tauber would mark the high-water mark of our advance. Division and corps cavalry forces would soon be assuming positions along the river to provide a covering force and early warning of the impending counterattack. Our mission was to remain on the high ground overlooking the bridge until the cavalry was in position and then to withdraw to defensive positions five kilometers to our rear.

Because our present positions were well known to the enemy

units just across the river and to those who passed by us during the admin halt, I anticipated that the night would not be quiet. As soon as full darkness surrounded us, I moved the vehicles about five hundred meters to be safe from an artillery attack on our old location. Near our previous position, I sent one platoon equipped with the .50-caliber machine guns they had removed from their 113s to form a dismounted ambush in case the Blue Force dispatched a ground recon during the night.

About two in the morning, the area exploded with blank ammunition, artillery and grenade simulators, and aerial-illumination parachutes. Our ambush caught an infantry company infiltrating the area on foot. Although our ambush was outnumbered four to one, our prepared positions, artillery support and, in particular, the .50-caliber machine guns, combined with the element of surprise gave us such an advantage that the controllers credited us with more than fifty kills without a single friendly casualty.

Dawn had barely broken when we initiated another ambush—this time with the entire company and at an entirely different target. According to our SOP we conducted "stand-to," which meant 100-percent alert for thirty minutes prior to dawn and thirty minutes afterward. This procedure was repeated at sundown for what was known as "stand-down." The purpose of increased alertness during those periods was simple—tradition as well as strategy has always favored those times for attacks. "We attack at dawn" is not simply a good line from the movies.

The objective of our daybreak ambush was even more satisfying than the defeat of the infantry company the night before. Our target was a flight of eight AH-1 Cobra attack helicopters. For the previous several years, war games in Europe had featured the tank-killing helicopters which were credited with success ratios as high as twenty to one. In every exercise the Cobras flew close to the ground, using flying tactics known as "nap of the earth." Rising just above the tree line, they simulated firing TOW missiles at tanks and APCs at distances more than three kilometers away.

While these tactics worked great in war games, and made the helicopter-minded generals and the aircraft manufacturers (where many generals got well-paying jobs after their retirement) happy, I do not think there was an armor or infantry company commander in Europe who did not believe that by the second day of a real war we would be knee-deep in helicopter parts and pieces of helicopter pilots. War games simply did not take into consideration the proliferation of artillery on the battlefield. Cobras might hide from ground observation behind a tree, but leaves do not stop artillery steel. Any attack by either side would be preceded by a rolling barrage of flying shrapnel which would tear the thin-skinned choppers to pieces.

Our daybreak ambush exposed another vulnerability of the attack helicopters. The pilots obviously were unaware that any enemy units were still along the river. They flew at an altitude of no more than sixty feet, within one hundred meters of the tree line in which we lay under camouflage nets reinforced by tree branches and leaves. At my signal, the nets were dropped and infantrymen and tankers fired a few blank rounds and then in unison all raised a middle finger at the choppers and their pilots. The idea that a single combined-arms team could destroy eight Cobras in a matter of seconds was obvious, but it was a fact that the senior controllers could not accept. Instead of eight, we were credited with only four. That must have shot hell out of their kill ratio, nonetheless.*

After being "first to the Tauber," destroying most of an infantry company and four attack helicopters, we had worn our welcome pretty thin with the Blue Forces. It was time to begin our withdrawal to preserve our resources to fight another day. During the next forty-eight hours, we fought a series of engagements in which we traded space for time without becoming decisively engaged with the opposing forces. Every few kilometers we selected a position which was easily defended, with avenues of withdrawal covered by hills or masked by villages. We would then prepare and camouflage our positions, preplan artillery supporting fires, and wait for the enemy. As soon as we slowed their advance and destroyed as many vehicles and men as possible, we repeated the process at the next advantageous location.

Around midnight of the second day of our withdrawal phase, a misting rain began. It was followed by a fog so thick that observation was limited to less than twenty-five meters. Orders

---

*The army continues to profess belief that helicopters can destroy tanks and APCs, allowing the pilots to survive and return to the clean sheets and crew rest that pilots so expect and covet. Grunt and armor captains continue to disagree. Incredibly, the Soviets have also added tank-killing helicopters to their arsenal. Perhaps their military-industrial complex also makes a large profit on helicopters, or maybe their generals also need retirement jobs. Whatever the reason, all it means is that if World War III does occur there will only be more parts of helicopters and pilots for the tanks and APC to run over as they fight the real battle on the ground.

from battalion instructed us to find a good defensive position and wait for the sun to rise and burn off the fog. I relayed the orders by radio to the platoons and guided them to a wood line that paralleled a primary road down the middle of a valley.

As the tracks and tanks moved into position, I realized that a bit of high ground a few hundred meters farther down the tree line offered better fields of fire for the tanks. Bain delivered me to Lieutenant Spencer's command tank just as the huge vehicles prepared to back into the wood line. When Spencer saw me, he climbed out of his command hatch to see what I wanted. As I shouted over the engine noise for him to move two hundred meters to the west, Bain grabbed my web gear as he pulled and shouted, "It disappeared, the damn tank just disappeared."

I glanced over my shoulder, where not more than fifteen meters away I had seen one of Spencer's tanks just before I got out of my jeep to talk to him. Spencer jumped off his tank and joined Bain and me as we searched the fog in disbelief. Surely, the image of a tank had been an illusion. Nothing that big and weighing sixty tons could simply disappear. The three of us followed the tracks of the tanks toward the wood line. Bain grabbed me as I was about to step out into nothingness. He shined his flashlight into the fog. We could barely make out the tank at the bottom of a forty-foot cliff. Upside down, its tracks were still rotating in the air. It looked like a huge turtle that had been turned on its back.

Yelling to Bain to call for a dust-off (evacuation helicopter) and for as many M-88s (heavy-track recovery vehicles) as were available, Spencer and I began moving along the cliff looking for a way to descend. Not more than twenty meters to the west, the cliff changed to a gentle slope, and we were soon at the tank's side. Spencer lifted himself up into the driver's hatch to hit the switch that would shut down the engine and stop the tracks.

A smell of diesel filled the air, but a quick inspection revealed that the fuel compartments were holding fine; the leakage was just a small amount from the crew compartment's heater. Because the tank was resting on its turret, the tank commander's hatch was directly on the rock floor of the forest. We were finally able to reach the loader's hatch, which was on the side of the turret. Spencer squeezed his way in and immediately reported no movement in the crew compartment. He began passing me gear and equipment, as he searched the bottom of the turret, which until moments before had been the top.

Seconds later I had wedged my upper body through the hatch and in the dim light could see that Spencer had uncovered the lower torso of one of the crewmen. The shoulders and head were protruding out the commanders hatch and apparently were crushed between the turret and the ground. Spencer searched for a pulse at pressure points along the leg and thigh with negative results.

We had found one of the crewmen but were, by my count, still missing three. I feared their bodies had been hurled out of the tank and were trapped beneath it. Spencer quickly explained that the tank had been one crew member short, so only two men were missing. Much to our surprise and relief we found the tank's gunner standing alongside the tank as we exited. He was far from coherent, but the best we could understand, he had ridden the tank over the cliff inside the crew compartment. He haltingly explained that he had no idea how he got out of the tank but had apparently crawled out the loader's hatch before we had reached the tank and either briefly blacked out or became disoriented in the fog.

Other soldiers were joining us at the base of the cliff and Spencer's platoon sergeant had positioned two of the tanks so that their powerful searchlights fairly well illuminated the scene. As more light was added and we became more familiar with the area, it became apparent that we were in an abandoned rock quarry. It had been dormant for such a long period that trees more than a foot in diameter had grown up in its floor.

Just where we were and how we got there was not the current major problem, however. We had one man with injuries, one dead and one missing. A dust-off was soon hovering over the area, and the injured soldier was placed aboard. As the helicopter lifted off, Spencer shouted to me that he had found his driver, or rather the driver had found him. The man had heard the helicopter and had followed the sound to our location from deep in the woods behind the quarry. Apparently unhurt except for a few scrapes and bruises, the driver explained, "I felt the tank began to tip over as I backed into the wood line. Before I could stop, we went over backward, landed on the rear end of the tank, and continued on over. The impact threw me clear as it tilted on back. As soon as I hit I began to run. By the time I stopped, I had no idea where I was or how far I had gone. When I heard the chopper, I followed the noise to here."

The driver was sent to the battalion aid station by ground ambulance for a checkup. By the time the ambulance had departed, several other helicopters had arrived as well as Spencer's company commander, Gary Eldridge. Lieutenant Colonel King drove up with instructions to follow the original order to hold the company in place until the fog lifted or at least eased a bit. It took most of the remainder of the night to clear a path through the woods and to right the overturned tank. Although we had attempted to dig the tank commander's body loose, it was not until the M-88s turned the tank upright that we were able to free him.

Observing the process, making drawings and taking pictures, were members of the division criminal investigation division (CID) and officers of the exercise safety team—both of which were required to conduct an investigation of any training fatality. While both teams apparently knew their business well, they avoided the tankers and infantrymen except for official questions. We had little use for them, and they apparently felt the same way about us.

At daylight the body of Sgt. Terry Williams of Goldthwaite, Texas, was loaded into an ambulance and evacuated. A brief memorial ceremony was held alongside the quarry. By 0800 hours, we were back in the exercise inflicting and receiving casualties, which, unlike that of Sergeant Williams, were merely recorded on paper rather than in the blood of a young man sent to an early grave.

The investigation itself would drag on for several months after the exercise with particular attention being given the differences between the tank company's field SOP and the one for Alpha Company. Ours stated that before entering a wood line, either at night or during the day, that a ground guide would precede the track to ensure there were no obstacles and to make sure there were no soldiers in sleeping bags who might be run over. Nearly every major exercise marked up at least one soldier run over before he could escape his sleeping bag. The tank platoon attached to us, like most armor units, did not require ground guides in their SOP. This was because the tank commander sat so high in his cupola that he had excellent observation to all sides of his vehicle.

Another point in the investigation questioned why I had not noticed the quarry on the map. This was quickly put aside when the investigators found out that the maps issued to maneuver units did not show the old quarry.

Eldridge, Spencer, the surviving tank crew, myself, and many of the soldiers near the accident were included in the interviews which were conducted by individual investigators and before a five-man board. On my recommendation, the board returned to the accident site at night to see for itself the difficulty in spotting the drop off. It would also have been easy to point out that the quarry touched the wood line for less than a total of twenty meters. If the tank had gone ten meters in either direction the accident would never have occurred. What might have happened was, of course, irrelevant. A soldier was dead—that was what was important, and as in every other incident that occurred, or did not occur, it was the responsibility of the commander.

The death of Sergeant Williams was not the only training accident of REFORGER.* In addition to several injuries, one soldier had been killed in a traffic accident, and two others fell victim to their radio antennas' touching the high-voltage wires above the tracks of an electric train.** Any exercise of the magnitude of REFORGER could be expected to produce some injuries and even deaths, yet the command philosophy at all levels was that no incident was an accident—it was the result of negligence. This policy of "zero tolerance" usually meant that a fatal accident was cause for the relief of the company commander, the platoon leader, and the battalion commander if the negligence was blatant.

Although I was facing the possible end of my command and the resultant end of my career as well, I did not disagree with the zero-tolerance policy about training accidents. Command of American soldiers is the highest responsibility that can be awarded. Any commander who loses the lives of men placed under his responsibility—in combat or in training—has blood on his hands which can never be removed.

The names and faces of men killed in combat or training invade the mind of the commander in the midst of daily routine as well as during the dark recesses of the night. Although the sense of loss never completely fades, the good commander can

---

*Training for war is a dangerous business in itself. The deaths during RE-FORGER were not the only ones in 1975. During the year, 632 U.S. Army soldiers died in training and off-duty accidents, and another 6,700 were injured.

**The danger from high-voltage lines was so real that it was battalion SOP that before reaching any rail crossing, the company halted and platoon leaders checked each of their vehicles to insure all antennas were tied down. As a backup safety measure, Top or myself positioned ourselves at the crossing and visually checked each vehicle before it was allowed to cross.

but justify his performance with the hope that his caring and abilities saved the lives of others and kept the list of the dead to a minimum. The death of Sergeant Williams was a burden I would shoulder the rest of my life, yet at the same time, it was a burden without guilt. I had done my best. Whether or not the accident could have been prevented was moot. It had happened. All we could do was learn from it and work toward a safer future.

Being in limbo during the investigation was not really an issue. While my future might be in question, the present was not. There was more than enough to do to keep Alpha Company on the road to becoming a combat-ready unit. Surprisingly, the conclusion of the investigation came with no fanfare. In normal distribution, I received a copy of the findings. At the end of the thick document was a summary and recommendations. According to the investigators the accident was "beyond the control of commanders at any level" and was the result of "inclement weather" and the possible use of an SOP which did not consider all contingencies. It was several months later before I ran into one of the investigators at the club. Over a beer he said that they visited the accident site at night according to my recommendation. By happenstance, the night was rainy with fog, much like the night of the incident. According to the investigator, they had very nearly driven their jeep over the same cliff. From that time, there had been no doubt as to their findings.

After the memorial service and before we rejoined the exercise, I spoke briefly to the company about safety and the dangers of the exercise. I also noted that in training, as in combat, we must not dwell on the dead and injured but on the mission. While the troops were somewhat subdued, they remained aggressive and focused on the matter at hand.

Over the next day and night we continued our running fight with the Blue Forces. During the day we would ambush their lead elements and fall back before becoming decisively engaged. During the hours of darkness, we conducted limited counterattacks and ground recons. Most of the skirmishes went our way—particularly those with the units deployed from the States for the exercise.

Troops from a German panzer division were tougher opponents that would probably have broken through our battalion lines if not for a quarter-mile tank ditch prepared by the engineers. The ditch was tied into a hill mass which funneled the attacking Germans into a kill zone covered by tanks, TOWs, artillery, and tac-air support. Once we were across the earthen bridges left along the ditch, they were bulldozed, forcing our pursuers to go around and enter the well-prepared kill zone.

The survivors of the German units were reinforced by an American unit and were soon continuing the attack. Two days later, we were defending a road junction in a small German village, consisting of only a half dozen houses and an equal number of barns. Several times earlier in the day we had engaged a German unit which seemed not to want to play the game of the exercise. They did not slow or take evasive actions when we initiated fire but merely rolled on until the umpires stopped their advance and assessed casualties.

A few hours after midnight the skies cleared, and a bit of moonlight provided more illumination than we had had during the night exercises. Across the valley we could spot the glint of tanks and personnel carriers of the German unit which had been giving us trouble. From a ridgeline and a clump of woods just above the crossroads, we had excellent fields of fire but realized that the Blue unit facing us was unlikely to pay any attention to the rules of the war game. I decided that if they paid no heed to blanks and simulators, perhaps there were other means of getting their attention.

Quietly, I sent two infantry platoons on foot into the village and had them hide behind stone walls, hay stacks, and barns. Each soldier had his helmet and pockets filled with apples from the orchard just outside the village. It was not long before the German regiment's recon element came racing down the road. In the lead were four motorcycle scouts followed by two wheeled-reconnaissance vehicles. I waited until they were nearly on top of us before I popped an illumination flare above the crossroads, the signal to open fire—or in this case to "throw apples."

Motorcycles and drivers went every direction except any farther forward. Their retreat was even faster than had been their advance. Minutes later we were back at our vehicles and on our way to the next delay position. The controller made no comment except to say that he could assess no casualties from apples. I noticed that he did not respond to the calls which filled his radio net from the controllers of the other unit. Whatever the result of the "Great Apple Attack" at an unnamed crossroads, it is noteworthy that for the remainder of the exercise the attacking unit in our sector kept its distance and never again came within throwing range.

We continued our withdrawal and delaying actions for another day despite the lack of real pressure from the Blue Forces. The lull gave us an opportunity to repair a couple of tracks in need of maintenance. In both cases our prescribed load list (PLL) of repair parts towed on a trailer behind the maintenance deuce-and-a-half provided the necessary item. When one of the tanks broke down, Silva was able to make contact with Eldridge's company trains and secure the needed part as well as a tank mechanic to install it. As a result of these efforts and our pre-exercise emphasis on maintenance, we were one of the few, if not the only company, in the exercise to keep 100 percent of our vehicles operational. The size of this accomplishment was noted by anyone traveling the roads of the maneuver box and seeing the inoperative vehicles which lined the sides of the roadways.

Early in the evening preceding what was scheduled to be the last day of the exercise, we received orders to end our withdrawal and conduct a general counterattack. With the assistance of additional reserve forces, we retook in a few hours the ground we had given up over the past few days. The Blue Forces were pretty well decimated on the paper scorecards of the exercise as well as in the reality of the maneuver. Victory seemed to be very nearly in our grasp, as I reported to battalion that we were facing light resistance, and anticipated being back to the Tauber River in a few hours.

No sooner than I completed my report than a controller's jeep appeared over a ridgeline to our front. Two men jumped from the vehicle and set up a small barrel-like device which soon began producing a mushroom cloud of smoke. I had seen atomic-blast simulators before and realized that our part of REFORGER was over. A few minutes later the controllers who had set off the simulator approached me and explained that we were in the blast area of an intermediate range nuclear missile as well as the victims of multiple hits by nuclear shells from 155mm and eight-inch artillery. Our casualties were estimated to be in excess of 95 percent. Similar casualties had been inflicted on the rest of the battalion and most of the division. Almost as an aside, the controller assured us that our Orange Forces artillery and missile units had already responded with equal "success."

Within an hour, we received word by radio that "endex" or the end of the exercise had been declared. There was no further explanation about the nuclear exchange and whether or not the use of the weapons had escalated to strategic from tactical—attack on cities and homelands versus being limited to the battlefield. I was not surprised at the lack of information. The senior commanders had their opportunity to practice the procedures for securing release of nuclear stocks and permission to use them. REFORGER had ended in a fashion similar to every other large scale maneuver of the time—with the exchange of tactical nuclear weapons.

Commands of both sides of any exercise usually feel that they won the war. With no one actually hurt or killed in the fighting, it is, of course, impossible to declare a clear winner. Yet, a pretty good indicator of the victorious was the side that did not have to first resort to nuclear weapons. Using that criterion, I suppose we won. Still it was sobering and somewhat perplexing to realize that if REFORGER had been the real thing, all that would be left of us would be a bit of ash on the battlefield and perhaps a rally cry for those that might take up arms to avenge us.

Despite the way the exercise concluded and the tragic tank accident, the exercise was a success for the company. We gained much needed practice in maneuvers and in controlling the unit for an extended period. Every vehicle that had exited the Ledward Gate before the exercise returned in company formation and under its own power. Additional pride and confidence had been instilled in men, who less than a year before had neither cared nor been capable of performing their assigned missions nor felt pride and confidence in doing so. We were almost to the point that I had doubted we would ever achieve—combat readiness.

CHAPTER 11

TOP OF THE HEAP, OR EVEN THE BLIND HOG FINDS THE OCCASIONAL ACORN

November–December 1975

The anniversary of my first year in command of A Company arrived with no fanfare but with much satisfaction in the progress of the unit over the last year. While the preceding twelve months had passed with unbelievable speed, I could hardly recall a time before being in command of the company. "The Company," as it was referred to at work and at home—and at the rare places when I was in neither—occupied the largest part of my world. Still, other than my previous command, I could recall no time of more happiness, pride, and satisfaction.

By the time we returned to Ledward from REFORGER, Alpha Company's reputation was widespread: it was the best in the battalion as well as near the top of the heap in the division. Receiving the battalion honor company award for the eleventh consecutive month was a recognition that I felt we deserved.

Although I was extremely proud that we had come so far, I was well aware that, while we were looking good, we were in fact far from being good. Much of our reputation was based on the simple fact that while most of the units were still having problems, we were at least making progress. Regardless of the reasons, I was glad that the soldiers were getting some of the recognition for which they had worked so hard. So what if we were not really all that good? We would get better, and after all, even the blind hog finds the occasional acorn.

Once maintenance and cleanup were completed after the return from REFORGER, I continued efforts to get the soldiers out of the barracks to see the sights of Germany.* In early Novem-

*In addition to the company trips, I had a standing offer of a three-day pass to any soldier who produced a receipt that he had signed up for one of the Service Clubs low-cost, extended weekend tours of Paris, Vienna, Zurich, or other cities.

ber we again loaded civilian buses for a two-hour journey to the south to Rothenburg ob der Tauber. The troops seemed to enjoy the luxury of the buses as opposed to our last transportation in the area, our M-113s. A few shouts of "first to the Tauber" when we reached the river reminded me that the soldiers were very aware of our recent accomplishments.

The Rothenburg visit began with an hour-long guided tour by a member of the local tourist board. The attractive guide held the soldiers' attention at least as much with her looks as with her information. She explained that Rothenburg was the best preserved example of a medieval town in Germany: its walls, gates, and sentry towers were all intact. Her story of how the town was saved from being destroyed in 1631 was also a tale that the soldiers enjoyed. It seems that the conquering force was about to put the town to the torch, when the enemy commander informed the city council that he would spare their town if they could produce a citizen who could empty a three-liter mug of wine in a single draught. The mayor of Rothenburg stepped forward, emptied the huge container in one long drink, and saved his city. An annual festival commemorating the event, with wine tasting a natural focus, had been held ever since.

To one of the soldier's questions about what had happened to the town in World War II, our guide smiled as she explained that they had been fortunate in avoiding any damage. Since it had no industry, the town had not been bombed. However, in the final days of the war, its gates and walls were nearly stormed by Patton's armor forces. A small garrison of young boys and old men were assigned as a home guard for the medieval city. When the Americans approached, they closed their gates in the belief that the ancient fortifications would again protect them. Under a flag of truce, the Americans explained that the stone walls would not stop their tanks or artillery and suggested that, in the interest of preserving the town, the garrison surrender. It did, and Rothenburg remains one of Germany's top tourist sites.

At the conclusion of the tour, I told the men of the company that we would be departing in three hours and the remaining time was their own. Many headed for the town's many gasthauses and wine shops to see if they could repeat the feat of the seventeenth-century mayor. Others took the maps provided by our guide to continue their tour of the walled city. Later, on the way back to Schweinfurt, one of my soldiers told me that he had visited the Holy Blood Altar in Saint Jacob's Church. He was still awestruck as he explained that a picture of the altar was in his Catholicism training books, and he had always thought it was a beautiful site. He added that he never dreamed that he would "see it for real."

With Rothenburg and fun behind us, it was time to resume training. For a week, however, we left our weapons in the arms room and our tracks in the motor pool while we underwent classroom lectures and group discussions on race relations. Officially titled "The USAREUR Phase III Race Relations Educational Seminar," the sessions were conducted by NCOs from the division Equal Opportunity Office. The Phase III part of the title meant that it was the third year of the training. Like any commander, I resented time taken away from combat-readiness training, but I had to admit that the seminars seemed to do some good. Conflicts surfaced and were discussed, and attempts were made to solve problems and misunderstandings between the races.

I sat through all the sessions and participated as much as possible as a student rather than as the company commander. The only time I put my "captain hat" back on was near the end of the week. One of the instructors spent nearly an hour explaining that anyone who felt he was discriminated against or was being harassed for racial reasons should report the incident directly to the installation Equal Opportunity/Race Relations Office. He added that there was no requirement to go through normal command channels. When he asked for questions, I raised my hand and walked to the front of the classroom. As pleasantly as possible, I explained to the sergeant that regardless of EO/RR policies, in A Company the chain of command was used for all things, and no member of the company was authorized to go outside the chain or to skip any link in it. I then turned to the company and told the men that what the sergeant had really meant was that if the chain of command could not solve their problems, then they should try the EO/RR route. As a conclusion, I added that my open door policy was another avenue of pursuit to solve any problem before a soldier went elsewhere outside the company.

I later learned that the instructors wrote up the incident and forwarded their report to the division commander. In the paper, they expressed their disagreement with my "overruling" of their policy. The division commander responded by calling in his

G-1, for whom the EO/RR office worked, and telling him that my interpretation of the use of the chain of command was correct and that the race-relations instructions would immediately reflect the proper use of the chain of command.

Race-relations training was followed by a week "away from the flagpole" for range firing with our German sister unit at Millrichstadt. Our hosts, the 2d Battalion, 352d Grenadier Battalion, 12th Panzer Division, provided German-issue 7.62mm rifles, ammunition, and firing-range supervision. We each got to fire for zero, familiarization, and finally for qualification. Those who scored well enough were awarded German shooting medals.

Following the shooting, our German hosts held a party for which they provided the food and we the beer. German and American soldiers got along fabulously, especially as more and more beer was drunk. The only negatives I heard at all were from several soldiers who asked me why the Germans were billeted in new, modern barracks with all of the best living and training facilities, while we were billeted in pre-World War II facilities which received only the maintenance which we provided ourselves. One soldier went so far as to ask, "Who in the hell won the war anyway?"

Regardless of the hard feelings about living accommodations, the range firing and the party did much to cement relations with our NATO ally. What had happened, or who had won, in the last war was no longer relevant. If there were a "next war," German and American would stand, and very likely die, side by side while facing the massive divisions of the Warsaw Pact.

After our return to Schweinfurt and a brief cleanup, we were back in the field at a bivouac site along the Main River. For a week we conducted small-boat drills for river crossings, worked on infiltration procedures, and rappelled off the cliffs along the waterway. We ended the training with a twenty-five-kilometer, night-infiltration maneuver on foot, which brought us back to Ledward. Despite the demanding training and long hours, there were no discipline problems whatsoever.

Thanksgiving week provided time for maintenance, a day off, and then the excellent holiday meal provided by the mess hall*—

*This praise for army mess hall holiday fare is no exaggeration nor is it intended sarcastically. There is likely no better meal prepared anywhere in the United States than that by the U.S. Military at Thanksgiving and Christmas.

for everyone except Top, troops in the mortar platoon, and me. Range time for the mortars at Wildflicken, the nearest ranges where live-fire could be conducted, was limited and had to be used whenever available—including holidays if that was the only option. Formal testing was scheduled for the mortars in the spring for the first time in several years. The only way to qualify was to have ample live-fire practice time in advance.

Lt. Gary Gaal, with more than a year in the company, was now one of the most experienced platoon leaders in the battalion. Although he had no experience beyond a few hours' training in mortars in the infantry basic course, I was not surprised that he had welcomed the new challenge when I had offered him the platoon. After a few weeks, he had reported that he needed two things to ensure the platoon's success—maximum range time and the assignment of two qualified fire-direction-center (FDC) specialists.

The first I could get for him; the second was much more difficult. Mortarmen carry military occupation specialty (MOS) code 11C (light-weapons infantrymen are 11B). Only the best 11Cs are proficient at using the M-1 calculating boards which convert information from the forward observers to elevation and deflection settings for the mortar tubes. After unsuccessful efforts at securing FDC specialists through normal replacement channels, Gary and I reviewed the company records for men with the highest GT (similar to an IQ test) score and selected the top five from the infantry platoons. With a guarantee of early promotion and promises of lots of live-fire range time, all five eagerly volunteered to join the mortar platoon.

The five were then sent to Vilseck for special training. They were also attached briefly to the battalion heavy mortar (4.2-inch) platoon to work with their FDC during actual live fires. After six weeks, the top two were assigned to the company FDC section. The other three were transferred to the almost as difficult jobs of acting as mortar forward observers for the infantry platoons. By the time Top and I—and a jeep trailer full of Thanksgiving dinner—visited the platoon at Wildflicken, we could see great strides had been made in reaching qualification proficiency.

December found us tasked with an unusual mission. Officially designated an Immediate Reaction Force (IRF), we had to provide a platoon of infantry to be on two-hour notice to deploy anywhere in the corps area of operations if ordered. What made the mission extremely unusual was that we were never officially informed of the purpose of the alert—not that it was all that difficult to determine. The tasking required the platoon to be proficient in radiation detection and monitoring and meet specific areas of testing and evaluation standards. It was clear the platoon would be involved in nuclear weapons security. A bit more investigation revealed that the platoon was on alert to reinforce security forces at storage sites for nuclear artillery shells and atomic demolition munitions (ADMs).* Another component of the mission would be to seal off and secure any accident sites where transportation of the nuclear weapons were involved.

Problems in preparing for IRF were immense. First, the requirements for a platoon meant a full strength unit—not the usual 90 percent or so that we had present for duty. Several soldiers and NCOs had to be attached to the 1st Platoon, which I assigned the duty. A more critical problem, however, was that before the platoon could assume the IRF mission, it had to be validated by division and corps evaluation teams. The oral questions and in-ranks inspections were of little trouble because they were similar to the IG drill. Assembling and being at a nearby location in less than two hours was easy to meet—the entire platoon was restricted to the barracks and prepared to move out with minutes' notice.

Once the ground rules were established, I had difficulty figuring out why no unit had passed on the first validation test, and only one had been successful on the second try. Several platoons had, in fact, never validated the requirements and had had to be replaced by other units—much to the embarrassment of their commanders. I understood the difficulty better after our first try at validation, when we flunked solely because we did not have bolt cutters with us at the practice accident site. I knew the mission was critical and that bolt cutters might truly be critical for rescue of objects from locked containers. Still, the inspection seemed ''chicken shit'' and more the result of our inspectors' enjoying their rare chance of fucking with the infantry than

*ADMs, some of which came in containers as small as suitcases, were to be used by the engineers to crater roads, destroy airfields, and blow up bridges. Although it was little discussed, the primary purpose of ADMs in Germany was to destroy what we left behind when we began our anticipated withdrawal—trading space for time—in the event of a general Warsaw Pact attack. Bridges and restricted roadways were constructed with ADMs in mind; sites were prepared for implacement of the charges.

in any real deficiency on our part. Regardless of our feelings, at the second attempt we produced our bolt cutters—along with the same scores of items we had the first time. Passing the validation on the second try tied the Corps record and added to our list of accomplishments.

The reward for the IRF was to remain on two-hour alert for the next month—including Christmas and New Year's. I suppose the good news—and good news was damn hard to find at the time—was that, except for several practice alerts, our services were not needed for any actual nuclear accidents or security threats.

The arrival of December also brought the two-and-a-half year anniversary of my arrival in Germany and of my departure from the United States. The long separation was as bad, or perhaps worse, for those we left behind. Both sets of grandparents were missing their grandchildren's childhood. A letter from my parents, back on their West Texas ranch, reminded me that, with my brother having recently transferred to the 2d Infantry Division in Korea, they had sons serving on both sides of the world and about as far from home as we could get.

The arrival of my parent's letter about my brother brought an interesting observation from Linda. She had just returned from suffering long lines in the commissary and the usual shortages. After she read the letter she remarked, "You know Vietnam is the only damn war we ever won. Thirty years after World War II, here we are in Germany. Twenty years after Korea, your brother is there. Not a single American soldier or family is stationed in Vietnam—nor is there any chance they will be in the near future. Don't tell me which wars we won and which we lost."

I had no answer at the time and have none today. Tours of duty in remote overseas locations were rough on everyone. Economic conditions, extended field duty, distance from family and support groups, and the restrictive living conditions of government duty were not conducive to happy, normal lives. While most of us muddled through the difficulties, for some they became too much to endure.

One evening I got a phone call from the Military Police that the wife of one of my sergeants was at the station swearing out a complaint against an MP for rape. After some investigation, it came to light that she had not been raped but had consented—until the MP brought his handcuffs into their affair. By the time that all that was revealed, however, the news of the "rape" was all over Schweinfurt. When what actually happened was made public, it was not the end of the case. The married MP had been on duty during their most recent meeting. Charges were soon brought for dereliction of duty and for adultery. Quite possibly, the military is the last legal body in the United States to make adultery a crime for trial, but it did and still does. Found guilty of both charges, the MP was busted to private and sent to prison.

Since the army had limited legal control over family members, even overseas, no charges were brought against my sergeant's wife. After the court-martial of the MP, I met with the NCO whose wife had made the charges. He said that they had worked things out and intended to stay together. At his request, I arranged a transfer to a unit on the other side of Germany, where both of them could get a new start. My primary reaction to the whole episode was regret that the company had lost a fine NCO.

The transfer was no sooner completed than a late-night phone call informed me that the wife of another of my NCOs was at the MP station swearing out a rape complaint—this time against one of the company's enlisted men. Top joined me at the MP station, and we met with the woman and with the accused soldier. The desk sergeant, one of the MPs I had become well acquainted with over the months, suggested we might want to take care of it on a company level without it getting onto the blotter. When all the facts were gathered, his advice was well supported.

I was aware that the woman making the accusations had been sleeping her way through the Company—both NCO and enlisted. Her husband seemed either not to care or not to be able to do anything about his wife's extramarital activities. Questioning of the woman revealed that the "attempted rape" was really a forced kiss in a hallway of the enlisted club. As for the soldier, he admitted the kiss but denied any attempt at rape. He pointed out that rape in a crowded enlisted club would be difficult at best. Once the man started talking, all we had to do was listen. I had read his Article 31 rights to him, and he waived his right to remain silent or to have a lawyer present. All in all, the soldier, other than being scared that he was in trouble, seemed upset that the woman who had been liberally spreading her favors around the company evidently was not interested in him.

Top and I again met with the woman and her husband, asking them if they wanted to proceed with the attempted rape charge.

The answer from the now much-more-sober wife was "No." Her husband seemed surprised that he had a say about anything concerning his wife, but nonetheless agreed with her. The next morning Top and I processed another transfer. Several members of the company seemed sad to see the sergeant's wife leave.

A week before Christmas, the company again boarded civilian buses and motored to the city of Nürnberg for a visit to its world-famous Christmas Market. Despite my efforts to get the IRF platoon released for the day, they had to remain in the barracks on two-hour alert. I promised them that once their duty was completed they would have a make-up tour of their own. In Nürnberg, we toured the expertly reconstructed medieval buildings and walls, which had been destroyed by American's dropping bombs instead of arriving on tour buses.

We completed our bus tour in a parking lot near the Christmas Market. I emphasized the location of the market to the men before reminding them not to be late returning to the buses. I also warned them that anyone visiting the "Wall" should take proper preventive measures. They laughed and cheered, well aware that the "Wall," with its bars and legal houses of prostitution, was as famous as the Christmas Market—and perhaps even more so among American soldiers. I was not surprised that I did not see many of them among the market stalls the remainder of the day.

Everyone made it back to the buses on time; some, however, had to be supported between two buddies. Wherever they had been and whatever they had done, they must have followed my advice. Sick call the following weeks revealed no unwelcomed souvenirs of Nürnberg.

As soon as we returned to Schweinfurt, we were once again assigned duty as a part of the installation support battalion. Rather than the usual month, our tour on ISB was to be only a week; someone at division had finally gotten smart. However, like the year before, we drew the duty on Christmas Eve and Day.

If there was anything good whatsoever about having ISB for the second consecutive Christmas, it was in observing the continued improvements in the appearance and discipline in the company as compared to the previous December. Once again we did our best to maintain morale by keeping available coffee and hot soup along with homemade cookies from the wives. For Christmas dinner we delivered hot turkey meals from the mess hall and brought along Protestant and Catholic chaplains for brief services for those soldiers inclined to participate.

In another repeat, several bachelor lieutenants showed up at my quarters to assemble toys and drink the liquor cabinet dry—at both of which they had reasonable success. For my three- and six-year-old daughters, not having daddy home for Christmas morning was becoming routine.

CHAPTER 12

. . . BUT WHAT HAVE YOU DONE LATELY?—TRYING TO HOLD OUR OWN

January 1976

Awaiting us after the holidays was another challenge—one in which we had absolutely nothing to gain in doing and all the accomplishments of the past year to risk. Even though we had undergone a complete inspector general inspection only six months previously, and had done extremely well, that had been considered only a reinspection. According to the calendar, we were due for another annual IG. We were back in the barrel with all the focus and pressures on us to prove that the great results of a half year previous were not a fluke.

The only good news about the inspection was that it would cover maintenance areas only. Barracks and in-ranks inspection would not be included. That meant that instead of having two opportunities to fail, there was only one. Of course, one failure was all a company was allowed anyway, so there was no real lessening of risk.

If half an inspection was the good news, timing was the bad. With the inspection beginning on January 5, we had no chance to enjoy what little remained of the holidays after ISB. Even during ISB, every available soldier spent every available moment preparing for the inspection. We worked eighteen hours on and six off as a routine—and many of us couldn't manage that much off time. The only exception was New Year's Eve, when we shut down the company at 1800 hours. In allowance for New Year's celebrations, and the large heads and sick stomachs they produced, we did not resume our preparations again until noon on New Year's Day.

There was, of course, plenty of complaining about the grueling hours and deprivation of holiday activities. Still, with few exceptions, the company worked as a team and everyone made an honest effort to do his best. Complaining is a basic part of being a soldier, and as long as complaining was accompanied by pride in themselves and the Company, I had no problems with it whatsoever. If there had been anyone for me to complain to who would have helped make a difference, I might have joined in myself.

Throughout the holiday season, I held daily company meetings to explain what we were doing and how we were going to go about passing the inspection. I continued our efforts to develop an edge by doing our homework on the inspection team members and the specific areas they had been checking in other units. As long as the men understood why they were being driven so hard and felt they were doing it for "our" company, they worked well toward a common objective. For many of the soldiers, their assignment to A Company was the first time in their lives that they had been part of a winning team. They liked being number one and had no more intentions of letting our status diminish than did I.

With the scores on our last maintenance IG and the performance of the vehicles during the rigorous REFORGER exercise, I felt reasonably confident about the inspection. Confidence aside, I was still nervous as hell that something could go wrong. Regardless of how good our maintenance program really was, if we did not prepare carefully, we still might not achieve satisfactory results.

I continued to look for anything that would give us an advantage. During my first months of command, I had carefully read the USAREUR maintenance regulations and guidelines, which had revealed that any M-113 with over a certain number of miles logged could be turned in for rebuild. In exchange for the turn-in, a track fresh from the rebuild depot would be issued. My excitement over the discovery had soon been dampened by the discovery that the rebuild depot had been out of operation for several years due to a lack of funds.

Despite that my XO or I called almost weekly to find out when the depot would reopen. When we finally received an affirmative answer in late November we hand carried our turn-in documents to the facility. Shortly before Christmas we had been able to trade two of our oldest M-113s, including the "dog" track from the ammo dump, for as-good-as-new rebuilds. In addition to having the new tracks, there was an added benefit. Before turning in the two old 113s we were allowed to strip any parts we needed—which we interpreted to mean any we needed for ourselves, the rest of the battalion, or for general trading purposes.

A few days before the IG, Lieutenant Colonel King made a preliminary inspection. King had not supervised us closely since the critical reinspection of the previous August, yet plenty was at stake. With only weeks before the completion of his command tour, his efficiency report would reflect the final test. Apparently King had confidence in his company commanders. After his inspection, he told me we were looking good and A Company would be the lead unit in the IG. That was an honor with no rewards. With inspection criteria and areas of emphasis changing from battalion inspection to battalion inspection, being first in the barrel brought unwanted surprises and emphasis on areas previously thought not to be important. From the notes we kept during the inspection and the out-brief that followed, succeeding companies would benefit. The advantage to being further down the inspection roster was that as each company completed its inspection, their mechanics and maintenance specialists reported to the next unit in line to assist in any way the commander desired. By scheduling the best first and the least-prepared last, a battalion ultimately ended up with each company's achieving approximately equal scores. King's recognition of our being the best was satisfying. At the same time, it added more pressure to the basic load of tension that accompanied every IG. Now we were not only struggling to preserve our company reputation but also in a position to be responsible for much of the rest of the battalion's as well.

The IG team arrived early on the morning of January 5 and immediately after we exchanged the two biggest lies in the army—them by saying they were there to help, and my responding that they were welcome—the inspection began. As always, rumors of varying degrees of credibility drifted back to the orderly room and my office, but all in all, there was little to do but wait. The phones were amazingly silent. Everyone in the battalion and the brigade knew that the inspection was ongoing. No other item of business or pleasure was important enough to worry about on IG day.

Most of the morning I spent staring out my window, interrupting myself only for a few half-hearted attempts to do a little paperwork or to read the daily edition of *Stars and Stripes*. While I was concerned with all areas of the inspection, one area provided particular worry. Shortly after the last IG, my communications chief had rotated back to the States. Despite promises of a replacement, none had ever arrived. The commo chief position, normally filled by a signal corps staff sergeant (pay grade E6) was occupied in the interim by an infantryman who had expressed an interest in communications. PFC Louis Smith (pay grade E3), a tall, rifle-barrel-thin black from "the projects" in Providence, Rhode Island, assured me that there was "no sweat" and that he would get us through with a satisfactory. Despite the infectious enthusiasm of Smitty, I did not really share his confidence.

My feet were propped on my desk, and I was again staring out the window when the word came in midafternoon that the IG team was ready to present its out-brief. Along with my officers and senior NCOs, I reported to the company classroom. With no words of introduction, the team chief began his briefing by flipping a chart displaying the communications score. I skipped the intermediate scores to check the bottom line—88 points. I noticed that Smitty, standing at the back of the classroom, had the same confident smile that he displayed when he had told me "no sweat."*

The rest of the scores were revealed rapidly. None were below eighty, some were in the nineties. On the average we were eight to ten points above the August inspection in every area. The team chief concluded by saying he had few comments to add other than many of the inspected areas were the best he had seen in three years in the office of the inspector general and that A Company could stand up to any unit in the division. He concluded, "It is my privilege to inform you that the overall rating of A Company is satisfactory. If we were allowed to award a rating of commendable, it would be yours."

When our satisfactory rating had been announced in August, there had been yells of happiness and excitement. This time was different. Beyond a few nods of the head and a smile or two, my officers and NCOs appeared fairly unmoved. Like me, although relieved with the results, they knew we were good. Most of us felt that we had proved what did not need to be validated.

After the IG team departed, I spoke briefly to the company leaders and expressed my congratulations and appreciation for their long hours and hard work. I explained what they already

---

*PFC Smith's score stood up as the best in the battalion during the remainder of the inspection. A few days after the IG, I was able to secure a special promotion allocation and to pin the rank of Specialist Fourth Class (pay grade E4) on Smitty's collar.

knew—the week was not yet over, we still had to help the other companies in the battalion in their inspections. In closing, I told them I had requested a training holiday for the following Monday and promised that over the next few weeks, we would make up for some of the holiday time we had spent in the motor pool.

A few minutes later, before I had even left the classroom, I found out that my promise of off-time was premature. When I finished my remarks, the battalion and brigade operations officers (S-3s) entered the room and called me into the hallway. The Brigade S-3 handed me a folder filled with checklists and sternly informed me, "Captain Lanning, this is your formal notice that A Company is alerted for an annual field test. Within the next twenty-one days the company will be notified to move to an assembly area for testing and then into a maneuver area for tactical evaluation while engaged with an aggressor force. Upon notification, you will have two hours to cross the line of departure, which will be the back gate of the motor pool. The tests will be of five days in duration. Do you have any questions?"

I had no questions about the company maneuver test. We could handle it and do well. What I did want to ask was who in the hell had done such a magnificent job of scheduling to put us right back in the barrel only moments after a pressure-packed IG. Evidently the two S-3s, both majors, were aware that the notification did not fall into the category of "good news." In unison they explained that the training schedule was so filled that the test had to take place in the next three weeks. Whatever they thought I would say, they did not hear. I took the pretest briefing packet, turned wordlessly, and went back into the classroom to catch the lieutenants and NCOs before they departed.

In my mind, scheduling us for a field test so soon after an IG and everything else we had been doing in the last months was a combination of several things—poor planning, poor leadership, and a lack of concern about troop morale and welfare. However, I expressed none of these thoughts before the reassembled Alpha leaders. The attitude of the company commander is reflected in the attitude of the company. It was not the time to complain, whine, or express indignation.

I began my remarks by saying that Alpha Company had been given another chance to excel and to prove once again that it was the best. I explained and told them I would schedule a meeting of the chain of command as soon as I learned more details and had enough information to issue a warning order for the exercise. In closing I assured them that I did not think we would be called out until the rest of the battalion completed the IG. They were to continue to help our sister companies while beginning preparation for the test. I did my best to remain upbeat and to act as if the test alert was the best news I had heard lately. Beyond a few head shakes and audible "oh shits," there was no complaints. A year before, the company test alert would have caused a riot or a mutiny or both. Now there was no hint of either. The only reaction was the resigned acceptance of the responsibility of being a soldier by a group of tired but unbowed professionals.

Our first action was to up-load all equipment except weapons and sensitive items on the tracks so that we could be on the move within the two-hour limit. Recall rosters were checked to ensure telephone numbers were current. Soldiers who lived off-post and did not have telephones had to submit a written plan on how neighbors would alert them to return to the company. For the men "shacking" downtown with German girlfriends, the options were limited. Either come up with a plan for recall notification or move back into the barracks. Whatever the plan, everyone in the company was made aware that there was no excuse not to be present for duty and prepared to move within two hours of notification. The consequences of missing a movement would be an Article 15 or a court-martial.

By studying the brigade training schedule, it was fairly easy to determine on which days during the next three weeks the test would not occur. Although we remained at the ready at all times, I was reasonably sure that the alert would be called in the final days of the twenty-one-day standby period. Normal training and company business continued, but at no time was anyone in the company not aware of the impending test.

When the actual alert came, it was no surprise. A full three weeks had passed since the issue of the twenty-one-day alert. When the call came at 0500, the only real news was that rumors that the test had been indefinitely postponed were incorrect. By the time I grabbed my alert bag of extra clothing and equipment and made it into the company, only twenty minutes or so had elapsed. I would have made it even sooner but freezing rain mixed with snow was steadily falling from the still dark sky. An AFN radio forecast said that a blizzard was sweeping across Eastern Europe and would last from three to five days. It was beginning to sound like we would have even more than the usual opportunity to excel.

When I arrived at the company, weapons were already being issued from the arms room and soldiers were moving from the billets to the track park and motor pool. NCOs living in the barracks had the company moving just as we had rehearsed on two occasions during the twenty-one-day alert period. Specialist Bain had had our jeep dispatched from the motor pool and had checked my weapon out of the arms room. Within forty-five minutes of the initial alert call, the platoon sergeants reported 100 percent present. At sixty-three minutes into the test, we were ready, loaded, and lined up at the back gate prepared to move.

A half an hour later the sun was just coming up—at least, according to our watches, it was supposed to be doing so. We really had no real proof of daybreak except that the blackness of the night changed to an equally impenetrable white from snow swept by a thirty-five-mile-an-hour wind. Despite the weather, we made final checks of the men, vehicles and equipment as we waited for the designated 0700 time to move out.

Shortly before H-hour, word came that due to the heavy snow and forecast for more, all activities other than "mission critical" were canceled. The local exchange, commissary, dependent schools, and normal workplaces were to be closed. I was trying to determine if our company test fell into the definition of "mission critical" when the brigade S-3 pulled up in his jeep. It seemed to me that if the roads were unsafe for driving to work, then surely they were as unsafe for field maneuvers. I was wrong. Obviously the decision had already been made at a level much higher than the company—at "echelons beyond caring" as the troops said. The S-3 said that the training schedule was so filled for the next two months that if we did not continue with the test, that there would be no other opportunity. Despite reservations, I followed the only course of action available in such a situation. I saluted and gave the order to move out.

We had moved only a few hundred meters when it became apparent that "continuing the mission" was not a fortuitous idea. The rubber pads on the tracks—designed to decrease wear on the steel track sections and to prevent damage to hard-surface roadways—could not gain traction on the iced asphalt leading out of Ledward to the training area. Slight changes in the slope of the roadway sent the thirteen-ton tracks skidding like hockey pucks.

One of the greatest advantages of having experienced NCOs is that there is rarely a situation or occurrence which they have not seen before. Sergeant Arford with the lead platoon and Sergeant Liebrich following him both halted before I gave the order. Two tracks were already in the ditch and several more were sideways in the roadway. Both NCOs had their crews dismount and were beginning to remove every third rubber track pad by the time I reached them. As soon as I saw what they were doing, I understood that the metal edges on the tracks would cut into the ice and provide traction. Minutes later the other platoons were following my orders to mimic the efforts of Arford and Liebrich.

Removing track pads is a fairly effortless task in the motor pool on a nice day. It is not as easy in a blizzard with temperatures hovering near the zero-degree mark. Despite the weather, by spelling "wrench turners" every five minutes to let them warm themselves inside the 113s, we were ready to resume the move in a little less than an hour. With the track pads removed, traction was much better, and only occasionally did a vehicle skid off the roadway. By maintaining a speed of less than five miles per hour, we were able to proceed. At steep inclines, we moved slightly off the roadway to place one track in the paralleling ditch. The heavy tracks, with every third pad missing, easily cut into the frozen ground, providing even more stability.

A kilometer or so short of our assembly area was a 10 percent downgrade, with a hundred-foot sheer drop-off on one side. Arford himself took the controls of the lead vehicle, after unloading the squad from inside the carrier. With one track of the 113 off the roadway opposite the drop-off, Arford eased the vehicle down the incline. The squad of soldiers walked alongside, pushing the 113 back straight when it began to slide. When Arford safely reached the bottom of the hill, a cheer went up from the soldiers at the top.

Over the next hour we "walked" each track down the incline. Once the last 113 had made the journey, we again moved out in column to the assembly area, arriving eight hours after departing Ledward on what would under normal weather conditions have taken only a bit more than an hour.

The assembly area represented a site to the rear of the battle lines where we would receive our upload of ammunition and our cross-attachment of tanks, engineers, and a fire support team. We simulated the receipt and storage of ammo with sand-filled boxes to equal the weight of ammunition. We received blank ammo to use against the aggressor force in the actual tests. In the assembly area, I learned that during the test we would be "infantry pure"—no tank platoon would be exchanged for one of our mechanized subunits.

We remained in the assembly area overnight. The storm continued as temperatures dropped into the double digits below zero. By midnight there were sixteen to eighteen inches of snow, with drifts of six feet along fences and embankments. We snatched sleep during the night in quarter- and half-hour naps. Leaders at all levels made continual checks for frostbite and proper ventilation to ensure that the heated crew compartments of the M-113s kept a hatch cracked open to prevent asphyxiation. Dawn brought an end to the winds, but the below-zero temperatures continued under a sky that threatened more snow.

The two officers and two NCOs from brigade who were serving as evaluators had returned to Schweinfurt an hour after dark. We were eating a hot breakfast prepared in our mobile mess truck the next morning when four different evaluators arrived. The major in charge seemed somewhat embarrassed when he told me that the evaluators would be changed every twenty-four hours because of the weather. Exchanges of evaluators would be accomplished by helicopter if the weather cleared enough to fly. He said that Ledward and surrounding bases were still to be closed to all but essential duty.

I informed my chain of command about the "short tours" that the evaluators would serve while we remained in the field for the duration and added that we were the only unit in the Schweinfurt area that was not snowed in their barracks. When the chain of command passed this word to their soldiers, the result was as I expected. There was, of course, the usual bitching and complaining—normal infantry procedure—but the overall reaction was one of superiority and "Let's show the bastards how it's done."

Our first task of day two of the test was for the company to negotiate a compass and map-reading course. Eight different sites, varying from five hundred meters to two kilometers apart, had to be found on foot using a map and compass. Operating in two-man teams, the company would begin from a half-dozen starting points. The cold and snow already offered an environment where the soldiers felt challenged to do their best and prove they were in the top company in the division. While I was convinced by this point that Alpha Company no longer needed an edge, the current conditions offered too good of an opportunity to let pass by—and they also offered direct assistance in our achieving the most outstanding record on the compass and map course in the history of the division company test.

On my instructions, each two-man team beginning the course from the six start points was composed of two senior NCOs or one senior NCO and a lieutenant. Each team, therefore, had more than twenty-years' experience and/or a graduate of the army's Ranger School, to find its way through the course. In the deep snow, the lead teams left trails that even a Pentagon clerk could follow. What was even more amazing was that the part-time brigade evaluators never figured out why Alpha Company was so good with map and compass. In their final report, they gave rave reviews stating, "The company did outstanding on the map and compass course; all but two teams maxing the tests."

On that issue, I had only two thoughts. First, any commander who does not take advantage of a situation offered is not taking care of business. Second, an edge is an edge is an edge.

Preparation for movement and the tactical road march phases of the test were evaluated during our move to the assembly area. Once the map and compass course was completed, we moved into the rest of the tactical test which included occupation of the kill zone, defense of the kill zone both in day and at night, withdrawal from the kill zone and occupation of a blocking position, and finally, a counterattack to retake our original positions.

According to the official, as well as the experimental, doctrine of the time, the mission of all these phases of offense and defense was to "destroy the enemy." The kill zone was further defined as "A designated area in which all available fire, both indirect and direct, have been coordinated with obstacles and terrain for the purpose of defeating a numerically superior, tank-heavy force. Kill zones are normally established along good armor avenues of approach with sufficient open areas to permit all antitank weapons available to be used at their maximum range."

Control measures of the kill zone included the "decision line," where the kill-zone commander makes the determination if the enemy is progressing into the kill zone in the most advantageous manner to be engaged, and the "trigger line," where the total firepower of the defending force is initiated.

The kill-zone concept was the same doctrine that we practiced in our forward GDP where we actually anticipated an invasion by the Warsaw Pact forces. Kill zones offered the only means by which our greatly outnumbered units could hope to stop, or even slow, the vast number of enemy tank divisions. By concentrating all our assets and by beginning to attrit the enemy at maximum range, we might be able to hold our own. At the very best, the kill-zone concept provided us a narrow edge. At its worst, it provided a small amount of confidence that the defense of Western Europe was not absolutely a terminal occupation.

A front-line trace, showing the simulated forward positions of the brigade, was provided as a part of the test operations order. My first job was to perform a reconnaissance of the sector assigned to the company and to determine the best location and method of defense. I also had to coordinate with adjacent units. Since in reality there were no other units actually in the field, I accomplished this with one of the evaluators representing the other companies.

My recon revealed a five hundred-meter-wide valley bordered by ridgelines of two to three hundred meters in elevation. A natural dogleg would allow the majority of the company to set up in an L formation. On the far ridgeline were good positions for one platoon, which could, if necessary, initiate the kill zone to force the advancing enemy into the sights of the remainder of the company. A small tree-covered hill in the middle of the valley would have provided a more advantageous position for one platoon and/or a TOW missile section, but I discounted its overall value. Although it was perfectly situated for the defense, there were no covered avenues of withdrawal. Any unit set up on the isolated hill would have to fight to the end because there would be no way to safely retreat.

Within a half hour of my return to the assembly area, I had composed my order and was prepared to issue it to my platoon leaders. Using a mock-up of our kill zone, made with sand, twigs, pine cones, and expended ammunition brass on ground cleared of snow, I briefed the platoon leaders, leaving enough time for them to have several hours to prepare their plan and men before moving out.

A part of the concept of the operation for the kill zone included the alternate position to which we would pull back if we were not able to hold our original defenses. Another sand table showed each platoon its location and sectors of responsibilities. I diagramed routes from the first kill zone to the second. Each platoon leader was responsible for conducting his own recon of those routes once the initial kill zone was established. A third sand table displayed the location of the mortar platoon about five hundred meters to the rear of the rest of the company, where they could plot fires to cover dead space—gullies and areas behind small ridges where our direct-fire weapons could not reach. The fourth and final sand table represented their alternate support position.

Before and after issuing the order, I continued to coordinate by radio and in person with evaluators representing supporting fires and forces. I called for mine fields, delivered by air drop and artillery, to be laid in to channel the enemy into the strength of our kill zone. Additional fire was planned to help attrit the enemy from the time it came within observation until it came too close to our positions to safely call in the artillery. I requested to have a section of Cobra gunships to overwatch our kill zone from a hill mass three kilometers to our rear; my request was denied. Since my opinion of the potential lethality of tank-killing helicopters and chopper pilots had improved not one bit since REFORGER, I did not really care that the Cobras were not available. Nonetheless, the evaluators did give us credit on their checklist for asking.

After my order, the platoon leaders left to prepare their plans and brief their squad leaders who, in turn, briefed their men. By the time we began to move to the kill zone, every man in the company knew the current enemy and friendly situation, possessed a general idea of the company and battalion operations plans, and understood specifically how he and his responsibilities fit into the plan.

Our maneuvers were backed by days of practice in the local training area, at Hohenfels, and during REFORGER. As a result, everything went in precise, clockwork fashion when we moved into our kill-zone positions. Within seconds security was posted, wire was laid between positions to minimize easily detected radio traffic, and vehicles and individual positions were prepared and camouflaged. Except to check the exact location of our TOW section and make a few reports on the radio, there were few demands on me during that phase of the test. Like an athletic coach, I had prepared the team. On game day, all I could do was watch from the sidelines until something unanticipated occurred which needed my guidance and/or orders.

The brigade evaluators rushed from squad to squad and platoon to platoon with clipboards and checklists. Often we were already well into the next phase before they had completed looking at the former portion of the test. Although the temperatures never rose above zero and we struggled through snow varying from a foot deep to over our waists, the occupation of the kill zone phase went so smoothly that it appeared to be almost without any real effort. Every leader and soldier knew his job and went about his task as if the enemy were from across the border rather than weather and guys from brigade with red pencils.

Late in the afternoon the aggressor force sent a platoon of tanks on a reconnaissance to attempt to pinpoint our positions. We responded only with simulated artillery fires and turned them back without the knowledge they sought. During the lull that followed, a new team of evaluators arrived by helicopter relieving the old team who seemed quite happy to be headed for a warm brigade headquarters. The new major informed me that Schweinfurt military installations would be open for business as usual the following day.

While the snow had not melted and the temperatures had not risen, the main roads were clear. The major added that any aggressor tank we spotted would have to simulate a section of three. It seemed that only one tank company had been committed to our "test war." Poor maintenance and the brutal weather had reduced the seventeen-tank company to nine operating vehicles. Since there was no doubt that we could whip nine attacking tanks on our own, the force ratio had to be artificially enhanced to ensure we would have to withdraw for the other phases of the test.

By midnight the aggressor tank force had made several probes on our position with little results. An hour later they made a high speed approach en masse down a narrow road in the middle of the kill zone. The dark hulks of the sixty-ton tanks stood out starkly against the snow in the dim moonlight from the clearing sky. When we initiated the entire firepower of our kill zone, I added several parachute flares which lit the valley like daytime. With fire striking them from two sides, the tanks turned in attempt to escape—only to run into the firepower of the single platoon positioned across the valley. Again they turned in an attempt to escape the kill zone and ran directly into one of our prelaid mine fields. Twenty minutes into the battle, the tank company was in disarray as it turned back down the road on which it had approached.

The senior evaluator said a few words including "good job" as he credited us with killing all nine of the tanks. He added, however, for us to remember that each aggressor tank had to be multiplied by three and that despite the results, we should consider the present kill zone untenable and withdraw.* A short radio call set the company in a carefully orchestrated maneuver to the fall-back position. Within minutes wire had been rolled up, camouflage nets collapsed, and, with platoons covering each other, the retrograde movement began.

In our alternate position, labeled position Tango in the company order, the platoons repeated the occupation of a kill zone with the same speed and proficiency which had characterized the first. The evaluators were surprised to find that the company mess truck had been at Tango for the past few hours and had hot coffee and soup ready for everyone as they finished their tasks. The major in charge accepted a cup of coffee with a murmur of thanks and the usual silence maintained by staff officers in the presence of field commanders, regardless of differences in rank. His NCOs were not as silent. Ice crystals glittering in his mustache, one master sergeant approached me saying, "I've been all over this company looking for something bad to write up. Damned if I've been able to find anything. I've been on more of these goddamn tests than I care to remember, and you guys are the best I've seen. Except for this fucking weather, it's almost a pleasure to be here."

During the next hour, I planned for the withdrawal to a third position as well as for a counterattack to retake the original kill zone. I even managed to sleep for an hour or so before the senior evaluator ordered us to counterattack at dawn. Since sunup was only a hour away, it was good that I had already prepared my plans. Issuing a quick order, again with the aid of sand tables, we were ready to move at the assigned time.

Apparently the evaluators failed to let the aggressor force know the counterattack was underway. We caught the tank company in the midst of breakfast, with no security or early warning posted. With little resistance, we retook the original kill zone and once again destroyed the nine tanks opposing us. After we had consolidated and reorganized on the objective, the major approached me saying, "Captain, the report will not be finished for several weeks, but I'm sure you know the final evaluation will be 'combat ready.' The report will also highly commend

---

*Our domination of the "enemy" was so complete that the evaluator had to include in his final report "an artificial situation had to be created to justify Company A having to uncover their kill-zone position."

the company on your level of maintenance. It's hard to believe that you have been able to keep everything operational in this weather. Now let's get the hell out of here and go home.''

CHAPTER 13

NAPOLEON WITHOUT THE TALENT

February 1976

Our army would be invincible if it could be properly organized and officered. There were never such men in an army before. They will go anywhere and do anything if properly led. But there is the difficulty—proper commanders.

Robert E. Lee to
Stonewall Jackson, 1862

Clear roads and warming temperatures allowed us to return to Ledward in an hour rather than the eight it had taken on day one of the company test. Leaving the platoon leaders and sergeants in charge to begin cleanup and accountability, I headed for the battalion headquarters. One of the best things about the test had been that it kept us in the field during the battalion change of command ceremony. It was almost worth four days in subzero conditions to miss the indoor parade.

I had been surprised that neither the new battalion commander nor any of his staff had visited us in the field, but I had chalked that up in the plus rather than the negative column. My opinion continued to be that the less supervision was the best supervision—exceeded only by no supervision at all.

Regardless of my feelings, a new battalion commander was on board, and it was time to meet him. My intelligence work had turned up no one who knew the new commander or had previously worked for him. All I had been able to learn before the company test was that he was coming from some job in the depths of the Pentagon—not much of a recommendation. While Lieutenant Colonel King had been good at letting his company commanders command with a minimum of supervision, at the same time he had not lent any great inspiration or set a note-

200

worthy example. Still, the known was preferable to the unknown—and I was about to learn why.

Before reporting to the new battalion commander, I stopped by the battalion adjutant's office to see my old friend Bill Morrow. The adjutant is generally a unit's repository of rumors, lies, facts, and other bits of information, and the position is usually filled by a captain awaiting command or just completing his command tour. When I stuck my head in Bill's door, he was gathering up a pile of papers and mumbling about another meeting at brigade. When he spotted me, he made remarks about hearing we had done well on the test. Nothing seemed unusual until I asked him about the new Old Man. Bill replied, "Not now, Lee. Got to go to brigade, but gee whiz, uh, dad gum, uh, well, golleywoggles, I wouldn't know what to say. You'll figure him out pretty quick anyhow." With a "Got to go, late, late, late," Bill was out the door and down the steps like the white rabbit in the story about a girl named Alice.

Bill and I were on our second tour together, having spent a couple of years training students in the Infantry School's Ranger camp at Eglin Air Force Base, Florida. In addition to being a good buddy, he was the only soldier I knew who had taken on two North Vietnamese with only a .45-caliber pistol and lived to wear the Silver Star he was awarded for his valor. Bill was not hesitant to admit that as an advisor to a South Vietnamese Airborne battalion he had become separated from his counterpart during a night attack. When he fell into the foxhole of a two-man .51-caliber machine-gun crew, he found the .45 to be the better weapon in such a confined space.

Between growing up in the woods of northern Idaho, that experience in the Vietnam foxhole, the years as a Ranger instructor, and a half-tour in the VOLAR Army in Europe, Bill had learned a few profanities which were a bit more severe than "gee whiz" and "dad gum." As for "golleywoggles," that was a new one on me, but it did not seem in character. Minutes later, in the battalion commander's office, I began to understand Bill's new vocabulary.

I knocked on the battalion commander's office door and after hearing a faint "enter" advanced to the front of his desk, saluted, and reported. Lt. Col. James B. Motley returned my salute and extended his hand without getting out of his chair. After his limp, sweaty handshake, I took the chair he directed me to at the side of his desk. The meeting was exceedingly formal in comparison to those of my previous experience, but he had the rank, and we were on his home turf. All I could do was play his game. Although Motley had not stood, I could tell that he was considerably shorter than six feet and carried himself like a little man who wanted to be taller. His bulging, rosy cheeks, thinning hair, black-rim issue glasses, and rumpled fatigues did not better the impression he left.

When the new battalion commander began to speak, I realized that my initial impression had been much more generous than he really deserved. Thinking that Motley would begin our conversation with congratulations on the successful company test or some of our other recent accomplishments, I was surprised to hear his first words, "God's last name is not damn. I will tolerate absolutely no profanity by an officer or anyone else in my command."

As the battalion commander spoke, he pointed to a sign under a glass protector on his desk that backed up this declaration about God's last name. I stifled a chuckle and refrained from asking if it was "bless" or even "Smith." The best course of action seemed to be to keep my mouth shut. I was well aware that profanity was often the indication of a limited vocabulary and that there were certain groups who professed that it was a sin to use God's name in vain, yet giving orders to soldiers not to cuss was like asking them to be happy about getting up early in the morning. Whatever this new, confusing order really meant, it did make a little more sense of Bill Morrow's "gosh darn and golleywoggles."

I was still attempting to understand the no-profanity order when I realized that Lieutenant Colonel Motley was continuing to speak. By this time, like any good military subordinate, I had my green issue note pad out and was furiously taking notes. Although I may have missed a few words of wisdom while contemplating God and golleywoggles, Motley regained my attention when he exclaimed, "Never trust your NCOs, they will lie to you every chance they get. I know because long ago I was an enlisted man in the Marine Corps."

The new battalion commander then went into a long diatribe on what constituted good training. He went into great detail about the importance of a well-developed and coordinated weekly training schedule. I tried convincing myself that perhaps Motley's comments about God and NCOs were just a nervous reaction to suddenly being in command of an eight hundred-man battalion and that perhaps he would improve on acquaintance. He soon put that hope to rest by going into a tirade concerning the importance of neatness in preparing the training schedule and how he would not tolerate misspellings or typographical errors. Each week's schedule would have to be perfect or it would be unacceptable.

I started to point out to the colonel that my training sergeant, as well as those in the other companies, was an infantry buck sergeant who typed the document with two fingers on a mimeograph master and had been selected for the job because he was "well educated" with a single semester of community college under his belt. Again, however, I realized that the best course of action at the time was no action at all. My listening and keeping my mouth shut, accompanied by an occasional nod of acknowledgment, seemed to be all that Motley was interested in.

In the months ahead, I would learn that Motley had other ideas about training that had little to do with the actual performance of the battalion. Style seemed to be much more important than substance. In addition to perfect training schedules, the battalion commander placed great emphasis on training aids such as professionally reproduced wall charts; elaborate, larger-than-scale, wooden models of weapons, and compasses; as well as printed wallet cards, notebooks, and diagrams of all types.

Apparently Motley had worked in training-aid production in the Pentagon or in the Heidelberg headquarters before reporting to Schweinfurt. Training aids were of such importance to Motley that the day after our first meeting he gathered all five of his company commanders and his operations officer for a day-long trip to a warehouse full of such items. It seemed strange to take a complete day away from the company and stranger still that Motley wanted to visit a warehouse before he had even met the soldiers of his battalion.

Unfortunately, before our exciting trip to a dimly lit, cold, dirty warehouse full of charts and mock-ups, I had to endure the rest of Lieutenant Colonel Motley's initial briefing. Now that we had discussed training—with a focus on glitz and glitter rather than on preparation and readiness—Motley turned to more personal matters. Motley explained that in the army it was a two-for-one system and that by employing the soldier the service picked up the wife as a worker at no addition expense. He continued that his wife had volunteered to help manage the local thrift shop and that each officer's wife in the battalion would "volunteer" to assist her. Other projects such as fund drives and clean-up campaigns would receive equal "volunteerism."

As almost an afternote, he stated that wives would, of course, be expected to attend regular meetings of the battalion Officers' Wives Club which would be chaired by his wife.

Motley's next subject seemed to be a part of the previous one, but I was unsure if he intended it to be so. According to the battalion commander, he had been in Schweinfurt for several Sundays prior to assuming command and had been "disappointed, no outraged" that none of the battalion officers had been at Sunday services. While he did not mention wives' attendance, I assumed that he meant that this was to be another "two-for-one" effort.

We had now been talking, or at least Motley had been talking and I listening, for well over a half hour. During the entire time he had never smiled. His expression remained one that reminded me of young ROTC cadets or new second lieutenants attempting to look serious and "in charge." When Motley finally relaxed a bit and leaned back in his chair, I hoped that he might finally reveal a part of himself and his command style that might lend at least a bit of promise for an enjoyable or productive future. Again, I was wrong, absolutely wrong. Motley said a few words about the good things he had heard about Alpha Company while at the same time adding, "The entire battalion has a long ways to go to meet my standards." Then he dropped the "big bomb" when he explained that since A Company was doing so well that he was going to transfer several of my officers and NCOs to other companies in need of leadership. With that comment he indicated our talk was over and that I was dismissed.

The company test, completed only hours before, seemed far in the past. Except for the bone-weary exhaustion resulting from the pressures of the test compounded by the weather and the average of only two hours' sleep a night for the past four days, I felt as if the recent exercise had happened to someone else.

By the time I walked back to the company, the cleanup and accountability were well under way. By 1900 hours that evening, things had progressed to the point where we could secure quarters until the next morning. Before dismissing the company, I held a brief formation in front of the barracks. For several minutes I commended the men on their test performance and noted several distinguished efforts by platoons, squads, and individuals. I closed by stating that I had met with the new battalion commander and repeated the few words of praise he had given the company, making a much bigger issue of the comments than Motley had really conveyed.

I followed the company formation with a meeting of my first sergeant and platoon leaders. After outlining my plan for recovering and refitting from the company test, I pointed out that while we had a new battalion commander with some new ideas, the tactics which had led to the company's being the best in the division would continue. I noted Motley's disdain of profanity and told my subordinates to be sure they warned their men. Because my guidance to the enlisted men in the company had always been to limit answers to what was asked and not to ad lib or elaborate, the "no God's last names in front of Motley" would be fairly easy for them. As for myself, Top, and the platoon leaders—who had much more direct contact with the battalion commander than the troops—I emphasized that we would have to be on our best behavior around the new commander. I made no mention about wives' volunteering or of mandatory church attendance. The reason was simple: these were not lawful orders, and there was no requirement to follow them. Motley had made the mistake of the greenest officer—giving orders he could not enforce. Even lawful orders are useless unless the commander can ensure they are carried out.

Although I had grave doubts concerning Motley's ability to successfully command the battalion and to earn the respect of his officers and men, I made no comment about my thoughts to my chain of command. One of the most important characteristics of any subordinate is loyalty to his commander. Any difficulties I had with Motley would have to be worked out between him and me. As far as the soldiers were concerned, they would hear nothing but positive comments from me and the other officers. Unfortunately, or, perhaps, most fortunately, soldiers have minds of their own. It would not take them long to see that our new leader was a Napoleon without the talent.

For the next couple of weeks, Motley did little to lead his new command. Either the pressure of his new job, or some strange virus that affected no one but him, had Motley so ill his first two weeks of command that for days he was unable to come to work. When he finally did show up, he cloistered himself in his office with the lights off and a towel wrapped around his neck. In any conversation he quickly broke out into a sweat which he constantly mopped with a green towel.

During these initial days of command, Lieutenant Colonel Motley was an obvious topic of conversation among his five company commanders. After his first week on the job, we five began meeting on Friday nights for a poker game where drinking beer and laughing at the latest Motleyism was every bit as important as card playing. We were in agreement that the new battalion commander was the most inept officer whom we had encountered in our combined total of fifty years of service. Still, all we did was talk. There was never any discussion of not following the legal orders of the colonel. As for the illegal orders, we did not respond to them—because of common sense and experience, not through collusion on any of our parts.

A topic around the poker table was one on our minds whether on duty or off. What would Motley be like in actual combat? Could he lead any better on the battlefield than he could in garrison? The two references most commonly repeated about Lieutenant Colonel Motley indicated that no one had any hope for the new commander in either environment. One compared Motley's unique ideas about training schedules and church attendance to Captain Queeg's interest in counting strawberries in the movie *The Caine Mutiny*.

The second reference was even worse and began with the question, "What would happen to the battalion if there was Russian artillery at the end of a long valley and an English poet by the name of Tennyson was sitting on a hillside where he could watch and write?" The answer was, "Onward would charge the light battalion, onward into the valley of death. We in the lead and Motley to the rear, and we would all die, motherfucker, we would all die."

Despite the lack of confidence we felt in Lieutenant Colonel Motley, we shared a belief that the system itself had sufficient checks and balances to ensure that one poor commander could not tear down the entire organization. With Colonel Creighton as the brigade commander and a succession of able division commanders—including E. C. "Shy" Meyer—Motley might make life uncomfortable for those of us in his command, but he would not be able to maintain his position without giving us some latitude to lead our companies.

To have achieved his position as battalion commander, Motley had to have paid his dues with long service and difficult assignments. Somewhere along the line, apparently in the halls—or basement—of the Pentagon or on some other assignment, he had earned the right to command. As long as he did not significantly reduce the readiness level of the battalion, fail two IGs, or go head-to-head with the brigade or division commander, his job would be safe. In peacetime, commanders are usually given some latitude to fail in the hope that they will learn in the process. If combat actually came, he could be replaced quickly with someone who could gain the trust of the command.

In the meantime, we lived with Motley's orders and directives that belied any semblance of leadership. During his first barracks inspection, the new battalion commander ignored the immaculate rooms, knife-sharp creases in uniforms, mirror-shined boots, and knowledgeable, motivated soldiers to go into an absolute temper tantrum upon finding pictures of nude women on several room bulletin boards. With face red, sweat popping out on his brow—which he wiped off with the still present green towel—he demanded to know why such pornography was openly displayed.

I was tempted to respond that I thought that most of the pictures were quite good, and that if good, they were not pornography, but obviously in Motley's mind all nude pictures were smut. At least he listened while I explained that the company policy was that anything sold in the post exchange book store was considered acceptable for display. Sweat by then pouring from his forehead, he angrily replied that the new policy was that no pictures of nudes whatsoever were to be displayed.

With more than a year in this, my second company command, I, of course, felt a mixture of emotions about the antics and policies of the new battalion commander. Along with anger and out-and-out disbelief, I kept in mind that he was, in fact, the battalion commander. No army, or company for that matter, can exist for any length of time without a viable chain of command where lawful orders are carried out without hesitation or question.

A soldier is allowed only one opportunity to unreasonably question his commander—and this is known, appropriately, as "falling on one's sword." The connotation is not in jest. Questioning a commander's order or attempting to undermine his authority is simply suicide. One's job, career and, indeed, possibly one's life are on the line when the orders or authority of a superior commander are questioned. If the situation is perceived as dire enough—and generally only when the safety of the subordinate command is in the balance—then obviously job and career have to be put on the line.* Even if one is right,

---

*Another way of dealing with the ineffective or dangerous commander received much attention in the Vietnam War, though it was just as common in previous conflicts. Fraggings in Vietnam were a bit more direct than the "accidental" or "friendly" fire that killed commanders in previous wars, but they accomplished the same purpose.

falling on the sword may be "fatal"—either immediately or in the long run. As much as I disagreed with Motley for both his tactics and his censorship, I was not going to fall on my sword over a few pinups. I had looked down the sharp sheath during my first command, and survived. I might not be so fortunate this time.

All commanders are charged first and foremost with training and leading their commands so that they will be able to accomplish whatever missions were assigned. Congruent and equally important, is the responsibility to take care of the soldiers entrusted to those commands. In the worst of times, a commander must risk the safety and lives of his men to accomplish the mission. His ability to successfully train and lead is measured simply by the amount of death and carnage that are sustained to take the objective or to hold the line. Such is the nature of the business, and any potential commander not prepared to assume the responsibility is in the wrong profession.

In the midst of battle there is little or no room to question orders. This is not to say, however, that a commander should lead his precious soldiers to certain death if he perceives that an order is given in error, or if from his on-the-ground position, he can determine a safer alternative.

During my Vietnam company command, I questioned an order. It was not gallantry on my part, for my life was at risk as well as those of the men under my command. After three days of almost constant combat in an attempt to overrun a North Vietnamese unit dug into deep bunkers, I had seen nearly half my company killed or wounded. After each unsuccessful attempt, we withdrew, evacuated our wounded, received a resupply of ammunition, and attacked once more under the cover of artillery and air support. Promised reinforcements for two days, the company was exhausted, in a state of constant reorganization from the loss of key leaders, and then outnumbered by an enemy protected by excellent defensive works.

Late on the third day, an order came from the battalion commander, orbiting above the jungle in his command helicopter, to attack once again. My radio operators looked at me in disbelief and tears came to the eyes of my company medic. It was time to "fall on my sword." After a long pause I responded on the radio, "If you want us to, we will. But be advised, we have been fighting for three days. You know how many we've lost. We're outnumbered and outgunned. If we go back in, this will likely be the last transmission from us. I don't think we can survive another attack.''*

There was a lengthy silence on the radio before the battalion commander came back on the net and said that a reinforcing company was finally approaching from another direction. We were to take up a blocking position instead of attacking. His change in orders was, to say the least, most welcome. However, if he had come back and repeated his order for us to attack, my response would have been "Roger." We would have attacked once more and likely died in the process. Such is the nature of the business.

As Motley settled into command, it was apparent that the only option available was to follow the rules for working with a poor boss. From all indications, Motley was not going to be relieved of his command unless we, his subordinate commanders, did so poorly that the battalion could not function. Like my four contemporaries, I certainly was not going to jeopardize our mission and our men—two interchangeable priorities. All we could do was to perform our duties to the best of our abilities and to continue to demand the best from the soldiers. While Motley gained no respect for himself, we still maintained a respect for the rank and position he held.

My first major confrontation with the battalion commander came when he had another "innovative" idea about training. According to his directives, classroom training inside the barracks was not conducive to learning nor was it in the "tradition" of the infantry. All classroom training would take place in the open air, outside the Ledward Barracks cantonment area.

While I agreed in principle that field training was much better than classroom, the new directive served no real purpose except to harass the troops. We spent ample time in the field at the local training area, at Hohenfels, or in the German countryside on various exercises. Marching a half hour each way for the sake of getting off post and then sitting in the winter temperatures so we would be outside a classroom made no sense. To my mind, we would only be wasting time, degrading training, and offering the little needed opportunity to practice being cold, wet, and miserable.

*See *Vietnam 1969–1970: A Company Commander's Journal*, New York: Ivy Books, 1988, pp. 173–174.

I questioned Motley's new training order as respectfully as I could, hoping that he had a logical explanation. His response, while possibly not logical, did make sense when one considered that a lieutenant colonel battalion commander far outranks a captain company commander. According to Motley, his new training procedures were the way they were because he wanted them that way. No explanation was necessary. In rising anger and cracking voice, he concluded that he would tolerate no more questioning of his orders.

My second confrontation with Motley was over a much more important issue, but it ended with the same results as the first. As I had noted in my early days of command, the 2d of the 30th benefited from the advantages of being the worst or, at least one of the poorer, units in the division. Because of this, for months we had received more than our fair share of officers and NCOs. Now that the battalion was out of the cellar and near the top, this special attention ended. Worse yet was Motley's own technique of assigning the "best to the worst and worst to the best."

Since A Company was doing so well (the nearest he ever came to saying anything positive, incidentally), Motley was transferring several of my officers and NCOs to other companies. Two of my lieutenants, Gary Gaal and John Lucas, were to be transferred to the battalion's combat support company. While each other company in the battalion would have four lieutenants, A Company would have to get by with just two. The only concession I could gain from Motley when I protested the transfers was permission to keep Gaal in the company through the mortar tests scheduled the following month.*

The worst news came when Motley informed me about Carrasco's replacement. Top had completed his tour and was en route to Fort Carson, Colorado, to an assignment as first sergeant and, later, a promotion to command sergeant major.** Carrasco's departure represented the loss of an absolutely superior NCO as well as a good and respected friend. The accomplishments of the company were very much a reflection of Top's

---

*One week before the mortar tests, Motley relieved (fired) the combat support (4.2-inch mortar) platoon leader and ordered Gaal to take his place.
**Sergeant Major is the highest enlisted grade in the U.S. Army. Some Sergeants Major are selected as Command Sergeants Major to serve in troop units as the senior NCO.

personality, leadership, and hard work. Despite Motley's opinion of NCOs in general, I would have much preferred sharing a foxhole or a beer with my old first sergeant than with the new battalion commander.

While I had hoped to receive one of the experienced first sergeants arriving in-country, Motley informed me that my new top NCO would be one relieved from another company in the battalion. I had worked with the man, and although I had seen some potential, I was not surprised that he had been fired.

My apprehension was well founded. Despite much work with the new first sergeant, he failed to earn the respect of the men in the company and never really was able to take charge. Some are born to be a first sergeant, a few others are able to develop the skill. Many cannot. After several months, I, too, was forced to transfer my first sergeant out of the company. By that time no other first sergeants were available, so I appointed Sergeant First Class Liebrich as the company first sergeant. Although Liebrich was not the senior sergeant by date of rank, he was, in my opinion, the best qualified for the job—and that is what the soldiers deserved. The other NCOs must have agreed, because none of them questioned the order or came to knock on my "open door" (an opportunity I offered when I announced that Liebrich was the new Top).

February, like any other month in the infantry, did not provide bad news only. In the midst of the personnel changes came word through the chain of command that I had been selected as the 3d Infantry Division's representative to the Commander in Chief, United States Army Europe and Seventh Army Company Commander's Discussion Program to be held at Heidelberg on the 24th and 25th of the month as one of thirty company commanders chosen from across Europe. According to the formal letter of invitation, the purpose of the conference was to "discuss and exchange ideas and information of mutual interest between the participating company commanders and the USAREUR staff." In addition we would have the opportunity of meeting and talking with the USAREUR commander in chief, his deputy commander, and his command sergeant major.

The idea that the commanding general of all U.S. Army forces in Europe would be willing to sit down and listen to a group of his company commanders seemed to many a strange idea. It did not seem that way to me because I was aware that Gen. George Blanchard had received his fourth star and had moved from VII

Corps commander to his new job as commander in chief of USAREUR and Seventh Army. I had learned at Kelley Barracks that Blanchard was the kind of man who listened as well as gave orders, usually accomplishing the former before proceeding with the latter. I also knew that the new program was in no way grandstanding on his part but represented a legitimate effort to learn more about his command and to determine how to increase combat readiness and to improve his soldiers' quality of life.

During the two days, Blanchard and his staff chiefs, representing operations, logistics, personnel, legal, medical, and education, presented briefings and answered our questions. On the whole, they were well informed about the problems in the trenches, and under Blanchard's leadership they were doing their best to be of assistance.

Several of the company commanders were fellow students from the Vilseck Company Commander's Course or the advanced course at Fort Knox. Hearing the stories of challenges and woe experienced by my contemporaries was entertaining as well as informative, making for an overall outstanding two days. The best part of the conference was having a brief break to see that the Motleys were in the minority and that the Blanchards were still present to lead and command in the manner we expected and deserved.

CHAPTER 14

NO PROBLEMS, JUST CHALLENGES: STRIVING TO BE ALL WE CAN BE

March 1976

For [Douglas] MacArthur, military life may be symbolized by '. . . faint bugles sounding reveille,' but for many if not most of his countrymen it is something else: it is reveille. It is training manuals and twenty-mile hikes, stupifiying lectures on platoon tactics and the use of the Lister bag, mountains of administrative paperwork, compulsive neatness and hideous barracks in Missouri and Texas, sexual deprivation, hot asphalt drill fields and deafening rifle ranges, daily tedium unparalleled in its ferocity, awful food, bad pay, ignorant people, and a ritualistic demand for ass-kissing almost unique in the quality of its humiliation.

William Styron
New York Review Of Books
October 8, 1964

Early March brought no hint of spring as we moved back to Hohenfels under cold, gray skies. This third rotation to the major training area since my assumption of command was a repeat of the live-fire training and maneuver of our earlier visits. The repetition of training in no way represented a waste of time or resources. During each interval between visits to Hohenfels, the company experienced many changes in leadership and responsibilities. Several men who had been drivers or riflemen during previous exercises had been promoted to sergeants and team leaders. Transfers, completion of tours, and new assignments brought other new faces to Alpha Company.

The only way we could maintain our proficiency and the training edge that we would need in actual combat was to practice those skills in the most realistic environment possible—and Hohenfels was the best we had. Like the quarterback who practices tossing the same pass thousands of times in hopes of using it once in actual competition, or the batter who takes a hundred cuts in practice for every at-bat in a real game, we could expect to be only as good as we practiced. Of course, the difference between athletes and soldiers is that the soldier hopes that game time never arrives. The man in uniform is also well aware that regardless of the reality of training, combat is a different game altogether, and only those who have actually experienced it have any idea of its realities and how they will act under fire.

Despite the repetition and routine of Hohenfels, it continued to offer some of the most exhilarating and satisfying days of my command. Without the distractions and mundane housekeeping chores of garrison life, we were free to train with a focus on nothing but increasing our combat readiness. The only bad point to this stint at the major training area was our battalion commander. Motley soon proved to be no more proficient at leading the battalion in the field than he was in garrison. Mechanized infantry and combined task force warfare seemed as foreign to him as charisma. On two occasions that the entire battalion was aware of, and others I am sure we were not, Motley committed the ultimate infantry sin of getting lost. The mistake of being a poor map reader and of not properly using a lensatic compass were errors that might be forgiven a green second lieutenant, but for a lieutenant colonel battalion commander, getting lost was a lapse that removed any shred of respect we might have retained for him.

Prone to issuing orders without allowing sufficient time for proper execution, Motley zipped about the training area in a helicopter giving and changing instructions as if he were above the guerrilla-infested jungles of Vietnam rather than a tank-heavy Central European battlefield well supplied with antihelicopter missiles. If the situation had not been potentially so lethal, the tirades of the battalion commander would have been comical. Often excited and overwrought, Motley could barely scream his displeasure. Calm was not one of his attributes. We all wondered what he would do if real bullets were in the air, or even a misspoken goddamn or two reached his ears.

Unfortunately, Motley's solution to his own ineptness was to use a tactic common to commanders who are having trouble—fire a subordinate or two. The target of his wrath was the newly assigned operations officer. The major was a West Point graduate and former Academy faculty member who had a distinguished record in both peacetime and combat assignments. His dozen years of service were abruptly terminated when Motley relieved him from his position and wrote a damning efficiency report. The major's career was over without his even having the opportunity to "fall on his own sword."*

Our final challenge at Hohenfels was a week-long evaluation called an ARTEP (Army Training and Evaluation Program). This program set the new army-wide standard by which all units were rated in annual tactical field tests. Much of the exercise repeated the attack, defend, and delay portions of the no-notice test of the previous January. I was not surprised that we received Sats on all fifteen of the tasks and subtasks—the best score in the battalion.

When we finally concluded our training and returned to the Parsberg railhead to out-load for Schweinfurt, we were greeted by the unexpected. Our train had not yet arrived. Despite the set-your-watch punctuality of the German railway system, we had to wait more than two hours for it to puff into the station. The wait was not bad, as it offered an opportunity to clean weapons and equipment. More important, it provided the unheard of opportunity to harass the German railroad staff. Every half hour or so one of us would wander into the station and ask when the train would arrive. Before departing, we mentioned that we did not understand the delay because back in the States "the trains always ran on time." The stationmaster, called "Herman the German" by the troops, was nearly in tears when our transport finally arrived.

When we pulled into the station back in Schweinfurt, I noticed out the window that many of the battalion wives and children and several German girlfriends were there to meet the train. To one side I could see Linda with a daughter firmly grasped in each hand. Reunions at the railhead were held to a few minutes because of all the work required to unload and move back to garrison, but those few minutes were always nice nonetheless.

Before our departure for Hohenfels nearly three weeks earlier, my six-year-old daughter Reveilee had asked me why I was

*The major completed his tour in Germany as a minor staff officer at brigade and then resigned his Regular Army commission. I ran into him a decade later at a Stateside field exercise and was pleased to find that he was a vice president at a Fortune 500 company and a full colonel in charge of a U.S. Army Reserve Special Forces Unit.

going away and why I was never home. As her three-year-old sister Meridith listened with some apparent understanding, I explained as basically as I could that the world was made up of good and bad people. I told them that to protect the good people, special men were selected to be soldiers, and it was necessary for us to practice so that we could fight the bad people and win. When she asked if that included guns and shooting, I nodded in the affirmative and was grateful that she had not inquired about the requirements of killing.

My departing explanation to my daughters was far from my mind as both girls ran to meet me with a hug. Lifting one in each arm, I leaned over to give Linda a kiss. When I turned back to the girls, I boosted them up to gain a better grip, causing Reveilee to bump against the .45 pistol I was carrying in a shoulder holster.* Her eyes widened as she pulled her hands away from the holster to under her chin as she anxiously inquired, "Who was bad, daddy, who was bad?"

Once everything was sorted out, cleaned, and accounted for on our return, we continued to focus on maintaining our level of discipline and readiness and to concentrate on areas that would make us a better company. Physical training had been an integral part of building discipline from the beginning days of my command. Daily in garrison, either early in the morning or at the end of the duty day—depending on the time of year—we began with an NCO or lieutenant leading the company in exercises that followed the *Physical Training Field Manual* and were known as the daily dozen. In each exercise, individuals had to follow the exact commands of the leader and conduct repetitions of the exercises by the count. Errors, by anyone of any rank, were paid in push-ups. This included—much to the enjoyment of the soldiers—myself, Top, and the rest of the chain of command. Once the exercises were completed we went on a double-time run for two to five miles.

As time passed, PT became a time not only to exercise but also to build team spirit. Although the sweat was real, for those in any kind of condition at all, PT was often more fun than work. While the benefits of physical training have always been understood by armies of all nations, the fitness craze and interest in running in the mid-1970s more than spilled over to the military.

---

*Our shoulder holsters were not worn in an attempt to imitate gangsters or John Wayne. Holsters worn on waist belts interfered with rapidly and safely getting in and out of tank and M-113 hatches.

Units were soon running farther, faster, and more frequently. The greatest disadvantage to the increased emphasis on running was that the army had not acknowledged that there were many better types of footgear for PT than combat boots—so away we ran, boots and all.

Several months earlier, the division commander decided that there should be a PT standard for all units to achieve. Quarterly, each company in the division would be required to run two miles, in formation, with 95 percent of the men completing in seventeen minutes or less. Units could test only once a month and had to repeat every thirty days until the standard was met. Initially this validation of PT standards seemed easy enough to accomplish. However, we failed on our first two attempts to validate. The problem was that on each try we had more than 5 percent drop out or fall back too far to be considered part of the finishing formation. Our only consolation was that no other company of the more than one hundred assigned to the division had been able to achieve validation, either.

On return from Hohenfels, we had renewed our efforts by running farther and faster each day. As with all other tasks, however, I knew we needed to develop an edge. The most critical part of the edge was to convince the company that we could meet the standard. Pointing out that we could be first to do what no other company had accomplished provided reinforcement. To sharpen the edge before our attempt to validate at the end of March, I added a few things. Soldiers who were in the poorest condition and usually fell out of the formation were put in the front rank. At the rear of the formation were the senior NCOs. On the flanks were the lieutenants who would lead jody calls and generally offer encouragement. At the front would be myself with one of the company's best runners who would carry the company guidon.

My position at the front was not just because I was the company commander. In each of our earlier tries to validate the PT requirement, the company had run too fast. Finishing in sixteen rather than seventeen minutes counted for nothing unless 95 percent were still in the formation. By setting the pace myself, we could use every second allowed to complete the run. The final edge on the edge was allowed by the division regulation, which stated that each company could conduct its run at a location of its choosing. Rather than running around Ledward Barracks, we marched to a nearby German park. Now the soldiers could see new sites as well as show off in front of the fräuleins who frequented the park. That would also offer potential embarrassment to anyone who thought about dropping out. With evaluators from battalion and brigade looking on, we began our run. Carrying my own stopwatch, we ran the first quarter mile in a little less than two minutes and then slowed to an eight-and-a-half-minute pace. At the end of a mile, several of the soldiers in the front rank attempted to drop back only to be pushed along by those behind them. The farther we ran, the louder the cadence became. With jody calls ringing off the surrounding German apartments, we were gathering a fair audience as we neared the finish line. Rather than speed up, we slowed in the final hundred meters to get the ranks and files neatly dressed. As the last rank crossed the finish, the evaluator shouted 16 minutes and 55 seconds. Only two men had failed to finish. We had validated with 98.5 percent finishing in less than 17 minutes.

Letters of congratulations soon arrived from the division and brigade commanders and a nice article appeared in the Marne Division newspaper. Late the next month, we repeated our validation of the two-mile run. By that time, only one other company had been able to match our effort, and by quarter's end, we were still the only company to accomplish the feat twice.

Riding the momentum of "first to validate," we next went after an even more difficult objective. For well over six months, division had been attempting to have a company-size unit "drug free" for thirty days. To meet the requirement, each man in the unit had to sign a pledge that he would not use or condone the use of illegal drugs. In addition, during the thirty-day period, there could be no drug busts, no drugs or paraphernalia found in the barracks during health and welfare or other inspections, and no positive results in the command-directed random urinalyses.

When the first mentions of a drug-free company were made, like most commanders I had paid little attention. It was one of division's "want-to" programs rather than an order or stated requirement. At the time I would have been happy to go a week— even a day—without a drug bust or finding drugs freely lying around the barracks. However, a challenge was a challenge, no matter how slim seemed the chance for success. Like everything else, we would give drug-free a shot.

The first step in the program was to hold company command information meetings where the dangers and pitfalls of illegal drugs were discussed. Since volunteer soldiers of the mid-1970s were very much a product of their civilian environment, where drugs were glorified in the media and condoned in many circles, there was no effort in these sessions to bullshit the troops. When questions arose about "What is wrong with hash?" and "What does a little marijuana hurt?" my response was that I did not make the rules but I was sworn to enforce them. Cannabis in any form was illegal. To properly perform their duties, soldiers had to be disciplined and follow orders. Use of such drugs was a form of undisciplined behavior and was in direct conflict with published orders. Enough said.

The next step was for "little feet to take little steps," or in the vernacular of the time, "its easier to eat an elephant one bite at a time than all at once." Instead of a drug-free company as a goal, we began with drug-free individuals and then expanded to drug-free fire teams. Since the four- and five-man fire teams usually shared a room, a drug-free room and drug-free fire team went hand in hand. Top and I began the drug-free room objective by signing the drug-free pledge, submitting to a urine test, and—when it returned negative—declaring our offices drug free. To mark the accomplishment, we stenciled a boar's head— symbol of the regimental mascot—above our doorways.

Beyond the obvious benefits of ridding the barracks of junkies who harassed others and stole to support their habit, we needed to offer additional perks to get the soldiers solidly behind the program. Two of the most important things to a soldier are his off-time and the ability to maintain a bit of privacy in the communal barracks. As company commander, I could have an impact on both of these items.

Off-time was easy. I promised a day off to any fire team/room that met all the specifications of being drug free for thirty days.

The issue of privacy was just as easy to handle. My policy had been that each room had to be arranged according to the company SOP, which required bunks and wall lockers to be set against the walls. In addition to traditional military uniformity, this arrangement allowed unannounced inspections to check for drug use because, upon entering, one was to be able to see the entire room with no obstructions. There was no way a man could hide, swallow, or otherwise get rid of evidence without being seen.

I announced that any room meeting all drug-free criteria for thirty days could rearrange the furnishings any way suitable to the occupants. Wall lockers could be used as partitions and doors could be locked when the room was occupied rather than left open (as had to be done under the SOP).

Another reward for a drug-free room seemed counter to the purpose of the campaign, but I approved it nevertheless. The new volunteer army regulations permitted booze in the barracks; local directives allowed company commanders to suspend the privilege—which I had done during my first week in command when confronted by drunks, fights, and sick soldiers nightly. I reinstated the right to possess and consume alcoholic beverages in quarters for occupants of drug-free rooms.

During the first six months of our implementation of the drug-free program, several rooms had qualified for the benefits of the status. As expected, when the other soldiers saw their buddies getting a day off and rearranging their rooms, they, too, became interested. The more rooms that met the requirements, however, the more pressure we applied from the command level to ensure that drug-free really meant an absence of drug use, not just free of getting caught. We increased health-and-welfare-inspection frequency from once a month to every two weeks. We followed no schedule—often holding an inspection only days after an earlier one. Drug dogs continued to sniff out the barracks. The number of random urinalyses—based on the last digit of social security numbers—and command-directed tests of suspected users increased. A single positive urine test now placed a man in a rehab program and initiated concurrent action to discharge him from the army.

Punishment and reward are tools of improvement, but the real key to any long-term success is peer pressure—which we increased by making the group responsible for the individual. If one man made a mistake, his fire team/room, and in some cases his platoon and company shared the punishment. Any indication of drug use—a positive urinalysis, actual bust for possession, or the discovery of drugs or paraphernalia in a room, on the person, or in an assigned vehicle or equipment—was cause for the drug-free status of a room to be removed. Furnishings immediately went back to the walls, and all other privileges were suspended.

Furthermore, the room had to be "sanitized." The occupants had to empty their quarters and wash, clean, and/or GI each item before it was returned to the room. This meant a complete washdown of walls, floor, ceiling, and windows. Linens had to be laundered, and all uniforms sent to the cleaners at the soldiers' expense. The sanitation process, which usually took twenty-four to thirty-six hours, had to be completed before the occupants slept or rested.

On the surface, sanitation of a room would seem to qualify as unlawful orders. Sanitation, however, was voluntary—and the only way to begin again the thirty-day process toward drug-free privileges.

The sanitation process, which I found as objectionable and demeaning as did the soldiers, served its purpose—it created a tremendous amount of peer pressure. After five men stayed up all night sanitizing their room because one of them had brought into their quarters a little hash or a roach clip with residue, the innocent four tended to discourage the guilty fifth from such action.

By mid-March, we were nearing the status of drug-free. In the closing hours of the thirty days with every room and man meeting the standards, I ordered the most detailed health and welfare inspection yet conducted. A drug dog spent half a day going through the barracks, motor pool, and personal vehicles. Every man who had a previous drug bust on his record was directed to take a urine test. In every case, the tests were negative, and the barracks and surrounding area as clean from drugs as a convent.

We submitted the documentation declaring the company drug-free, and within a few days the division commander awarded us a certificate, an embroidered streamer for our guidon, and an additional training holiday. The division newspaper ran a long article on the first two companies to reach drug-free status. (An engineer company had matched our accomplishment a few days after us.) Although I sat by my phone for days with the apprehension that a dozen or so of my soldiers would be busted for all manner of drug use and possession, it remained silent. As much to my surprise as anyone else's, we had done what had seemed impossible only six months before.

The attainment of drug-free status was, of course, not created in a vacuum. Without the methodical team-building, discipline, and training readiness performed over the previous sixteen months, it would not have been possible. Slowly, yet surely, the soldiers had learned that breaches of discipline were punished severely and that satisfactory performance was richly rewarded.

Over the next two months, we maintained our drug-free status until a soldier was busted downtown by the MPs for being in possession of a small amount of hash and a smoking bowl. The feelings in the company were so negative toward the man that he was not returned to his fire team except to assist his bunkmates in the sanitation ritual. He remained in the custody of Top or the charge of quarters (CQ) until his discharge was completed.

Although the soldier's bust marked the last official drug incident during my time in command, I was not naive enough to think that we had ended drug use in the company. As I explained to the division commander and several of his senior staff members, we had met the division requirements of being drug-free to the letter of the directive. However, I explained, I did not want him or his staff to think that there was a total lack of drug use in the company. We had been successful in getting drugs out of the barracks—as proved by inspection—and eliminating the use of morphine derivatives—as supported by urine tests. Yet, there was no doubt in my mind that some soldiers assigned to the company still smoked hash and marijuana. Hidden from fellow soldiers as well as the chain of command, the users probably indulged off post—usually in the apartments of German girlfriends or outdoors in the many public parks.

The division commander nodded. Although he did not seem too happy about my admission, he did seem appreciative of my candor. Like me, he was well aware how difficult it had been to meet the written standards. At least in A Company drug use had become the exception rather than the norm. Another first for Alpha Company had been achieved, but more important, we had taken another step in accomplishing our mission and preserving the lives of American servicemen.

CHAPTER 15

IT WAS NOT MUCH, BUT IT WAS HOME: WE MOVE TO THE PARKING LOT

April 1976

Dear Captain Lanning,

Last October you said I should write to you if needed. I am worried because I haven't heard anything from my son, Private ____. He usually writes regularly. I am concerned that he might be in trouble. Please let me know if anything is wrong or if he has just forgotten his Mom.

Thanks for your time,
(signed)*

April opened with the mortar platoon test at the Wildflicken live-fire ranges. Over the past sixteen months, the company had made great strides, going from passing nothing to passing everything. Mortar testing would be the last big evaluation of my command tour and represented a tough challenge. No such test had been conducted in recent memory. Insufficient ammunition had been the excuse, but a more likely explanation was that it had been years since the training level of mortar platoons in the division was adequate to safely allow a live-fire examination.

The men from each of the line companies' 81mm mortar sections, along with those in the 4.2-inch mortar platoon from the battalion's combat support company, were to be tested over a period of a week. Eleven tasks were scheduled for evaluation, including such areas as occupation of a position, registration missions, live fire, shifting fires, night fire, illumination missions, and operating in a chemical/biological environment.

---

*Such letters, usually from mothers—but occasionally from fathers, wives, or girlfriends—came fairly often. In each case I would call in the soldier and suggest that it might be better for him to write home and let them know he was all right rather than for me to do so.

Beyond dispatching the A Company mortars to Wildflecken a week early to practice for the test, I had been unsuccessful in developing an added edge. Nevertheless, I was confident. With the hard training the platoon had undertaken, the overall discipline of the troops, the leadership of Gary Gaal before his transfer, and the guidance of the platoon sergeant, SFC George Arthur, the mortar test should yield another positive first for the company.

Although I visited my mortar section during its practice sessions, I deliberately stayed away on the day of the test. I saw no reason to place the added pressure by having the Old Man present. All I could do was to observe from the sidelines. I calculated my arrival to coincide with the completion of the test. The eleventh task was just about over as I drove up to the firing point. Sergeant First Class Arthur saw my jeep and with a big grin gave me the thumbs-up.

A few minutes later, after completing the fire mission, he reported that they had received ten sats out of the eleven tasks. Charlie Company had passed nine tasks while the other two companies had managed to get sats on only four and six of the subtests. Our ten sats was the best score thus far in the division and over the weeks, as the other battalions were tested, stood up as the best score. Another "best" for Alpha had been established. More important, we now had a confident, proficient mortar section which could provide organic indirect firepower and illumination. The mortarmen's reward for their fine performance—once they had thoroughly accounted for and maintained their equipment—was a day off with a keg of beer and a cookout.

Shortly after the return of the mortar section to Ledward, we were faced with an unusual mission, even for infantrymen who expect, and generally receive, the unexpected. The German government had authorized expenditure of funds for the upgrade and refurbishing of our barracks. Wiring would be redone; latrines and showers modernized from their original pre-World War II condition; floors, doors, and windows replaced; new light fixtures added; and a fresh coat of plaster and paint would be applied to everything.

The advantages of the modernization efforts were obvious—better living conditions would be enjoyed by all. Achieving the end result would not be so easy, however. Living space was at a premium at Ledward and nearby Conn Barracks. There was not enough excess space for a company, much less the three companies that usually occupied a barracks. The solution was about as old as armies themselves. Since soldiering began, a tent had often been the only protection between man and the elements. So it was to be for Alpha Company and the rest of the battalion.

Reconditioning the barracks would take four to six months. In the meantime we would occupy Tent City, which had been established in the post exchange parking lot. The only advantages the acres of canvas had to offer were an asphalt hardstand, a central location, and a home that was better than nothing at all. Portable showers and latrines in trailers provided the other amenities, unless one counted the rolls of concertina wire which gave our new home a bit of a boundary. Soldiers, supplies, arms, and orderly rooms all took their place in the tents. Fortunately, the mess hall was scheduled for later refurbishing, so an adequate dining facility remained operational.

The initial reaction of the troops was what is to be expected of soldiers of any army under any conditions—they bitched like hell. Below the surface of the complaints, however, there was no real hostility. One of the most welcome occurrences in any soldier's life is something that breaks the monotony and repetition of daily military life. Moving to a parking lot and living in a tent managed to meet that objective.

Because Tent City was to be used by a series of battalions as their barracks were renovated in turn, the usual poles and support ropes were replaced by a rigid wooden framework. A plywood floor and electrical wiring made the tents almost comfortable. We added a little to the austere conditions by stripping our old barracks of doors, light fixtures, and anything else that would make the tents a bit more livable. Since our move into the tents began with the arrival of spring, we did not install the issue diesel-burning stoves, allowing more living space and eliminating the risk of fire from the often dangerous heaters.

Designed for a squad of ten men sleeping on cots, the tents easily held the larger bunks we moved out of the barracks for the four- or five-man fire teams assigned to each structure. Drug-free rooms now became drug-free tents with the same occupants, same rules, and same boar's-head stencil above the door to indicate status.

The troop tents, like my orderly room and office, were a bit cool in the early morning and often hot in the afternoon. Our only system of temperature regulation was to roll up the tent sides or let them down. Rolling up the tent sides did sometimes provide a cool breeze, but at the same time, it also eliminated any privacy, especially for those whose tents bordered the area where families and soldiers walked on their way to the Exchange. Regardless of the temperature and the relative lack of privacy, the canvas roofs kept the rain off and the inside of the tents dry. What more could an infantryman really expect? Despite the upheaval of the move from barracks to tents, we maintained a challenging training schedule to practice individual and unit skills and to maintain vehicles and equipment. Still, the soldiers found time to play, have fun, and on occasion, get into trouble—regardless of the long hours and hard work. The infantry is a young man's game. Except for a few of the senior NCOs who were over 30 and myself, who was nearing that age, the average soldier in the company was 18 to 20 years old. Most had matured into men—damn good men—in training and while on duty. When off duty and out of the barracks, their youth on occasion caught up with them.

Checking the company late one night, I entered a tent occupied by four buck-sergeant (E5) fire-team leaders. They had just returned from downtown and were obviously feeling no pain. All of them were giggling like children and making reference to tattoos, asses, and gorillas. Finally, after much encouragement from the other three, one of the sergeants lowered his trousers to show off a six-inch-high, full-color gorilla tattoo on the cheek of his ass. He insisted that I notice that the gorilla was smiling. I joined the laughter of the sergeants—however, I am not sure if it seemed that funny to the tattooee the next morning or for the fifteen odd years since he awoke with a smiling gorilla on his buttocks.

With the many maintenance personnel assigned to companies in a mechanized division, it was not unexpected that their interest in mechanics and vehicles would spill over into their off-duty time. Under the leadership of a warrant officer who headed a battalion maintenance operation, a group of soldiers received permission to have the engineers scrape out a half-mile oval dirt track at nearby Conn Barracks.* Pooling their money, the men in nearly every company in the area bought old Volkswagens and other German small-engine cars to race on Sunday afternoons.

*We were not the only American community in Germany with our own racetrack. Troops in the Nürnberg area bulldozed theirs in the same stadium where Hitler made many of his speeches to massed formations of soldiers and party members prior to and during World War II.

The Alpha Company maintenance section helped operate the track and entered a car of its own. Fortunately, they were much better at maintaining military vehicles than they were at keeping their tired old VW running. Despite their poor record on the track, I was most pleased to join them on Sundays. Prominently displayed on the side of the car was the name selected by its crew and owners. "Lanning's Loonies" seemed most appropriate.

Although time was always in short supply for accomplishing essential tasks and conducting required training, time for leisure and family activities came up even shorter. Social obligations for a commander took up much of the little time off that we had available, but that was part of the business. In addition to Sunday afternoons at the races, I frequently received invitations to attend ball games and concerts where sons and daughters of my soldiers were playing.

Formal social activities—such as monthly battalion officer hail-and-farewells and quarterly parties for the brigade officers—were functions where attendance was not optional. Much better were the occasional promotion parties or gatherings at someone's quarters or a downtown establishment. The mid-1970s were still several years away from the Army's emphasis on "responsible drinking." In Germany at the time, "social drinking" was a near art form among U.S. Army officers. Even Lieutenant Colonel Motley did not have the nerve to attempt to curb the flow of booze—although he participated little or not at all. The only rules were no drinking and driving and no visits to the company area after any serious drinking. If an officer passed out and had to be carried home by fellow officers, we looked upon the action as a well-deserved attempt to let off a little steam and relax from the daily pressures. As long as one was able to make the company the next morning for the early morning PT run, the night before was viewed as just an effort to make it through another day in green.

Regardless of how good it becomes, a company is still 150 individuals. Officer and enlisted alike have problems adjusting to the military life-style and discipline. Being a good soldier on duty does not necessarily lead to a happy home life off duty. During April there were two distinctive examples of this "not everything is great all the time" axiom of military service.

The first was a young private from New York. Formerly a member of his state's National Guard, the man had not liked being a weekend warrior, or any other kind of warrior for that matter, and quit going to his meetings. Unlike its civilian coun-

terparts, the National Guard did not fire employees who failed
to come to work—his unit dusted off the man's enlistment contract, showed him the fine print wherein he agreed to go to the
Regular Army if he failed to attend drills, and sent him off to
anxiously awaiting commanders such as myself. Our challenge
was to turn a National Guard reject into our country's finest—
not exactly an easy task or one that I welcomed.

The former New York Guardsman found the Regular Army
no more to his liking than part-time soldiering. A few nights
before our move to the tents, he drank a couple of beers, climbed
onto the barracks roof, and began screaming that he was going
to jump. I arrived within minutes to find a couple of bored MPs
and a "meat wagon" ambulance from the aid station standing
by. I quickly climbed up the stairs and pulled myself to the roof
from a fourth-floor window. From a few yards away, the soldier
assured me he would jump if I came any closer.

I had only begun to talk to the soldier, trying to get him down,
when the battalion sergeant major appeared on the street below. He looked up at me, saluted, and, after I had acknowledged,
most courteously asked if he could send the MPs and ambulance
on their way. Seconds after I answered in the affirmative, they
disappeared down the street. The sergeant major then directed
his attention to the soldier. Looking up he yelled, "Jump, you
little son of a bitch, I don't think you have the balls for it."

The soldier looked at me, then at the sergeant major, and
finally the asphalt street below. Without a word, he crawled to
the window, let himself down, and returned to his room. The
sergeant major was correct: the man did not have the balls for
it. After I followed the soldier off the roof, I went downstairs to
see the sergeant major. All I said to him was that apparently he
knew more about getting a man off a roof than I did.

A few days later, the soldier received his wish. He got out of
the army. The bad-paper discharge did not seem to bother him.
He might have made a fine civilian back on the streets in New
York, but in Schweinfurt we were glad to be rid of him.

On the officer side, the situation could be just as difficult.
Problems in marriages were nothing new to the army of the mid-
1970s, and we in Schweinfurt were certainly faced with our
share of marital strife. Some of the wives went home to file for
divorce or to wait for a more pleasant future Stateside assignment where the hours might not be so long or the work so
intense.

A wife of one of the battalion's lieutenants took yet another path in dealing with a troubled marriage. Apparently, her conflict was neither with Schweinfurt nor the U.S. Army, but rather strictly with her husband. Instead of going home, she moved out of their apartment and in with one of the battalion's single lieutenants. Eventually she divorced the first and married the second. Other than a change of names, she seemed to have changed her situation little—except, unlike many of the other wives, she did appear to be quite happy. Of course, Motley was much less than impressed with the entire episode.

CHAPTER 16

THE FINAL DAYS—
DEMOCRACIES DO NOT NEED
FENCES

May 1976

> In spite of everything, I still believe that people are good
> at heart.
>
> *Diary of Anne Frank*
> Amsterdam, 1944

By the arrival of the spring of 1976, it was difficult for me to
recall a time when I had not been in command of A Company.
With regret and relief, I began to realize that my tour with "the
company" was nearing an end. Much like a love affair or a
marriage, command had brought extremes of happiness and of
frustration—often in the same day and occasionally during the
same hour. I would be leaving, but a part of my heart would
always belong to the months when I had the absolute honor of
leading American soldiers.

Command tours for company commanders were eighteen
months at the time, which was considered to be adequate to
maintain a sense of continuity—the merits of which were obvious when considering the condition the company was in after
having had three commanders in six months, before I assumed
command—and short enough to allow most captains the opportunity to take their turn in the barrel. When there was a shortage
of available captains or when a particular unit needed continued
leadership, a few officers were allowed to extend their command
tour for up to six months.

I strongly considered extending but did not for three reasons.
First of all, there was an abundance of captains—good captains—who wanted a company with the same intensity that I had
felt during my time in Stuttgart with the VII Corps staff. Second,
I had received orders to report to graduate school at East Texas

230

State University in August to begin work on a master's degree in journalism before assuming duties as a public affairs officer.

The final consideration was the battalion commander. Motley seemed to learn nothing from experience, and the only respect he commanded was that merited by his position and the silver oak leaf of a lieutenant colonel on his collar. The battalion commander continued to mask his own inadequacies by destroying the careers of others. Another major, this time the battalion executive officer, was his next target. Motley seemed to delight in announcing at a meeting of his company commanders and staff that he had given his departing executive officer an evaluation report that "will guarantee that he will never be allowed to command a battalion." On the surface this did not seem like the information that should be shared with junior officers. More important, it seemed amazing that the major had received a poor report rather than a "max" evaluation. The battalion XO had been the stabilizing force, who had often been the cohesive factor in keeping everything on track when Motley was making almost deliberate efforts to destroy morale. I would miss the company and the battalion. Motley I would not miss. All I had learned from him was what not to do when properly leading and training soldiers.*

With the end of my tour in sight, there was no time to half step. The company had come a long way, and I intended to leave it in the best possible condition for the next commander. We reevaluated several marginal soldiers, allowing a few, with stern warnings, to remain in the company; a couple of others we processed with bad paper back to the States. Inventories of weapons, vehicles, and equipment revealed that shortages did not exist and that my replacement could readily and quickly account for everything. We inventoried the excess as well.

I was pleased when I learned who my replacement would be. Capt. Bill Steiger had the experience and wherewithal to continue the company on its way to becoming even more combat ready. Still, it seemed strange that in a matter of days Alpha Company would no longer be my company. While I felt that I

---

*It would be more than a decade and dozens of commanders later before I would find an officer who rivaled Motley in ineptness and lack of any identifiable leadership characteristics. Unfortunately, Edmond S. Solymosy, by some flaw in the system, reached the rank of brigadier general. The only solace to those of us who worked for him was that he had achieved his rank in the air defense artillery rather than in the "real" combat arms.

had left my mark, I was well aware that passing the guidon of companies, battalions, regiments, and armies has continued through the ages, and commanders are forgotten by the units long before the units are forgotten by us. Although it was difficult to accept, I knew that commanders come and commanders go. Such is the nature of the business.

The day before the change of command, I held my final meeting with the company. I began by saying how proud I was to have served with them and that I looked forward to our paths' crossing once again. On a portable briefing flip chart, I then began turning pages as I read to the company their accomplishments over the past eighteen months: two satisfactory maintenance inspections with one praised as the best in the division, a commendable rating on the annual general inspection, battalion honor company twelve of sixteen months awarded, best scores in battalion on mortar test, first company in division to validate PT standards, first company in division to be drug free, lowest blotter-incident rate in battalion, consistently highest vehicle operational rate in battalion, lead company in REFORGER and "first to Tauber," and outstanding results in the annual company no-notice test despite extremely adverse weather conditions.

I concluded by saying, "These accomplishments have all led to the combat readiness and fighting spirit which will allow this company, if ever called upon, to fight and win against any force which we might face. You are the best soldiers in the best company in the best army in the world. Citizens of our country will continue to enjoy the finest quality of life ever known on this planet because of the umbrella of protection that you provide. The rest of the world looks to you to defend those perilous freedoms which have been won by the blood of those who have gone before you. Regardless of your reason for being here or whatever you may do in your future, you can look back with pride that you served your country in a difficult time when being a soldier was neither an easy nor a popular profession. Most important, you have done it well. I will miss you and charge each of you to continue the march."

These words were repeated one last time as I scratched them into my journal late that night. Unlike my journal from Vietnam where the pages where often splattered with mud and, occasionally, bloodstained, the diary from Germany was fairly neat and clean. Only the words indicated the long hours, late nights, and hard work which, without a doubt, had been well worth it. The company was now capable and able to fight, but more significantly, by being ready we likely would not have to. An army that has to fight has already lost its most important objective— to deter any enemy from wanting to meet it on the battlefield. For eighteen months we had "enjoyed" peace. My hope had been what nearly fifteen years later would become a reality— the Cold War never became a hot war but rather began to develop into a warm peace.

At midmorning on May 29, 1976, the 2d of the 30th Infantry assembled on a grassy area in front of the battalion headquarters. The division band played a few songs, Motley made a short speech, and in a very few minutes, the battalion commander marched out with new commanders for A, C, combat support and headquarters companies. Stopping in front of the company, Motley returned my salute and then he and Bill Steiger took positions to my right and left. Liebrich stepped forward, took the guidon from the bearer, passed it to me, I passed it to Motley who passed it to Steiger. I assumed the position at Motley's side, and Bill took his place at the head of Alpha Company. I marched with Motley to the other companies as we made the other exchanges of guidons. When we had completed the company changes of command, we returned to the head of the formation. The band played "Dog Faced Soldier," and Motley dismissed the battalion. Colonel Creighton was there to shake my hand, along with many other staff officers and friends from other units, Linda gave me a hug, I sought out Bill Morrow, to wish him well in his new command of the combat support company, and Bill Steiger, to again congratulate him on taking command of "his" company.

After a brief reception in the mess hall, I went home. For the first time in a year and a half, there was no reason to worry about a phone call or what was going on at the company. I felt relief, satisfaction, and a nearly overwhelming sense of loss.

The next morning, Linda and I left the girls with friends and drove to Rhein-Main Airport where we caught a "hop" on a C-141 transport for Adana, Turkey. Our intent had been to take a week in Athens, but that flight was full. When they announced that seats were available to Adana, I quickly calculated that if Greece and Turkey were close enough to fight a war, then Athens must not be too far from Adana.

Not until we were on the aircraft and met several families returning to their home base did we discover that Adana, in southern Turkey, is much closer to Syria than to Greece, and no one, I repeat no one, ever went there on vacation. Although everyone on the plane seemed to think we were a bit strange, it felt like an adventure to Linda and me. With no company to worry about, the girls in good hands, a bit of change in our pockets, and a week on our own, we were ready for anything.

Over the next two days we rode buses with Turks across mountains and desert and stopped at places where they acted as if they had never seen a Westerner. Because we spoke no Turkish and no one we met spoke English, we did a lot of pantomime and picture drawing. By the time we crossed the Bosporus bridge at sunrise of our second day on the bus and pulled into Istanbul, we were sad to leave our new-found friends.

After a day in Istanbul and the discovery that ferries had not resumed their routes to Athens since the Cyprus War, we were back at the bus station. Two more days riding through country not mentioned in the usual travel brochures and we arrived in Athens. A couple of days on the beach and visiting the various sites that house the remains of the cradle of democracy, we caught another U.S. Air Force hop back to Germany.

My final weeks in Schweinfurt were spent at brigade assisting the operations officer. Little was asked or accomplished during that brief period. The day before we flew back to the States, Linda and I drove the girls north from Schweinfurt to the East German border. Stopping at the one-kilometer limit of approach, we looked down from a hillside at the double fence, watchtowers, rolls of barbed wire, a deep ditch, a mine field, and roving patrols accompanied by attack dogs. From our distance the border appeared to be a black line snaking across the countryside. For a half-hour or so Linda and I pointed out the fence to our three- and six-year-old daughters, explaining to them as much as to ourselves that that was the reason we had been in Germany for the past three years.

APPENDIX A

Organization

2d Battalion, 30th Infantry, 3d Infantry Division
1975–1976

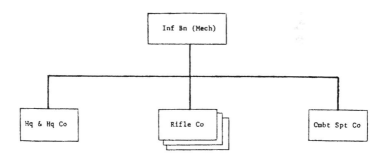

Mission and Capabilities

2d Battalion, 30th Infantry, 3d Infantry Division

MISSION: To close with the enemy by means of fire and maneuver in order to destroy or capture him or to repel his assault by fire, close combat, and counterattack.

CAPABILITIES:
1. Provides a base of fire and maneuver elements.
2. Seizes and holds terrain.
3. Conducts independent operations on a limited scale.
4. Provides antitank protection.
5. Provides indirect fire support for organic and attached units.
6. Conducts long range patrolling when properly equipped.
7. Provides a high degree of cross-country mobility to successfully exploit the effects of nuclear and nonnuclear weapons.
8. Provides a force that complements and enhances the inherent capabilities of tank elements, when employed in tank/infantry teams.

9. Provides a force that can participate in airmobile operations when provided air transport.
10. Maneuvers in all types of terrain under all climatic operations.
11. Participates in amphibious operations.
12. Provides limited air defense.
13. Participates in counterinsurgency operations as elements of brigade-size back-up forces.

Organization

Company A, 2d Battalion, 30th Infantry, 3d Infantry Division
1975–1976

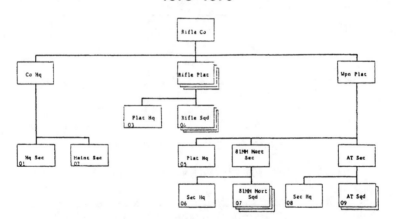

Mission and Capabilities

Company A, 2d Battalion, 30th Infantry, 3d Infantry Division

MISSION: To close with the enemy by means of fire and maneuver in order to destroy or capture him or to repel his assault by fire, close combat, and counterattack.

CAPABILITIES:
1. Provides a base of fire and maneuver.
2. Closes with the enemy in order to destroy or capture him.
3. Repels enemy assaults by fire, close combat, and counterattack.

4. Seizes and holds terrain.
5. Maneuvers in all types of terrain under all climatic operations.
6. Capitalizes on all forms of mobility.
7. Provides limited antitank protection.

Personnel Allowances*

PARA	LINE #	DESCRIPTION	GRADE	STRENGTH
01		HEADQUARTERS SECTION		
	01	Company Commander	CPT	1
	02	Executive Officer	LT	1
	03	First Sergeant	1SG	1
	04	Supply Sergeant	SSG	1
	05	Communications Chief	SGT	1
	06	Company Clerk	SGT	1
	07	Armorer	SP4	1
	08	Personnel Carrier Driver	SP4	2
	09	Radio/Telephone Operator	PFC	1
	10	Supply Clerk	PFC	1
			Para Total	11
02		MAINTENANCE SECTION		
	01	Motor Sergeant	SFC	1
	02	Sr. Recovery Veh. Operator	SP5	1
	03	Sr. Track Veh. Mechanic	SP5	1
	04	Equipment Records Clerk	SP4	1
	05	Field Radio Mechanic	SP4	1

*Based on Table of Organization and Equipment (TO&E) 07-047H at Level 2 which was in effect in the 3d Infantry Division in 1975–1976. At Level 1 the authorized strength increased by 10 percent to a total of 172 personnel and at Level 3 it decreased by 10 percent to 135.

06	Recovery Veh. Operator	SP4	1
07	Track Vehicle Mechanic	SP4	4
		Para Total	10
03	**3 RIFLE PLATOON HEADQUARTERS**		
01	Platoon Leader	LT	3
02	Platoon Sergeant	SFC	3
03	Assistant Platoon Sergeant	SSG	3
04	Personnel Carrier Driver	SP4	3
		Para Total	12
04	**9 RIFLE SQUADS**		
01	Squad Leader	SSG	9
02	Team Leader	SGT	18
03	Automatic Rifleman	SP4	18
04	Grenadier	SP4	18
05	Personnel Carrier Driver	SP4	9
06	Rifleman	PFC	18
		Para Total	90
05	**WEAPONS PLATOON HEADQUARTERS**		
01	Platoon Leader	LT	1
02	Platoon Sergeant	SFC	1
03	Radio/Telephone Operator	SP4	1
		Para Total	3
06	**MORTAR SECTION HEADQUARTERS**		
01	Section Leader	SSG	1
02	Forward Observer	SGT	3
03	Fire Direction Computer	SGT	1
04	Personnel Carrier Driver	SP4	1

	05	Radio/Telephone Operator	PFC	2
		Para Total		9
07		3 81MM MORTAR SQUADS		
	01	Squad Leader	SGT	3
	02	Gunner	SP4	3
	03	Mortar Carrier Driver	SP4	3
	04	Ammunition Bearer	PFC	2
	05	Assistant Gunner	PFC	3
		Para Total		14
08		ANTITANK SECTION HEADQUARTERS		
	01	Section Leader	SSG	1
		Para Total		1
09		2 ANTITANK SQUADS		
	01	Squad Leader	SGT	2
	02	Gunner	SP4	2
	03	Assistant Gunner	PFC	2
		Para Total		6
		TOTAL AUTHORIZED STRENGTH		156

APPENDIX B

Organization and Station Property*

Company A, 2d Battalion, 30th Infantry, 3d Infantry Division

Organization Property

ITEM	NUMBER AUTHORIZED	UNIT PRICE $	TOTAL PRICE $
Aiming Circle M-2 (Mortars)	1	1,267.00	1,267.00
Antenna AT-784	2	50.87	101.74
Antenna RC-292	2	106.00	212.00
Body Armor (Flack Jackets)	153	27.75	4,245.75
Bag, Barracks	153	2.53	387.09
Bag, Waterproof	153	3.92	599.76
Barber Kit	1	117.00	117.00
Bayonet, M-7	153	5.48	838.44
Belt, Individual Equipment	161	2.74	441.14
Binocular, M-3	7	191.00	1,337.00
Binocular, M-17A1	10	195.00	1,950.00
Bipod, Rifle, 5.56mm M-3	18	5.00	90.00
Blanket, Wool	278	12.00	3,336.00
Boots, Cold Weather	161	35.90	5,779.90
Cabinet, Tool	1	118.00	118.00
Cable Reel, Wire WD-1, Small	21	15.70	329.70

*Organization Property includes those items required for accomplishment of the unit's combat mission. Station Property includes "household" items necessary for garrison living. All dollar amounts are in 1976 prices.

Cable Reel, Wire WD-1, Large	8	44.96	359.68
Camouflage Screen	40	580.00	23,200.00
Camouflage Screen Supports	40	162.00	6,480.00
Canteen, Water Plastic	153	.44	67.32
Cap, Cold Weather	161	4.11	661.71
Carrier, 81mm Mortar M-125A1	3	37,444.00	112,332.00
Carrier, TOW	2	40,028.00	80,056.00
Carrier, Personnel M-113A1	15	34,678.00	520,170.00
Case, First Aid	153	.52	81.09
Case, Ammo	278	1.61	447.58
Charger, Radiation Detection	3	12.00	36.00
Coat, Cold Weather	161	17.20	2,769.20
Code Changer, KY-38	1	395.00	395.00
Compass, Lensatic	48	14.79	709.92
Compass, M-2	6	44.32	265.92
Compressor, Air	1	446.00	446.00
Cover, Helmet	153	.97	148.41
Cover, Canteen	153	1.96	299.88
Coveralls, Mechanic Cold Weather	30	16.60	498.00
Coveralls, Mechanic Cotton	17	8.11	137.97
Cup, Canteen	153	1.31	200.43
Decontamination Apparatus, M-11	23	65.18	1,499.14
Demolition Set, Explosive	1	331.00	331.00
Desk, Field	1	118.00	118.00
Detector Kit, Chemical, M-15A2A	5	55.99	279.95
Field Pack, M-1972	153	14.25	2,180.25
File, Visual Index	4	38.13	152.52
Gloves, Barbed Wire	10	3.93	39.30
Goggles, Sun-Wind-Dust	90	3.01	270.90
Headset, Commo, H-182	5	25.94	129.70
Heater, Space	1	91.00	91.00
Helmet, Armored Vehicle	37	226.00	8,362.00
Helmet, Combat Crewman	9	75.00	675.00
Helmet, Type 1	153	5.10	780.30
Hood, Cold Weather	153	20.10	3,075.30
Individual Channel Alignment Meter	1	317.00	317.00

Intrenching Tool	153	8.00	1,224.00
Intrenching Tool Carrier	153	.91	139.23
Launcher, Grenade, 40mm M-203	24	89.32	2,143.68
Launcher, Tubular Guide, TOW, M-220	2	25,888.00	51,776.00
Liner, Coat	161	7.07	1,138.27
Liner, Parka	161	8.85	1,424.85
Liner, Helmet	153	6.50	994.50
Liner, Trousers, Cold Weather	161	6.19	996.59
Machine Gun, .50 Cal, M-2	21	1,767.00	37,107.00
Machine Gun, .50 Cal, M-2 HB Ground Mount	1	1,775.00	1,775.00
Machine Gun, 7.62mm, M-60	15	1,081.00	16,215.00
Mask, Protective, Vehicle, M-25A1	38	77.57	2,947.00
Mask, Protective, Individual, M-17A1	115	57.75	6,641.25
Mattress, Air	153	9.89	1,513.17
Metascope, AN/PAS-6	6	275.00	1,650.00
Mitten Insert, Arctic	161	1.88	302.68
Mitten Set, Arctic	161	15.50	2,495.50
Mitten, Shell	153	3.80	581.40
Mortar, 81mm, M-29	3	1,260.00	3,780.00
Mount, Tripod, MG, Cal .50, M-3	21	343.00	7,203.00
Mount, Tripod, MG, 7.62mm, M-122	15	232.00	3,480.00
Multimeter, AN/URM-105	1	36.25	36.25
Net, Camouflage, Fiber	8	40.00	320.00
Night Vision Sight, Crew, AN/TVS-2	21	2,650.00	55,650.00
Night Vision Sight, Individual, AN/PVS-2	18	1,881.00	35,858.00
Night Vision Sight, Individual, AN/PVS-2A	3	1,800.00	5,400.00
Night Vision Sight, Crew, AN/TVS-4	1	4,447.00	4,447.00
Overshoes, Rubber	161	5.90	949.50
Pan, Mess Kit	153	5.20	795.60
Parka, Snow	161	16.90	2,720.90

Parka, Wet Weather	161	11.90	1,915.90
Pistol, .45 Cal, M-1911A1	14	57.00	798.00
Plotting Board, M-16 (Mortars)	3	43.46	130.38
Pocket, Ammo, Magazine, .45 Cal Pistol	14	.81	11.34
Poncho	153	11.20	1,713.00
Power Supply Assembly	2	693.00	1,386.00
Quadrant, Fire Control	3	143.00	429.00
Rack, Storage, Small Arms, .45 Cal Pistol	1	138.00	138.00
Rack, Storage, Small Arms, M-16 Rifle	12	82.57	990.84
Radiac Set, AN/PDR-27	1	148.00	148.00
Radiacmeter, IM-93/UD	12	12.91	153.92
Radiacmeter, IM-174/PD	7	43.00	301.00
Radio Set, AN/GRC-160	10	1,325.00	13,250.00
Radio Set, AN/PRC-77	5	943.00	4,715.00
Radio Set, AN/VRC- 46	1	1,491.00	1,491.00
Radio Set, AN/VRC- 47	4	2,158.32	8,633.28
Radio Set, AN/VRC- 64	13	1,040.00	13,520.00
Radio Set, AN/GRA-39	2	295.00	590.00
Radio Accessory Kit MK-1266/V	3	156.25	468.75
Radio Accessory Kit MK-1291/G	3	180.00	640.00
Radio Accessory Kit MK-1296/G	1	81.85	81.85
Radio Installation Kit MK-1402/G	2	118.53	237.06
Radio Installation Kit MK-1306/VRC- 47	1	274.00	274.00
Range Finder, AN/GVS-3	1	11,912.00	11,912.00
Receiver, Radio AN/PRR-9	15	109.00	1,635.00
Recovery Vehicle, M-578	1	110,040.00	110,040.00
Reel, Cable RL-159/U	7	6.97	46.69
Reel Equipment CE-11	2	37.93	75.86
Reeling Machine RL-39	14	6.86	96.04
Rifle, 5.56mm, M-16A1	139	142.00	19,739.00
Rifle, Recoilless, 90mm, M-67	6	2,758.00	16,548.00
Safe, Field	1	161.00	161.00
Scarf, Neck, Wool	153	2.09	319.77
Screen, Latrine	1	80.00	80.00
Shelter Half, Tent	159	14.40	2,289.60

Shirt, Cold Weather Wool	321	6.66	2,137.89
Shoes, Gym	161	2.14	344.54
Shoes, Mechanic, Safety	8	11.50	92.00
Sight, Bore Optical	1	505.00	505.00
Sleeping Bag	161	38.50	6,198.50
Sleeping Bag, Carrier	153	1.90	290.70
Sleeping Bag, Case	153	8.91	1,363.23
Special Security Radio TSEC/KY-38	2	5,400.00	10,800.00
Strap Assembly, Field Pack	153	1.03	157.59
Submachine Gun, Cal. 45 M-3A1	2	111.00	222.00
Suspenders, Field Pack	161	2.96	476.56
Suspenders, Trousers	153	.65	99.45
Sweat Pants, Blue	161	2.09	336.49
Sweat Shirt, Blue	161	1.82	293.02
Switchboard, Telephone Main SB-22/PT	1	602.00	602.00
Switchboard, Telephone SB-993/GT	1	53.25	53.25
Telephone Set, TA-1/PT	25	32.30	807.50
Telephone Set, TA-312/PT	3	53.77	161.31
Tent, General Purpose, Small	1	504.00	504.00
Tent, Liner, Small	1	99.00	99.00
Tent, Vehicle Maintenance	1	443.00	443.00
Test Set, Electronic Tube	1	179.36	179.36
Tool Set, Auto, No. 1	1	1,455.00	1,455.00
Tool Kit, Auto, Mechanic	7	75.00	525.00
Tool Kit, Electronic	1	48.50	48.50
Tool Kit, Engineer	1	1,185.00	1,185.00
Tool Kit, Small Arms	1	85.00	85.00
Trailer, Cargo, ¼ Ton M-416	2	377.00	754.00
Trailer, Cargo 1½ Ton M-105A2	2	1,049.00	2,098.00
Transmitter Set Radio	15	160.00	2,400.00
Trousers, Winter, White	40	4.85	194.00
Trousers, Cold Weather	321	11.80	3,787.80
Trousers, Wool	321	8.50	2,728.50
Truck, Cargo 1¼ Ton M-561 Gamma Goat	1	12,312.00	12,312.00
Truck, Cargo, 2½ Ton M-35A2	1	13,502.00	13,502.00

Truck, Cargo, 2½ Ton M-35A1	1	8,458.00	8,458.00
Truck, Utility ¼ Ton M-151A1 Jeep	2	3,196.00	6,392.00
Trunk, Locker	1	10.40	10.40
Trunks, Gym	161	1.90	305.90
T-Shirt, Reversible	153	3.85	589.05
Typewriter, Portable	2	90.00	180.00
Vestibule Tent, Small	1	86.00	86.00
SUB TOTAL			$1,338,941.18

STATION PROPERTY

ITEM	NUMBER AUTHORIZED	UNIT PRICE $	TOTAL PRICE $
Bed, Ends Tubular	107	31.20	3,338.40
Bookcase, Metal	2	44.90	89.80
Bulletin Board	1	294.00	294.00
Cabinet, 4 Shelve	1	100.00	100.00
Chair, Easy	4	75.00	300.00
Chair, Straight	9	58.32	524.88
Chest, Ice Storage	1	157.00	157.00
Cleaner, Vacuum	2	94.00	188.00
Cleaner, Vacuum, Shop	1	441.00	441.00
Cover, Mattress	155	6.54	1,013.70
Desk, Double Pedestal	10	60.00	600.00
Desk, Single Pedestal	28	101.10	2,830.80
Desk, Typewriter	3	75.00	225.00
Dryer, Clothes, 16 lb.	1	105.00	105.00
Filing Cabinet, 5 Drawer	6	130.00	780.00
Guidon, Infantry	1	5.82	5.82
Lamp, Table	1	40.50	40.50
Mattress, Bed	127	31.10	3,949.00
Pad, Mattress	100	4.50	450.00
Pillow	108	1.63	176.04
Polisher, Floor	4	108.00	432.00
Pool Table	1	850.00	850.00
Radio/Phono Combination	1	279.00	279.00
Rug, 9 × 12	4	60.00	240.00
Safe, Field	1	161.00	161.00
Sheet, Bed	669	2.97	1,986.93
Table, Occasional, 28 "	4	32.25	129.00
Table, Occasional, 36 "	3	67.50	202.50
Table, Occasional, 60 "	4	129.00	516.00
Table, Occasional, 108 "	1	87.00	87.00
Table, Writing	4	42.00	168.00

Television, B&W	1	127.59	127.59
Trunk, Locker	41	10.40	426.40
Typewriter, 13″ Elite	6	218.00	1,308.00
Wardrobe, Metal	132	140.00	18,480.00
Washer, Clothes, 16 lb.	1	156.50	156.50
SUB TOTAL			$41,168.86

ORGANIZATION PROPERTY Sub Total	$1,338,941.18
STATION PROPERTY Sub Total	41,168.86

TOTAL PROPERTY, A COMPANY, 2D BATTALION, 30TH INFANTRY, 3D INFANTRY DIVISION	$1,380,110.04

*Organization Property includes those items required for accomplishment of the unit's combat mission. Station Property includes "household" items necessary for garrison living. All dollar amounts are in 1976 prices.

APPENDIX C

Personnel Roster*

Company A, 2d Battalion, 30th Infantry, 3d Infantry Division

Acedo, Abran M.	PFC	Clark, James B.	1LT
Albert, Jerry L.	SSG	Clark, Wade E.	PV2
Alexander, Terry L.	SGT	Coalburn, Donald F.	PV2
Ali, Hazrat	SSG	Cole, Clarence T.	PV2
Archdale, George E.	PFC	Colmenares, Thomas D.	PFC
Arford, Dick L.	PSG	Cook, Richard L.	SSG
Arthur, George A.	SFC	Cooper, Jerry C.	SP4
Aston, Stephen R.	SP4	Courson, David E.	SGT
Bain, Robert H.	SP4	Cox, Timothy M.	PFC
Banks, Larry L.	SP4	Crawford, Gary N.	SP4
Beal, Randy C.	SSG	Crow, Rickey W.	PV2
Beamer, Steven A.	SGT	Crump, James C.	SP4
Billingsley, Jay D.	PV2	Crutchlow, Larry D.	PV2
Blake, Daniel W.	SGT	Cruz, Eloy L.	SP4
Blum, David R.	SP4	Daggett, David A.	SP4
Boyster, Dennis R.	PV2	Davis, Freeman, Jr.	PFC
Brierley, James J.	SP4	Dean, Douglas C.	PV2
Brown, Gregory D.	SP4	Defuria, Richard G.	SP4
Brown, Thomas, Jr.	PFC	Dixon, Dalton G.	SGT
Bryant, Donald C.	SP4	Donald, Roy M.	SP4
Buirch, Wayne E.	SGT	Dover, Richard D.	CPL
Byars, James L.	SSG	Downes, Clarence L.	SGT
Cady, Patrick E.	SSG	Earle, Richard W.	1LT
Carr, Gene M.	SGT	Ebard, Edward	SP4
Carrasco, Pedro A.	1SG	Echevarria, Adolfo R.	SP4
Carroll, Timothy	PV1	Edmondson, George A.	SGT
Chacon, Jose B.	SP4	Ellis, Charles M.	PV2
Chappell, Marvin V.	PV2	Everheart, Benny, Jr.	PFC
Christia, Gregory	PV2	Fermin, Roy F.	SGT
Clark, Edward J.	SP4	Fernandez, Alberto C.	PV2

*Included are those soldiers on the company rosters compiled on February 4, 1975, and March 23, 1976.

Flame, Larry B.	SP4	Keene, Frankie	SGT
Fisher, Jesse	SGT	Kiker, Gregory D.	PV1
Fisher, Keith E.	PV1	Killen, Dennis M.	PFC
Fisher, Ronald W.	PV2	Kim, Young J.	SP4
Flores, Albert	PFC	Kimball, Marlin M.	PFC
Fluker, Joe L.	SP4	Krommenhoek, David W.	PFC
Fontejon, Jesus A.	SP4	Langner, Michael D.	PFC
Foster, Michael H.	SP4	Lanning, Michael L.	CPT
Foxworth, John, D.	SP4	Lambrecht, Lester C.	PFC
Frazee, Harry P., Jr.	PSG	Lenderman, Thomas W.	SP4
Gaal, Gary L.	2LT	Lessard, Pierre J.	SGT
Gibbs, Michael S.	SGT	Liebrich, Wolfgang H.	PSG
Gilbert, Barry J.	PFC	Lockhart, Dennis M.	SP4
Gillespie, Milton R.	SGT	Lucas, John W.	1LT
Goins, Gary L.	SP4	Lugaro, Luis M.	PFC
Gonzales, Mundo I.	SP4	Magaro, Thomas G.	SP4
Grimsley, Tommy J.	SP4	Marceau, Peter C.	2LT
Grubb, Coy, Jr.	SP4	Marcum, Douglas G.	PFC
Gulley, Phillip D.	PV2	Martin, Willie C.	SSG
Gunier, Michael L.	SGT	Martinez, William	PFC
Guppy, Edward L.	PV2	Mathis, Tony B.	SP4
Hall, Donald L.	SP4	McAdams, Joseph T.	PV2
Hall, Gene A.	PFC	McDonald, Derral D.	SGT
Hamilton, Wiley R.	PFC	McDonald, Lawrence A.	SGT
Harper, Cepheus, Jr.	SP4	Miller, Jack R.	PFC
Harris, Robert S.	SP4	Mullins, Timothy E.	PFC
Haynes, Gary D.	SGT	Musser, Douglas B.	2LT
Heben, Gonzalez E.	SP4	O'Malley, Edward, A., Jr.	SGT
Hebert, Marvin R.	PFC	Orban, John A.	PFC
Henderson, Allen D.	PFC	Ortiz, David L.	SGT
Henderson, Terry	PV2	Osborne, Michael V.	PFC
Hernandez, Humberto	SSG	Palmer, Terry L.	SP4
Herrig, Robert A.	SP4	Parker, James, Jr.	SP4
Hess, Stephen D.	SGT	Payne, William L.	SGT
Higgins, James N.	SSG	Payne, Michael F.	SGT
Hill, Richard L.	SP4	Pepper, Barry K.	2LT
Hodgkinson, David J.	SP4	Perkins, Royce D.	SP4
Holman, Roger D.	SGT	Peterson, Albert, Jr.	SP4
Horn, David E.	PV2	Peterson, Edward	SSG
Hornbeck, Raymond R.	SSG	Peterson, Joseph	SGT
Humphries, Dennis	SP4	Peterson, Robert W.	SP4
Igo, Curtis L.	SP4	Phelps, Walter M.	PFC
Jerauld, Lynn W.	SGT	Pillow, David J.	SP4
Jiron, Patrecio J.	SP4	Pino, Rivera C.	SGT
Johnson, Stafford, III	PFC	Porter, Roger D.	SP5
Jones, Donnie R.	SP4	Porter, Steven E.	SP4
Jones, James R.	1LT	Quackenbush, Donald J.	SP5

Rios, Joe R.	SP4	Taylor, Thomas D.	SP4
Rivera, Samuel A.	SP4	Teeple, Raymond F.	SP4
Rivera, Victor M.	PV1	Templin, Scott M.	SP4
Robbins, Olanda	SP4	Thielman, Frank E.	SP4
Roberson, Terry J.	SP4	Thomas, Delbert A.	SSG
Robertson, Wilburn R.	SP4	Thomas, Henry W.	SP4
Rodriquez, Hector L.	SP4	Thornton, Edward J.	SGT
Rojewski, Lloyd A.	SP4	Trotter, John C.	SP4
Romans, Gary D.	SGT	Trujillo, Daryl W.	PV2
Rosales, Castro J.	PFC	Trujillo, Ronald R.	SP4
Salas, Juan, Jr.	PFC	Tuiolemotu, Aniutea F.	PV1
Sanders, Kurt L.	SP4	Turner, Garland	SP4
Scarberry, Joseph B.	SGT	Underdale, Daniel K.	PFC
Schehr, Vincent D.	PFC	Valdez, Rudolfo G., Jr.	SP4
Sexton, Fred O.	SGT	Vaughn, Chester M.	SP4
Shirley, Earl E.	SGT	Vickery, James E.	SSG
Shockley, James J.	SP4	Voils, Ansel L.	SP4
Shono, David D.	SFC	Wedding, Jackie	SGT
Silva, Domingo	PFC	White, Frederick	PV1
Silva, James M.	1LT	White, Michael W.	SP4
Sims, Robert L.	SGT	Whitfield, Clayance T.	PFC
Sledge, Michael	SP4	Whitford, Roscoe E.	SP4
Smart, Christopher L.	SP4	Willett, Michael A.	PV2
Smith, John A.	SGT	Williams, David A.	SP4
Smith, Louis J.	SP4	Wilson, John P.	SGT
Solin, Jay R.	PV2	Wilson, Joseph M.	SGT
Spencer, Tony	PV2	Wilson, Thomas J.	SGT
Sprayberry, Victor	SP4	Wollam, Park F., Jr.	PV2
Stewart, Roy P., III	CPL	Womack, Phillip A.	SP4
Swift, Bill E.	SGT	Yarbrough, Billy W.	SGT
Tabor, Gary L.	SP4	Young, Tony R.	PV2
Tally, Jeffery L.	SP4	Zamora, Refugio, Jr.	SP4
Tate, Thomas L.	PFC		

APPENDIX D

History of the 30th Infantry Regiment

The original United States 30th Infantry Regiment was organized by an act of Congress on January 29, 1813, for service in the War of 1812 and remained on active duty until 1815. On May 3, 1861 at the outbreak of the Civil War, the 30th Infantry was reactivated by order of President Abraham Lincoln. During the reduction of active forces following the war, the 30th Infantry was consolidated with the 4th Infantry and redesignated as the 4th Infantry Regiment.

On February 12, 1901, the modern 30th Infantry was organized for service in the Philippine Insurrection. With brief returns to its headquarters at the Presidio of San Francisco, California, for reorganization and refitting, the 30th remained in the Philippines until 1909. After return to the United States, the 30th remained at the Presidio until 1912 before being assigned to the Territory of Alaska for two years. Back in San Francisco once again in 1914, the regiment remained in the Bay Area until being assigned to guard duty along the Mexican border in January 1917.

Preparations for World War I sent the 30th Infantry from the Mexican border to Syracuse, New York, on May 9, 1917, to provide cadre for training new regiments for transfer to Europe. Six months later, on November 21, the regiment joined the newly formed 3d Infantry Division at Camp Green, North Carolina. On April 1, 1918, the division sailed for France and by May 31 was occupying frontline trenches against the Germans in what became known as the Aisne Defensive Action. Two weeks later the 30th Infantry fought the Germans at Chateau-Thierry and by mid-July was occupying defensive positions along the Marne River near Mezy, France. From these positions the 30th Infantry, along with the 38th Infantry Regiment, withstood and turned

250

back the last great German offensive of the war between July 14 and 18. Although virtually surrounded by a numerically superior force, the two regiments held their ground and prevented the German plans to retake Paris. After the battle, the 30th Infantry became known as the "Rock of the Marne," and soon the entire 3d Infantry Division was designated the "Marne Division."

After the Marne River defense, the 30th Infantry participated in the Aisne-Marne offensive and remained on the front lines until October 27, 1918—a mere two weeks before the signing of the Armistice which concluded hostilities. From the end of the war until August 1919, the regiment performed occupation duty at Koblenz, Germany. Upon return to the United States, the regiment moved to several temporary stations before returning for permanent assignment at the Presidio, California, in 1922.

Over the next two decades the regiment trained and actively participated in the activities of their host city. The relationship between the regiment and the Bay Area was so close that the 30th Infantry became affectionately known as "San Francisco's Own." This partnership was recognized by the army to the extent that the regiment was officially authorized by the War Department to have its color guard carry the City of San Francisco Flag along with the Regimental Colors.

With World War II looming, the 30th Infantry was ordered to rejoin other units of the 3d Infantry Division at Fort Lewis, Washington, in April 1941. On November 8, 1942, the division landed at Fedala, Morocco. For the next thirty-one months, the 30th Infantry fought the Germans in Sicily, at Anzio, and across France from the Normandy Beachhead. Fighting up the Rhone Valley and through the Vosges Mountains, the regiment captured Strasbourg and then spent from December 1944 through March 1945 in heavy fighting at the Colmar pocket. In March the regiment broke out of Colmar, smashed through the Siegfried Line, crossed the Rhine River, captured the German cities of Nürnburg and Munich, and at war's end was poised for an attack on Salzburg, Austria. VE-day ended the regiment's nearly three years of combat in eight countries at the cost of 8,308 killed, wounded, or missing. Twelve men of the 30th Infantry had earned the United States' highest valor award, the Medal of Honor, while 58 had been awarded the Distinguished Service Cross, 925 the Silver Star, and 1,223 the Bronze Star.

After the war, the 30th Infantry performed occupation duty in Salzburg and later in Kassel, Germany. Returning to the United States, the regiment was briefly assigned to Fort Campbell, Kentucky, before being transferred to Fort Benning, Georgia, on December 1, 1948. In September 1950, the 3d Infantry Division was ordered to Korea. Due to shortages of personnel, the 30th Infantry provided replacements for the other regiments of the division. New recruits eventually filled the ranks of the 30th, but it remained at Fort Benning to support training for the duration of the Korean conflict.

In October 1954 the remainder of the 3d Infantry Division returned to Fort Benning from Korea and the 30th Infantry rejoined its ranks. From Georgia, the 3d Infantry Division and the 30th Infantry moved back to Germany in July 1957. There the division joined the VII United States Corps and assumed a mission in support of NATO efforts to defend Western Europe.

Despite its long and proud history, there were other regiments with even longer lists of accomplishments and campaigns than the 30th Infantry. In the late 1980s the army announced plans to more align soldiers closely with individual regiments. Called COHORT, the plan called for fewer regiments with more battalions so that soldiers could be transferred from one theater to another and still be in the same parent regiment. As a result, in June 1989 battalions of the 30th Infantry were redesignated the 15th Infantry Regiment. The 30th Infantry designation was transferred to Fort Benning, Georgia, as a parent unit of the Basic Training Command.

2d Battalion, 30th Infantry Campaign Participation Credit

Philippine Insurrection
—Mindoro 1901

World War I
—Aisne
—Champagne-Marne
—Aisne-Marne
—St. Mihiel
—Meuse-Argonne
—Champagne 1918

World War II
—Algeria-French Morocco
—Tunisia

—Sicily
—Naples-Foggia
—Anzio
—Rome-Arno
—Southern France
—Rhineland
—Ardennes-Alsace
—Central Europe

2d Battalion, 30th Infantry Decorations

Presidential Unit Citation (Army), Streamer COLMAR.
Presidential Unit Citation (Army), Streamer BESANCON, FRANCE.
Presidential Unit Citation (Army), Streamer SICILY.
Presidential Unit Citation (Army), Streamer MOUNT RO-TUNDO.
French Croix de Guerre with Palm, World War I, Streamer CHAMPAGNE-MARNE.
French Croix de Guerre with Palm, World War II, Streamer, COLMAR.
French Croix de Guerre, World War II, Fourragere.

2d Battalion, 30th Infantry Motto

"Our country, not ourselves."

About the Author

Michael Lee Lanning retired from the U.S. Army after more than twenty years of active service. His decorations include the Bronze Star for Valor with two oak leaf clusters, the Combat Infantryman Badge, Senior Parachute Wings, and the Ranger Tab. Born and educated in Texas, he currently resides in Tempe, Arizona. His previous books include *The Only War We Had: A Platoon Leader's Journal of Vietnam; Vietnam 1969–1970: A Company Commander's Journal; Inside the LRRPS: Rangers in Vietnam; Inside Force Recon: Recon Marines in Vietnam* (with Ray William Stubbe); and *The Bamboo Soldiers: Inside the VC and NVA* (with Dan Cragg).

Printed in the United States
by Baker & Taylor Publisher Services